The A–Z

of

Educational

Nonsense

Considering dysfunction
in our primary schools

BY THE SAME AUTHOR

Poetry
Makers and Destroyers
Love's Troublesome Journey
The Sex Doctor
Scotland's Saint
Wrong Ticket Home
Surveying the Wreckage
Let's go ahead, then!
Epiphany in Azure: Columba on Iona
Likabehandlingsplan: Sweden Considered in Verse

Education Series
The Belt Room
Curriculum for Excellence
Queens of the Reich
Relentless: The Death March to Educational Excellence
The Hateful Seven: The Good Ideas Ruining Our Children

Biography
William Wallace
Robert the Bruce
Janet: A Life in Verse

See other Big Ride titles at www.glenntelfer.me

See author blog at https://senecacaledonia.blogspot.com

The A–Z
of
Educational Nonsense

A true guide for parents and teachers

Glenn Telfer

Certain that someone out there likes this stuff

Published By
Big Ride
6/3 Pinkhill Park
Edinburgh EH12 7FA
Scotland

LEGAL DISCLAIMER

As a product of the author's imagination, any resemblance to actual persons or events is entirely coincidental. Really.

A catalogue record for this book is available from the British Library.

ISBN: 978-1-909297-36-4
e-pub 978-1-909297-37-1

Cover design by Glenn Telfer

Design by Wordsense, Edinburgh; wordsense.co.uk

Printed by CPI Anthony Rowe Ltd, Wiltshire; www.cpibooks.co.uk

Foreword

To the honest parents; be not amazed at the magic of the players, or the colourful banners they proclaim, but hark to the awful message hidden within.

The beginning of wisdom is to call a thing by its real name, this book is an attempt to do just that with the ideas and forces that are common currency within the world of education in my area of expertise, the Scottish primary school.

This is necessary because, although many are aware of the high level of lunacy combined with the low level of education evinced by our primary schools, few are aware that they have become nation-sised death traps. By this I mean that in the guise of social progress and educational relevance they are destroying the well-being of our children and the social pillars of our nation. This dictionary defines, entry by entry, what I mean by this claim.

I am sick of this hubristic dream of a better world achieved through the politicisation of our children and the relentless dole of would be improvements heaped on our plate. Tired too of the misdirection and bare-faced lies needed to advance this agenda, and how it both insults and sullies all who come into contact with it. This work replies to that feeling.

There are many ways of advancing my argument, I have chosen the one that is in accord with my own genius and the absurd spirit of the times, in which words have lost their meaning beyond reason, subjects and practices sabotage one another, and final effect is the opposite of apparent intention. I am optimistic, though, that by means of whimsy and irony, serious attention can be drawn to the subversive powers arrayed against us and that we will come to know them for the civilisational scale challenge they actually are. And by following, for those who dare, the money and influence trail to the real masters behind these strange happenings. Thusly forewarned, as parents and teachers, we can begin to resist. Failure to do so in time will oblige Providence to once again rise up, strike down the overreaching hand and deliver the balancing nightmare to the progressive dream. But by then it will be too late. Too late for us, that is.

I once reminded someone in a debate, I think it was with Humpty Dumpty, that you don't get to make up your own definitions as you go along, or write your own dictionary. Once again I've proven myself wrong in grand style.

Glenn Telfer,
Edinburgh, March 2020

The beginning of wisdom

is

calling things by their right names

A

A

Just because lots of people are really stupid should not mean that they are not entitled to get an A grade. All we need to do is increase the standards *downwards* to get higher level results. With these higher grades everyone can get a Ph.D. and become a professor; and thusly, academic excellence will have been achieved by the Scottish education establishment. With so many highly certificated chiefs, and so few indians, within the system, we risk running out of people to do the monkey work that keeps society functioning. Perhaps robots or imported Africans can do this; and monkeys too, if it turns out that they are not suited to the academic life.

AA Hire

Ref: Affirmative Action in schools.

AA being the process of giving unmerited preference across various domains in selection, admission, hiring and promotion of ethnic others; this to correct the claimed bias of White society and to better enable such ethnic others to feel more included in British life. The relentless Goodpressure™ by the same political pressure groups that brought us to where we are, now advocate for the introduction of refugee diversity hires to make schools even more full of cultural enrichment – all in the name of justice.

As the proportion of AA diversity hires increases, standards invariably drop, and in proportion to this drop the workload gets increasingly transferred to the remaining competent teachers – along with being the scapegoats for all inefficiency and resident tension! Collegiality, vocation and sense of mission is also eroded. This results in the more intelligent and potentially dedicated teachers being scared away from the profession – which has no choice but to recruit among even more sub-optimal AA hires to make up the numbers. Blame and disappointment metastasises. The profession is now in a death spiral. All of this was quite predicable on the original political decision to alter (i.e., lower) standards for the sake of Affirmative Action targets.

School Equality Oberführer: *I have a new batch of refugee teachers for your school.*

Head Teacher: *Excellent news. Do any of them speak English?*

School Equality Oberführer: *Not really. But two are 100% burka'd up and aren't allowed to speak to males anyway.*

Head Teacher: *Sounds good. I think our equity and diversity Pokemon factor has increased doubleplusgood. And I'm sure the children will learn a lot from them about tolerance.*

Once such programmes start, as we see, they can never be got rid of due to the fear of racism accusations, or phobia claims in the case of various sexual identities. Indeed, they always expand as pressure is exerted by other 'excluded' groups for their seat on the gravy train. Hard issues connected with competence, mandatory accommodations to employment law and work practices, and the wider impact of new cultural norms get kicked down the road by the political class, or sensationally exploited to illustrate some or other failure of White society. Subtle social as well as direct political pressure gets directed down the recruitment chain to pervert academic and other standards at both point of entry and graduation from university. Diversity is certainly increased in schools, but also lowered standards; for a corollary of such programmes is the impossibility of criticism of such hires. Further, a racial and/or sexual dimension enters into even the most mundane of interactions, and of necessity, staff tiptoe around such issues and thereby lose spontaneity and integrity. Thus arrives; denial, deceit, staff division as sides are taken and, finally, lowered morale. Even the AA hires are professionally compromised by being converted into dependent parasites of the supporting bureaucracies. AA, then, harms everyone in different ways. As for education; who cares – the schools will be all to pot then anyway!

Ability

While respected and required, ability always contains the potential to provoke envy and disfavour. This being especially true where peers are not able to form natural competence hierarchies, as is generally the case with females. When combined with high IQ, high ability is selected against in primary schools; such teachers usually leave the profession early.

The take-away message – don't be too able, less you provoke envy. Functional and low initiative is always a safe career bet with insecure head teachers.

Academic Research in Education

This has been a powerful force in shaping modern education in all its domains; whether pedagogy, psychology or policy. However, it has contributed almost nothing of value. Often regarded as a joke on the rest of us. Endlessly repeated, and at staggering cost, it has delivered chaos and nonsense in equal measure.

Whatever useful intention attended the founding of such departments quickly segued to busy-work on public purse for grade 2 bureaucrats masquerading as scientists and experts. Ranging from hopeless fluff to baffling word salads they operate in an intellectual realm beyond reason, and thus they cannot be criticised by it. Attempting to do so is to waste your mind against unresisting imbecility.

But worse than carrying no wisdom, they have been nefarious vectors for all the nonsense and destructive ideas now common in schools and in educational debates. Using their academic prestige and access they have advanced behind this seemingly legitimising shield all the anti-civilisational -isms that are by policy after policy relentlessly destroying our children in school by seeding their minds with ideas and attitudes that will not help them be useful to themselves. Some of these experts are just busy-work dupes, but some aren't. They are the warriors for their future, but their future is not ours. In a genius level pincer movement they have inculcated the impressionable, hopelessly naïve – when not actually stupid – young, mainly women teachers into their worldview, and (Ha ha) also been the principle means of undermining these same teachers' confidence. Highly intelligent teachers who have tried to make sense of the gibberish have suffered the same fate, although for different reasons.

Academia and their media allies have fulfilled their nefarious purpose well; this is what the end game of a decades-long, mind virus implant looks like. Defunding the university research departments would be the greatest accomplishment any leader who valued education and loved their country could ever have. It seems at present that no one would have the vision or courage to do this, but not to worry, comes the time soon enough when it will do it itself!

ACE

This sounds good. Well, it's ace! And being a child is ace. Well, not any more! Introducing our new school acronym, corrected for our times;

Adverse Childhood Experiences

Who would have thunk it, but apparently the more aces the kid has the worst the outcome. Ace is now a bad card. Check this out for inclusion in your kid's satchel with their playpiece: abuse, addiction, ADHD, anxiety, Attachment Loss Syndrome, attitude setting dysfunction, autistic spectrum, anger management issues, authority confrontational behaviour, Ariana Grande...and we're not even out of the letter A yet, FFS! Welcome to the 21stC.

Achievement Gap

That a more intelligent child does better in school than a less intelligent child may seem fairly obvious to a thinking person, but our schools have turned their face against nature and attribute this gap to unfair advantages or disadvantages. And have then adopted the social mission of 'closing the gap', without mention of the true cause of the gap. Of course, closing the gap fails again and again, but no matter the education bureaucrats and activists keep their jobs just the same. In reality, kids from poor family background do well in school if they are intelligent and the same holds true for more intelligent members of less intelligent races. Thusly, the achievement gap is in reality a manifestation of intelligence. One cannot say this, of course, as I have not said this here, as you can see.

If one wished to consider whether intelligence was the true factor in an achievement gap between different races, then one should express the question thusly:

The achievement gap in school and life outcomes between YDNA haplogroup R1a1 and YDNA haplogroup E1b1a.

Well, it will keep the handcuffs off your wrists while they look it up, and hopefully your escape taxi will have arrived by then.

Active Lessons

Yet another simple idea force-fed steroids until it becomes a monster. Rather than being something to consider in lessons as required, it has become something required regardless. And so we now have lessons engaging all the senses, activating all the target-oriented tickboxes, exchanging learning goals in dynamic settings, reinforcing skills through multiple pathways; but, honestly, it's just children wandering around not knowing what they are doing.

If you don't know what any of this means, don't worry, there's a training course for you.

Active lessons are the lesson philosophy for our ADHD age

NB, Active shooter and bomb drills are obviously exempted from this criticism. Nothing could be more important in your child's education than learning how not to get shot or blown up in schools. That's a real active lesson!

ADHD

Leon Eisenberg, the tribal inventor of this condition and, by an amazing coincidence, a friend of tribal Big Pharma, changed his mind about it and came to the obvious conclusion that it did not exist. That he was already in line at the loading gate for that big science conference in the sky, may have had something to do with his change of heart. That final ethics panel up there can bring down the deserving heavy judgement on him, hopefully ameliorated by his admittance of error. Still, damage done and shekels banked. Millions of boys are on Ritalin.

Alas, there's little money in health. All the money is in disease. Imagine the doctor said: *What your boy needs is fresh air and exercise, a hobby, real food and no TV or computer. His i phone is making him ill, get rid of it. Dump the energy drinks, they're poison. Make sure he gets a full night's sleep. He'll be cured in no time.*

Advent Calendar

As a sign o' the times, it is noted that this well-loved institution has, in the mind of the modern child, no known connection whatsoever to religion, being regarded exclusively as a pre-Christmas daily chocolate sweetie lottery. This has also become a human right (as per UN decree) to the extent that if a teacher (me) wishes not to do this, pupils complain and draw attention to other classes where this right is properly exercised.

NB, This refusal to issue the sweetie is due to loving concern about their metabolic health; the denial helping to reinforce the point – even if it only leads to a complaint. They'll thank me years later – although by that time I'll be dead. ☺

Advice

Re: multicultural benefits

'In the rare event of a firearms or weapons attack'

RUN, HIDE, TELL

For upper primary; Rally at muster point, Collect and prepare your firelock, Stand your ground, Return fire as commanded.

Re: for teachers

Good: see wise Seneca's entry under 'prepared'.

Bad: be yourself. This advice is independent of who you are.

Re: for pupils

Good: be yourself. This advice is dependent on who you are.

Bad: any advice given as advice. (Except this).

Re: for management

Your desires are unhealthy, your powers of resistance are weak, your plans are incoherent, your impulses are at odds with nature, and your system of values is false and confused.

AfL (Assessment for Learning)

An idea inherited from our monkey ancestors; you show another monkey how to use a stick, then provide appropriate level feedback on their efforts. Unfortunately, and I take full responsibility for this, the stick analogy has been interpreted literally by the educational establishment and they have used the AfL stick to beat, not pupils, but teachers for not using AfL resource packs provided by friends of the government minister who approved the attainment pack for enhancement, aka, APE Pack.

Assessment is for learning and if you don't learn better to assess your use of AfL resources, I'm going to take this stick and beat you with it at Friday's Anti-violence Assembly. (HT of Saint Francis's Primary, Drumchapel to anonymous P1 class teacher; the beating was figurative, but the threat was literal)

Now there is so much assessment going on that there is no time for learning as such. But this is a good thing because assessment is for learning anyway.

AfL, so that's what's what it means. Clever!

Africans

The gold standard in diversity. As monkeys would bananas, smiling faces and forever outstretched hands welcome our money and gifts, while temporarily providing protection against wicked guilt spells cast by witchdoctors in the BBC Newsround hut. Bad ju ju invariably makes the former disappear without discernible impact, while causing the latter to increase. Luckily, a cash top-up provides some more White privilege protection and those same endorphin-stroking smiles.

Paleface explorers are not always well received in the Dark Continent these days which unfortunately impacts on experiencing diversity directly, but something of the flavour of Wakandan culture can be experienced by import. It might be expensive, but in terms of the multicultural impact nothing can beat it.

We need many more happy jungle faces in our schools and universities to counteract the cruel, but true, charge that we are too pale and stale for a fair future, although even this benefit to us has a down side as the sub-Saharan space programme is losing some of its future rocket scientists. We can never be too grateful, literally.

Agency

The *word de jour* among educators. A mysterious thing that children lack, if lacking can get the teacher or school into trouble, or have it fully developed if having so can get the teacher or school into trouble.

Agenda, The

Here meaning the hidden intent, under the guise of something acceptable, to introduce something not acceptable. The talk is of love and inclusion, but the reality is hate and destruction of us.

Via the dysfunction and degeneracy you see now, with the chaotic end effect you can imagine by extrapolation from it, our children will arrive in a world at odds with their genetic and cultural heritage. And worse, by silently walking into demographic eclipse they will lack the numbers to defend their European civilisation and ultimately themselves. Many will say – indeed, they now openly do so – that they deserved this fate as they were racists and sexist and intolerant and anti-Semite. *So, good riddance!* This is the agenda.

This new world of sexual and racial 'justice' and multicultural replacement has been brought to the European world by Jewish controlled counter-culture in academia, entertainment and news media, and protected by the same group using their countless so-called charities, political control that spans all parties, war chest funding obtained by skillfully plundering state benefices and donated (tax deductible) by 100% controlled global banks, and the numerous organisations dedicated to this task

Its spear-point is aimed at women. This because of their conformist mindset; once flipped on any particular topic they become the footsoldiers of it and relentlessly police the domains for wrong thinkers. To this end, a generations-long campaign across all domains to present men as damaged and dangerous has been waged – and once the natural link between men and women is broken from the female side, it is broken no matter what men may think. This has been largely achieved and finds expression in attitudes prevalent among female primary teachers; and particularly so among the younger, childless cohort. Tacked onto this issue of male beastliness (the patriarchy), as a natural extension of the same fight for justice, were other aspects of the agenda relating to race, sex and all our history and cultural legacy.

Lawfare, backed by remote-control activists and bought political stooges, is permanently waged to demean and destroy traditional sources of national identity and succour. Perpetual racial outrage swirls around the public debate on anything, destabilising and killing trust between and within groups. This is the agenda's ambition. It seems to be working nicely. Any who disagree are publically marginalised or destroyed using tropes implanted in the public mind such as Nazi, sexist, homophobe, etc. Disagree further, and then you run into something that, although invisible, is gigantic.

As constitutionally naïve, transactionally trusting and non-tribal in our general mindset, it is very difficult for us as Europeans to understand this level of malevolence; of course, we can understand such at a personal level, as we may encounter jealousies, resentments and wickedness pathologised and directed towards the destruction of a irrationally hated subject, but scaled up to societal size and operating on an almost eternal timescale, our mind recoils from accepting it. Many understandably cannot counteract their lifetime of opinion programming and react emotionally by falling back on standard accusatory tropes – you hear them all the time now; a sign of the agenda meeting some resistance in its control of the public mind.

Why this agenda exists at all is a topic for another book, best left unpublished.

Megalomaniacal sociopathy; this apophthegm is here by mistake. Nobody's talking about it, and why should they? In fact, no one even knows what the saying means.

Agents for Change

Ever wondered where entitled, self-righteous, fantasy idealistic, opinionated, loud-mouthed, condemnatory, teen activists come from?

Another great idea from Wonderland to activate our children by means of this titled role (two per class) and a mandate to discuss and enforce justice initiatives in our schools. Their empowerment is faux, of course, and naturally they don't know what they are talking about because they are children, but the adults have to waste their time and degrade their integrity by pretending to take this seriously. Perhaps some do.

Some children, well primed by BBC Newsround, toxic home TV and the Scottish Government wish list, have morphed to macaws squawking back the party justice boilerplate. Disgracefully inflating their egos by allowing them to believe that their opinions have value and weight, we are actually preparing them, not just for the disappointment of reality, but for the tragic life of the opinionated tank girll, or the jaded, tweeting cynic by seventeen.

Luckily, many of the more sensible and less prolix little activist warriors thusly empowered, have no idea what all this is about and don't care. They aren't really agents and they aren't for change, unless it's a flume in the playground, or more chips and pizza at lunch.

These agents have no badges or guns yet, and so cannot enforce the world to come. But when they have, they will.

Agility

This is a quality that if it is not acquired young, it is not acquired. It should be a defining feature of being young (see, graceful), but is gradually becoming less so and increasingly replaced with disgraceful digital dexterity. This is of great consequence as it feeds into lifestyle and health options, and particularly future ones. The wheezing stiffy has trapped themselves into their life of wheezing stiffness.

The school solution is obvious – running in the corridor and leaping up and down stairs. Teachers could lead by example, perhaps chasing slow pupils along corridors, or tigging them at their desks to encourage a counter-tig around the classroom. The recalcitrant slow should be chastised as necessary:

Excuse me, you know the rules. No walking in the corridor. Now get going – quickly!

Certain suitable sections of the school building could be converted to parkour standard with money recovered from the class laptop budget. Weekly awards for top traceur in each class. Kids would love it. Teachers would fit into hot pants again; and what sort of man would object to that!

Allergens Advice

On milk carton; **MILK: 100% MILK DRINK. CONTAINS MILK. PACKAGED IN A FACTORY WHICH MAY HANDLE NUT PRODUCTS. CONSULT ALLERGENS TABLE**.

Evidence for the proposition that our schools are becoming more informed places. Now you know what a carton of milk contains.

Allergies

Allergies come in two forms, good and bad. Bad allergies are ones you don't have yet. Good allergies need action plans and training courses, inhalers and Epipens. The later of course have unfortunately short shelf lives and need constant replacement. Luckily, all these drugs are free up to the point you pay for them.

There is nothing suspicious in this, granted the presence of these hardly ever needed drugs reinforces the normality of drugs as prophylactics in the life of a child, and prepares the mind for more of the same later on. Cynics claim that this is a pharma scam of big fat hoor proportions; however, this jaundiced view is counteracted by the famous international kindness of global pharmaceutical companies, as can be ascertained by anyone who examines their conduct.

Amazing

How one essentially is, especially if a girl. There mere act of being born confers this power to our pupils regardless of ability, attitude or effort.

You are…! No questions asked, or even thought! How could there possibly be downsides to inflating children's opinions of themselves, as if there was a threshold effect from constant use of superlatives. Stupid question, silly you for thinking it!

By the way, Reader, you are amazing!

Anal Positive

Government minister demands more anal workshops in schools:

Scottish schools must be more homosexual positive. Tolerance is no longer enough. Our government is introducing curricular content aimed at putting the gay lifestyle at the heart of our future family policy.

Clapping is mandatory at conferences when the rainbow icon appears. Please return your conference buttplugs to the receptacle provided on exiting the bubble foam room. Remember to wash your hands, etc.

Annual Review

Crossed the t's and dotted the i's, met the targets; prove it. It is usually claimed this this potentially fraught meeting with management should be regarded as a coaching situation.

Head Teacher to annual reviewee: *I want you to regard this meeting as a coaching experience. There's a coach waiting outside to take you to Kinlochbervie, don't bother getting a return ticket.*

Anti-

Denoting a powerful force against, especially; racism, bullying, Semitism. Often partnered with -phobia, to double up on the White guilt.

If a word starts with this, then you know it's an idea whose end effect is the opposite of whatever is claimed. If it was only our money and time being wasted on assembly harangues, school initiatives, workshops and all the bin-bound paraphernalia that inevitably accompanies this futile journey to the promised land, then that would be maddening enough. But in fact the endless talking of how bad and dysfunctional we Whites are as a race worms its way into our children's minds, challenging their innate White decency and posits its apparent absence as a moral deficiency on their part. And thusly opens their mind to accepting their other apparent character and societal deficiencies, and then the necessary corrective therapies, workshops and funding. And, of course, the accusations and hypocrisies that always accompany such correctives to our moral deficiencies. Only we Whites need anti-.

This is where our children are taught to hate themselves. This is where our children are exposed to adult idiocy, betrayal and hypocrisy. All these antis are devouring us from within.

Luckily, built into the template of many children is a self-correcting mechanism that comes to instinctively recognise and resist attempts to manipulate them; it's called a bullshit detector. Such children come to embrace the opposite, and by their resistance become the torchbearers of God's simple truths in that anti-chaotic future.

On the other hand, if anti is spelt like this, AUNTIE, then it's probably ok. (Other than Auntie Beeb, obviously!)

Ella (P2): *I'm becoming an auntie soon!*

Teacher: **Are you sure? Your big sister's only fourtee....Oh, that's nice.**

Anti-bully

Ref: various initiatives conducted through the school year to prevent bullying. Here we are referring to the specific programmes with their attendant workshops, assemblies, anti-bully week, etc., and not the counsel of a wise teacher resolving a pupil dispute.

Anti-bully programmes, on the face of it, seem a nice idea. However, on thinking it through to consequences, it is revealed to be less than useless.

Firstly, all the programmes amount to (guess what?), conversations about feelings; and these always lead to misunderstanding about what constitutes bullying, which result in exaggerated claims and intentional misrepresentations as children access the currently popular victim culture – and thusly strengthen its hold. Another consequence of the constant reference to bullying is that the idea of such as a constant feature of school life, as opposed to an occasional problem, is planted deep with all its potential for anxiety.

All the solutions oblige adult intervention, indeed, many explicitly forbid self-solution. This is unfortunate as it merely postpones, probably until adult life, the necessary learning of self-reliance, and even courage, in facing up to bullying – and such qualities of the strong self are much harder to acquire as an adult! For boys in particular, this de-legitimises, as it denies them, the best recourse to resolving a bullying situation – the fight. Such need not even come to blows; squaring off to each other is often sufficient to resolve the problem. Each understands the limits of the other and, matching each other in the willingness to resolve the dispute physically, they can retire, honours even, and become friends again – as little boys typically do.

This last point illustrates a failing of many similar initiatives, in that they fail to account for differences in how males and females process life, and in this case experience and react to bullying. This being compounded by the mentors of such programmes being females, who do not understand, or are unsympathetic to, a boy's perspective. Their female social mind wants to put everything into a female social context; but this is overthinking it for a boy's more physical world. In a little boy's world, a fight is seldom the bad thing many females assume it to be. However, in taking away this option, they inadvertently take away a crucial aspect of his masculinity because it is this willingness to resort to the physical that makes a boy a wee man and worthy of the respect of his peers, and (when that time comes) the loving attention of girls.

Finally, such programmes do not do achieve their stated goals anyway; bullying is not lessened. And the implication of adult protection is a false one – another empty offer by adults! Once again, we meet with apparent nice ideas which turn out to be just talking and virtue signalling and training workshops – all wasting time and money. And offering to opt-out option. A bit like bullying actually.

Where are the ninja turtles when you need them?

Anti-privilege

This gets its own entry as the up and coming 'anti-'of school life. This new privilege is to be paradoxically achieved by joining the anti-privilege bandwagon; where one confirms the prior enjoyment of an, allegedly, unjust privilege of being born White in a White country, and one's public shame at so doing. One need not surrender the said privileges while denying them; as long as all the right things are said and tweeted publicly, all is ok. One has proven oneself brave.

Since many of the people preaching this are White, it makes anti-Whiteness of this phenomenon something like a suicide cult. Non-Whites, of course, logically participate in these anti-White pogroms for personal gain and racial vengeance, but the Whites are driven by something deeper. Anti-whiteness is the logical endpoint for White people driven by self-loathing. It is the ultimate form of self-abnegation

This supposed sign of being deep and, of course, virtuous, is proof of how easily tractored the mainly, in this case, female mindset is. All it takes is for the media to assiduously promote this idea until the tweets take over and make it a phenomenon. The calls for it to be incorporated into the school justice curriculum follow quickly, as they indeed have. It shows that without some limiting principle operating in society, there are no limits and no way to control fanatics created by our enemies in the global media.

The flagellants of the 21st Century are coming to school as instructors; and this mindset describes many younger primary teachers. It would not surprise if at some near future the little whips make a comeback as a fashionable accoutrement for the kneeling White pupil suppliant.

Anti-Semitism

In a primary school? Yes, Nazis are everywhere; but don't worry about finding them, someone will do it for you. In fact, they are doing it right now.

Despite not currently, nor ever having been, a feature of Scottish society, far less primary schools, anti-Semitism is coming fully armed and lawyered up to school, with the usual calls for loss of jobs, ruin etc. Whether one is an actual anti-Semite is irrelevant, any comment of any nature of anything connected to Jews, may be sufficient. This has happened many times recently in the Western world.

This state of affairs is predicated on the arrival of newly up-scaled Holocaust teaching materials and courses which will increasingly take the central place in the study of WW2, and following this, the putative lessons of the Holocaust which undergird the wider social justice message which our schools are dedicated to promulgating. The fun and games will start when the teacher training courses become obligatory and school-based commitments to combat (putative) anti-Semitic behaviours are demanded; for example, embedded within the school's mission statements, or extra anti anti-Semitic workshops. Such has already happened with the 'Never Again' Holocaust Education Act in the US. People (i.e., teachers and parents) may wonder where all this apparent White race anti-Semitic hate is coming from, as they never encounter it except in TV shows and news media; and that will be the first mistake they make. Should they question beyond this about anything connected to Jews, Israel, the Holocaust and the inclusion of such within the primary curriculum, then they may well find themselves considering it at Her Majesty's pleasure.

When this comes here, we expect that only in-class arrests of secret anti-Semite pupils (possibly even unknown to themselves!) and probable Holocaust-denier parents, will stamp out this persistent and apparently Gentile-exclusive scourge. This situation is, of course, unconnected to a pathologised victim-persecutor identity, wedded to an outsized, aggressive Levantine tribal power – which is why this has not been mentioned.

Ask not what your country can do for you – but ask what you can do for Israel.

Apologise

Sometimes you are made to, but often the obligation is tacit. If someone makes an issue about something to which you understand that you are somehow or other implicated, this creates the moral obligation to apologise for what you have done. As a race we are generally able to do this, as no loss of face accompanies the apology, nor resentment follows.

This simple situation is complicated if the alleged deed requiring apology is only attributable to you by association, for example by your race, religion, class or family; in other words, collective blame.

Thusly, by emphasising privilege and unfair advantage, does the secure and happy child feel a certain guilt for the disadvantage of the less fortunate pupil. Or the White child confronted with the unfortunate lives lived by slum, jungle or sandbox cohort equivalents elsewhere. This guilt is intended, of course; race hustlers, sex warriors and political class activists earn their bread and butter so. (The next layer of recidivism involves the end point of this guilt, but let us leave that cheery thought for another entry.) Having no possibility of personally apologising for collective blame, the child just has to live with this guilt and try their best to atone by symbolic acts of apology, which the school encourages by way of charity strong-arming.

In the future such charitable acts will be allowable against race and social class guilt quotas and help reduce the allotted punishment, and possibly even the need for anti-depressants. Certificates of Apology may be issued by special 'Apology Doctors', following payment of the processing fee and public sackcloth and ashes statement of contrition – this could be a yearly thing, like your insurance or favela protection money.

Unfortunately. those currently seeking protection from accusations by their apologies and thusly drawing a line under this topic, are finding that our new world of absolute moral truths is being extended by casting the new morality backward in time. Once our ancestors are anachronistically judged and condemned by time-travelling truths, these same judgements rebound back across the centuries to condemn us too. And it does not use to point to the absurdity and unfairness of this; for absurd and unfair is its point. Alas, there is a lot of White apologising still to come, and with it the modern version of Danegeld – Blackgeld!

The new school day shall start, not with a prayer or benediction, but with a formal apology for the guilt of ancestors that lives on in the present. Without even mentioning it, you already know what you are going to be apologising for. And you already know that the apology is not enough.

This power feeds on itself – it is nothing short of weaponised debasement.

Applause

The applause of posterity, that's the motivator for our educational overlords. In the real future, it will be curses instead.

Appreciation

A powerful force in developing positive emotions is expressing appreciation to others, a practice that is as beneficial to the giver as to the receiver. This can take many forms, a handwritten note, a card, a little gift, an e-mail, a call, or a conversation, but it has to be deliberate and set aside for this purpose; as a private moment. It also has to be unique to the receiver and specific, and the more so, the better the impact. Schools make much of using this power with respect to pupils. Alas, with respect to the teachers, other than generic 'so hard working' throw-aways at parent assemblies, appreciation is a rare visiting bird to Teacher Island.

Assembly

This institution has been co-opted by 'the agenda' to ensure that no opportunity is missed to collectively reinforce guilt via the problems of others. Whereas, in former time, the school assembly served to collectively celebrate some achievement or remember a calendar event, now it serves as a Banzai session for social justice. Pride too is evoked, but only where it pertains to the celebration of pupils accepting their guilt and atoning by various shekel-based activities. The unwitting children in this suicidal cult have their innocence mocked by being awarded traitor prizes.

HT: ...*and for raising nearly £600 to fund anti-sexist workshops for Homo naledi immigrants to Possilpark, Glasgow through sponsored monkey walking to school, P5 will get another 10 minutes playtime this Friday!* [Widespread cheers]

Translation in honest English: ...*and for raising through emotional blackmail and via insultingly trivial activities nearly 600 shekels for their UN overlords to spend encouraging more ancestral human families* in Pangaea Land to have even more children they cannot afford to care for, the P5 traitors will be marked for this shame by another 10 minutes left alone in the playground this Friday to contemplate their folly, while others are enjoying their classwork!* [Widespread cheers]

Assembly Spy

TURN IN ANY SUSPICIOUS-LOOKING CLASSMATES TO THE AUTHORITIES

This is a law enforcement idea to introduce and normalise the surveillance state to infants. The entire assembly thusly set up as spies, regular little grasses, kapos and victims. Every day is schadenfreude day when the school has assembly spies. Straight

---

* In real life the money does not go near any needy or pullulating Third World 'families'.

from the Stasi playbook, preparing the mind for full spy when one goes to university or surfs Faceborg.

Who is today's spy? It could be the person sitting next to you, or your best friend. So sit nice and listen to this video where Barney explains how wonderful gay marriage is.

TRAITOR TEACHER ARRESTED IN CLASS AFTER ASSEMBLY SPY OVERHEARS SECRET CONVERSATION CRTICISING PRIDE DAY

Attainment

This fashionable word always seems to arrive bearing a censure, for however much of it there is, is never enough. And of course, this failure to achieve the necessary level of attainment is ultimately the teacher's fault! Each use of this word is, then, equivalent to two canings on the teacher's bottom, or a slap on the face if they would prefer this.

Formerly denoting something which was achieved by effort and thus infrequently mentioned, this coin has flipped and attainment is now frequently mentioned, but unconnected to effort. And anyway, not successfully achieved in modern schools, except when being used by assorted taxpayer-funded educational parasites to self-congratulate. E.g., *The lager vouchers for parents scheme has, as we predicted, raised the attainment level of pupils in poverty by the same percentage as the alcohol strength of our sponsored super lager.* (Heineken Attainment in Action Conference 2018, The Bier Keller, Irvine)

Low levels of pupil attainment are often claimed to be due to low expectations. As to why schools have low expectations – well, obviously, some prejudice will be found, no doubt systemic, and of the sort that needs well-funded studies and workshops to correct. But whatever the cause, identifying nonsense pedagogy, low intelligence, deficient pupil application or rubbish parents, will always be the wrong answer to say out loud.

NB. In real life, attainment (or whatever you wish to call it) is raised in direct proportion to the amount of time the parent spends with their child at home supporting their learning. Who could have guessed this surprising fact?

Attention

1. What the child is supposed to bring to the lesson, and there was a time when they were *supposed* to bring this. Now its presence is entirely contingent upon the teacher being sufficiently entertaining, which itself is dependent upon a whizz-bang intro, flashy computer presentation, battery of pedagogic techniques, engagement, etc. However, I say to you that these conditions of success are in fact grounds for failure and that the child's attention actually comes from the teacher being worthy of it, as a person.

2. As in standing to; namely, erect, in line, still, neutral face. And quiet. And listening. This ability has apparently been bred out of the gene pool. Admittedly not needed for surfing the web or watching TV, nevertheless this is not a trivial loss to our children for it was an essential factor in developing self-discipline. Teaching and learning was so much easier when pupils could stand at attention, the same for delivering volley fire. The Iron Duke and Boney find agreement on this issue.

Avatars

Low artistic level, computer-generated artwork of cute alien humanoids, unicorns, monkeys and the like, which children in class are obliged to identify with in the promotion of some or other educational concept, or as a personification of a personal quality that the child has as a target. They are also used as personal markers for their work – like a sort of cartoon level signature. The modern equivalent of the olden times' illiterate's X mark!

These are really cool and fun, an idiot colleague once said. And therein lies the problem; no awareness of how these apparently trivial features, in turn trivialise the mind. For in, legitimising the IT world of which they are an essential part, in a *quid pro quo* the mind is led to further accept, identify with and eventually embed these computer symbols, which gives them the power of suggestion in other realms that connect with selling and manipulating opinion. Control needs its activating symbols, and these avatars are operant conditioning of our children on a gigantic, worldwide web, scale.

In creating this strongly visual mental landscape for our children, populated by digitalised and manic avatars, I wonder if their thought processes too become, as it were, pixilated, and that somehow this compromises their still developing literate culture? It seems not unreasonable, then, to regard the promotion of such avatars to our children as a sort of digital steroid boost to our future language of public discourse – Orwellian Newspeak!

The new world order unrolls their battle flag depicting the upside-down cross, the smiley and the 'cool' friendly unicorn avatar. You will have heard it said that computer avatars and emojis are just little cartoons and that their over-righteous opponents should 'lighten up', but I say to you that evil always wears a smiling face ☺ and always appears innocent. Until *that* time!

Awareness

'Raising Awareness'; the guise under which brainwashing is introduced into primary schools.

Here is a recent selection of topics from one term mentioned as issues to which our primary age children should be more aware;

child poverty, transgender rights, gambling addiction, child soldiers, domestic violence (against women), childhood depression, eating issues, chat room predators, homophobic bullying, sex grooming and woman's disempowerment. Learn this before your times tables, ye children of the Curriculum of Excellence!

Issues which are the domain of adults, and over which children have no transformative power whatsoever, are touted as central to a child's education. These are then proselytised by teachers whose gender instincts, training and life experience makes them uniquely unsuitable for the task they so willingly execute; being, as they are, generally incapable of considering the various topics in any terms, except that of extreme superficiality (i.e., that good intentions must surely lead to good outcomes). That primary age children cannot properly understand these topics, and anyway process them in a way quite different from that intended, is not considered. Indeed, considered even less, is the issue of the appropriateness of such topics being introduced in the first place.

Anyway, what is the child supposed to do with all this information about the world?

B

Bad Boy

The default position for the XY variant. Even if evidently 'good', this is a temporary state pending the evolutionary final form of patriarchal bully and sexploiter, just like the estranged father. It is a sad and sobering thought that your lovely little boy will become one of them whose deserved replacement by more coloured and tolerant varieties will all too soon be achieved.

Bad Deeds

A free society cannot function unless its members assume or are made to assume full responsibility for their actions. This must start as soon as. Misconduct must be challenged, however, the progressive ideas that inform current practice do not permit this. Bad deeds, however intentionally motivated, do not draw down the necessary incrimination, instead they are mitigated. Being viewed as due to factors, typically psychological or social, beyond the purview and control of the perpetrator. Following on from this, there is no culpability, no judgement, no punishment, no contrition and no forgiveness. Misplaced kindness in wishing to exculpate the guilty is a serious error here. The perpetrator needs the judgment. And so does their society, whether at adult level or scaled down to classroom size. With the absence of judgement and visible, but tempered, punishment, the moral order is mocked and a powerfully contrarian situation is set up which leads to more of the same. The 'therapeutic' interventions often exclusively mandated as solutions, make the situation worse. With no crime recognised and no punishment administered, why should a child NOT behave so again? Indeed, they may be led to this.

Some children not only need, but crave, judgement for their actions, and especially boys. These may keep repeating the same behaviours in a forlorn, unconscious attempt to get the judgement *and* the punishment; this as a sort of psychic atonement. This can become a dangerous situation for a boy, as it strongly contains the possibility of being misunderstood, especially so by female teachers and support service experts, who are also more likely to be women. These are in a position to make grave mistakes handling any boy unlucky enough to get into the telescopic cross-hairs of their psychological profiling.

Barriers

Ref: academic attainment;

to entry to STEM:IQ

to minority academic success: IQ

to attainment levels for children of poverty: IQ

to grade level recovery programme success: IQ

to success targets with new school initiatives: IQ

to lack of presence of minority teachers: IQ

to failure of profession to keep high IQ teachers: IQ

Barriers, Inclusion

Barriers to inclusion also includes barriers to; diversity, multiculturalism, equity, tolerance, gender, etc

In a primary school these barriers are typically a locked door with NOT WELCOME signs, or interlocking steel fences topped with razor wire. The attitudes which sustain these barriers are White racism and privilege.

In real life, of course, us being a rational and open-minded people, there are no, and generally never were, unfair barriers. Incompetence, entitlement and sporting a stinking attitude are not unfair barriers. If there had been any barriers at all, none of this barriers complaint would have been allowed. And you would not have to read this entry.

Beauty

Beauty brings and affirms joy, and in sorrow provides consolation. It is a great motivator. It is where we find awe and that connection to the transcendent which we all seek, knowingly or not. As beauty inspires the spirit, just as ugliness depresses it, one has to wonder about the intention behind the deliberate promotion of so much ugliness in public life; this effect reaches far beyond choosing less aesthetic, budget options.

As a child one is never more able to delight in beauty, innocently and for its own sake. And it is a great tragedy that while there is so much beauty that could be found and appreciated in primary school life, or drawn from the wider cultural and natural world, it hardly ever is. For example, I have never attended a school assembly in which something beautiful has been referenced directly and the children's attention directed to this beauty, and the wonderful gift that comes simply from the appreciation of it.

For many children, typically those who are most needful of it in their lives, perhaps it may seem as if beauty doesn't exist. Of course, the greatest motivator is a beautiful woman; proof of this is to be found in much of our great art, as muse and subject. But keep this a secret and don't tell women or wee boys.

Benefits

Ref: of being a teacher.

1. Material benefits of job; pencils, rubbers, paper clips, jotters, two packets of Blu-tak a year. These could be useful if running a Saturday morning car boot stationary business, or perhaps more randomly, odd sales one could make to a guy you met in a pub.

2. Career benefits of dedication and initiative; None.

Best, The

What's that? For your children; don't give them an i phone, play with them, read stories, no TV, walk, real food, family dinners.

Or, is it: *Sorry. No time, 'cause I'm too busy.* [tweeting and checking the status of twits like me.] *And anyway, the Celebrity Idiot Massage Parlour Challenge is coming on soon.*

If only the parish still employed a Cruelty Man, he would not lack for work.

Best Fighter

He's still there, although not necessarily known. Even to himself!
Likewise, the various subsidiary categories, right down to
school diddy.

Such a person served a purpose in a boy's world. This template by
which boys, for good or ill, independently ordered their own affairs
and hierarchies, has been replaced by adult female intercession; <u>the
worst possible outcome for the disputants</u>! Thus postponing, perhaps
even permanently, *that* moment when it's just the two of you, the
reckoning. Following which, even the loser is a winner too!

Betrayal

The myriad betrayals, catalogued in this work, that the primary
school effortlessly effects, corrodes the soul of adults and pupils alike.
It is in the nature of this phenomenon that even the beneficiaries
become damaged too, if only inasmuch as they connect to the wider
community; although, one naturally wishes for a consequence more
corporeal in nature. I have it on good authority that such a wish
will be granted; however, we must lay aside the exploration of this
pleasant thought or be subject to excessive delay in our cargo of
nonsense reaching port.

Bitey

See, benefits of diversity.

Along with spitty and knifey, this is the future world of multicultural
nursery and infant departments. Such a 'culturally alternative
response' to disappointment tends to die out in mid-primary, but

such deep traditions reassert themselves by secondary, allowing those teachers and pupils (especially female) who may have missed the opportunity to be enriched first time around to catch up on their diversity quota. What goes around comes around, as they say!

It has been suggested that it could be the case that biting is, rather than an alternative cultural tradition, more a case of mistaken identity with respect to food. The biter implying no censure, but is merely hungry and has confused the White child with the former contents of the jungle cauldron. Perhaps, 'currently former contents' is more accurate.

Blackmail

Although it's everywhere, pressuring all our children via guilt inducing videos and sponsorships, curiously the further you get from black and male the more powerful the effect, reaching its limbic zenith with White and girl. (*Thank you for noticing this clever pun*)

Almost like Supergirl and just as White, how many has she saved by sponsored kicking a ball for Africa or fighting for tolerance by selling packet mini muffins to her teacher and classmates, but always paying for the privilege? Rainbow tattoos – only 50p.

Blackmailed, really, into a world of suicidal kindness, by puppet-masters with the ethics of an insect who would squeeze her adrenals, and may yet, once the blackmail has done its job.

Blame

Follows the teacher with a mischievous grin;

1. Immediate unfair blame: child swallows (secretly and accidently) a whole mint and chokes without dying, child gets dirty on the way home *after* school; child loses coat *before* school day starts; child secretly swaps lunch ticket with classmate and eats meat lunch instead of vegetarian; child loses lunch change; child accidently wears other child's socks after swimming; child needs toilet but doesn't ask – stains pants; child forgets that the class did sing them a birthday song; child complains about being currently bullied by another child who left school the previous term!; child allegedly never given the chance to answer questions; boy child getting chased by girl classmates at playtime; child being forced to drink water; child not allowed to drink water, etc, etc. All subject to a written complaint.

It's catching and spreading:

Primary school teachers to blame for the First World War.

2. Final unfair blame: At the terminus of all the policies and practices, when the advocates and activists sneak away from the school shambles they have created, teachers will still be blamed.

3. Ultimate blame: At the ultimate level of recursiveness, arguably no one is to blame for the mess our schools are in. All the actors are just playing the roles assigned by history's big wheel. However, at the level at which humans operate, this blame amnesty should not be extended to those who sought office and leadership, but then betrayed it by lack of diligence, general incompetence, greed and moral cowardice. Few professions would allow such to escape consequence; this should start with returning the money they stole in consideration of a reduced secondment to the chain gang.

Blank Slate

The foundational element of a quasi-religious egalitarian belief system. Challenging this belief provokes believers into angry professions of faith and accusations of apostasy.

For safety, author recommends a daily profession of faith via the following catechism.

#1. There is no such thing as inherited intelligence.

#2. Any apparent manifestation of such is a result of prejudice.

#3. No platform to deniers.

Blessing

see under; just deserts

Blessed are the proud in spirit,

for theirs is the kingdom of Sheol.

Blessed are those who despise

for they will be forgotten.

Blessed are the opinionated,

for they will inherit the storm.

Blessed are those who hunger and thirst for deviance,

for they will be judged.

Blessed are the hateful,

for they will shown no mercy.

Blessed are the pure in dogma,

for they will see Lucifer.

Blessed are the bully,

for they will be called Social Justice Warriors.

Blessed are those who persecute because of feelings,

for theirs is the kingdom of this world.

NB. This clever, topical riff on Jesus' spoken blessing, as alleged by Matthew and Luke, is particularly apt for our school life. This adaptation was not composed by me, unfortunately and alas I cannot recall from whence it was copied, for I should very much like to acknowledge authorship.

Body Positive

We now have many 'body positive' children in primary school. The term itself is another example of the evil sophistry used to turn minds against themselves. Everyone knows what this euphemism means and how it actually connotes its opposite. Signs of beauty and reproductive fitness are innate to our understanding to such an extent that they can be immortalised in marble; no repeating of a lie can alter this. And it does our children, and particularly those sized like kitchen freezers, no good to delude themselves that they are healthy and look good; and should be encouraged to feel pride at their frankly appalling, physical condition. Let's agree to treat everyone with respect, no matter what they look like, but not delude ourselves with such deceptions and lazy justifications that act as an impediment to self-improvement. The body positive child and their parents should be motivated to change, not wallow. Fat ankles and breasts on boys should never be associated with 'positive'. If only for the sake of their future ruined health, the body positive could do

44

with a dose of body negative. An 8 year old should not look like the Ghostbuster's mascot.

For our own sake, too, we should resist the further intrusion of a deceitful lexicon into public discourse and not otherwise encourage the invasion of public spaces by more ugliness.

Bomb Duty Officer

Ref: benefits of diversity

One might expect this essential position to be paid out of the diversity fund, or at least a risk bonus based on the number of incidents, however, no financial compensation accompanies the post; a self-funded sinecure, as the saying goes. In compensation, it attracts the highest level of minimum level recognition from our political betters. As our education minister noted:

We are passionate about our BDOs. They are important part of our commitment to the future multicultural schools.

This praise is understandable, the future multicultural school is partly predicated on not having children blown up while learning about diversity. Most children would, of course, welcome their school being blown up, but not while in it.

This anti-tamper bomb is too complicated for me to defuse. We'll need to send for Ali in P4, he'll be able to sort this out! (overheard BDO remark to HT)

NB. Only BDOs, P7s and those children whose family background naturally includes such knowledge are permitted to attempt to defuse a bomb. This has to be done discretely, as alerting the whole school to the calamity could cause a panic and provide anti-diversity intolerants with tweeting ammunition.

Books

Books are like Kryptonite to children introduced to i life too early;
this now being almost all children. Alas, when children consume
video images for learning instead of books, effectively all they do is
consume images, for little to no learning occurs. A recently added
problem for those promoting children's books is the risk of otherwise
wholesome stories being identified as racist and sexist, and
possibly even by implication, anti-Semitic or transphobic. Indeed,
with *Biggles in the Jungle*, you could simultaneously cover all the
forbidden categories. Good old Biggles, forever flying into trouble!
None of these prejudice claims need be remotely true to have their
intended effect, of course.

For many children, perhaps most, the only source of books in their
life is school. However, one must keep in mind that children's book
publishing is a fully integrated part of the globalist media and
counter-culture propaganda effort, and so such titles as make it to
the classroom have already been vetted for the correct political and
sexual values. Should promoting such become oppressive to the
teacher, the perfect liberator can be found in *The Iliad*. And children
love it! Some, however, believe that Homer has been dining off his
White privilege for a few millennia too long. And as a harbinger of
what is to come, certain Phoenician Navy officers, currently seconded
as school teachers, recently celebrated by Tweeter LOLs their role
in the removal of Homer from their school's approved reading list –
this being in the interests of tolerance and anti-Whiteness, naturally.
Philistines? – not exactly, but close enough.

Boys

Boys are the best!

I wonder if it seems to them – as it does to me – that everywhere boys turn, society is against them? For it would not be unreasonable for a visiting alien lifeform, say from a Star Trek type future, on consuming our media to conclude that boys were an unfortunately gendered sub-species currently transitioning to an improved, less troublesome version, via beneficial drug regimes and UN-sponsored fem-ducation.* Of course, little boys cannot consider this as directly as I have expressed it, but perhaps they sense something hostile radiating from their teles and i phones. Certainly, the idea that your entire society was somehow against you, merely for being what you are, would have been literally unthinkable to boys of an earlier age. But now?

And this whimsy leads us to reflect on the long war against boys going on in primary school; partly; this is intentionally directed against their interests and natural proclivities, and partly as the unconscious expression of a hostile, feminist-inspired mindset natural to certain female teachers of our time. All this takes place against a backdrop of unrelenting attacks against White adult males in wider society, and so it is naïve to assume that such poisoned filtrate does not reach little boys. Although it may seem from the practical way they continue their activities, that such attacks pass them by, we must not confuse the absence of direct evidence for the evidence of absence.

Here we argue that this effect translates to a slow trauma of self-doubt, confusion and disappointment. The psychic weight of this builds up, eventually it must find its outlet. Here the tragedy continues, for at this moment they may well find no-one to turn to

---

* I am not commenting here on the aetiology of the trans phenomenon, but just referring to it as a little boy might understand it.

in their broken family landscape. And those potential surrogates in the media and sporting sphere that are often held up as templates, actually epitomise, and even proselytise, the very values that have led our boys to this killing field.

Making males more like females, and females more like males, will result in the ideal sterile and disposable worker drone that will serve its master's corporation, or just disappear as required by their shekel-sticky overlords. In this context, the current push for transgenderism may not be a coincidence.

What does it mean to be a Western boy in 2021? The world ahead does not look favourably on you. And no safe spaces, not even your own country. And certainly not your classroom!

Brain-damaged

Ref: of modern children.

In multiple, overlapping ways: a combination of poor diet, excessive sugars, heavy metals in bloodstream, little exercise, extraordinarily poor sleep patterns, absence of the natural world, confusing and excessive choices, artificial lighting, dehydration, failure to sanction improper behaviour, improper praise, hyper-sexualisation, too much device and screen time and other myriad forms of parental neglect typically contingent upon parents excessive personal access to social media and TV.

See, Sleep.

Brain Gym

Let's clear this up right away; there's no gym or brains involved. In practice this activity resembles a two year old waving goodbye to their granny, from which activity it was probably developed. One's brain actually gets the same 'neuro-physiological' workout as head scratching or tying shoelaces. A normal person would think that education department chiefs would laugh this head shaking nonsense out of the door, but to think this is to completely misunderstand the essential nature of such 'chiefs'. Actually, they can't wait to spend your money and waste teacher time with a six part ('career enhancing') course training this nonsense. The charlatan that made this up really must have been laughing all the way to the bank. (Would that it were the lunatic asylum instead!)

One may consider this a harmless nonsense. But the relentless conveyer belt of such pseudo-scientific baffle preps the mind for more of the same. Legitimises the advocates of such ideas, makes one indifferent to the costs and inures one to cons, so common do they become. The questions that should get asked, thus don't even get thought!

IDIOT TEACHER: *What questions? I don't even know what you're talking about!* [Takes out phone and checks status]

Brand Loyalty

Childhood education has been remodelled as the place for building brand loyalty. Alas, the only loyalty found in schools is to the IT products produced by the IT giants and placed in class by complicit administrators and previously conditioned teacher-dupes. Thusly is the future customer base developed among children, their brains rewired for computer input and the wider social message contained in the associated products promoted. The capture of hundreds of millions of minds hardly noticed, nor the implications considered.

Teacher-dupe: *Google have invited me to test their new laptop and the apps come free too, how cool is that! Oh, by the way, I've just won a speedboat in the Nigerian lottery.*

Of course, once out of school, the children can conveniently convert their school accounts to personal ones. There is no reason to be worried about the personality and marketing profiles they will have built up since childhood. It's Google, we can trust them; if you can't trust Jewish globalist oligarchs, who can you trust!

Breakfast Club

From: *You've Got to be Kidding me!*; Chapter 666

Another good idea, come to grief in its meeting with reality, represented in this case by dietary habits and nutritional knowledge.

In what way is Coco Pops, toast with jam and orange juice an improvement on nothing for the already plumping Scottish child? This entire breakfast consists of various forms of sugar. Spiking insulin is exactly the wrong start to the day. And why are children given low-fat milk?

Actually, the breakfasts typically proffered at the clubs (as carbohydrate and straight sugar) could be considered as evil metabolic training for a ruinous future of insulin management by drug. If a Satanic pharma corporation could choose the breakfast menu with a view to creating a future market for insulin products, this is what they would pick. Actually, maybe they do.

Broad General Education

The BGE was stomping about making a lot of noise recently, but he's been put back in his place and (by popular teacher vote) redefined as knowledge about: X factor contestants, Come Dine With Me contestants, Britain's Bake Off contestants, Wife Swap contestants, Love Island contestants, Strictly Come Dancing contestants, and ~~the glories of European culture, be they are scientific, engineering, arts~~. Twitter.

Honestly, so completely has TV shaped the world of reference among primary school teachers that there is no way such an idea could be meaningfully introduced. In any case, it risks running foul of the R word.

You may imagine a staffroom discussion about high art, or find teachers thrilled at the prospect of introducing such for its transcendental qualities in the lives of the pupils, but you will never see or hear it. ☺

Broken Families

The ultimately destroyers of society, effected at the practical level by the broken children of such families ruining the school experience for everyone else. Such families never attract censure, except secretly by the unfailingly based cleaners and the occasional clear-thinking teacher, but often enjoy sympathy and limitless support; the exact opposite of what they need. Indeed, when they come in holy form (the single mother) they not infrequently find themselves lauded as worthy recipients of the school's prime directive, tolerance.

Bullshit

Ref: The Curriculum for Excellence

Everywhere 'excellence' goes it leaves behind bullshit; bombastic claims, inflated egos, denials of reality, failure to justify, falsified results, hypocrisy. All the better, then, to prepare our children for more of the same; the empty words which make the lie.

E.g., Signs seen on class doors;

EXCELLENCE EVERY DAY (pressure starts at P2!)

and the ultimate mind implant – the rainbow poster.

NB. For those just returned to planet Earth: the rainbow does not mean what it used to mean.

Bully

It used to be a simple thing to identify a bully by their works, and just as easy to fix them by a dose of their own medicine:

One day these four ninja turtles saw a bully beating up a fat kid, so the ninja turtles kicked his ass.

Alas, such old school solutions generated no income for workshop meisters and the other collectors of the public purse. This has been fixed now:

The Respect Me! pen I was given free at the anti-bully workshop has had a dramatic effect on bullying in our school. When the bullies see it, they are stopped dead in their tracks.

However, in our age of the parent tweeter posse, public shaming of wrong opinions, puppet pupil enforcers of the orthodoxy, teacher targets, the 'intolerance of the intolerant', who exactly are the bullies now? As the poster says:

JOIN THE CURRIE ANTI-BULLY CLUB

YOU WONT REGRET IT!

(but you will if you don't!)

Burnout

...it's going to get you!

C

Cancel Culture

Ref: to the tendency to disrespect and challenge every aspect of established White culture from a position of total ignorance and employ threats, direct disruption, vandalism and assault in achieving this end.

The fruition of the all NLP and agitprop of the primary school years finds the pupil not just well-seeded for radical harvest in their teenie years, but the radicalism flowering early with all the correct opinions manifesting themselves as parroting. We got a first taste of this with the 'spontaneous' pupil reaction to Greta T's alarmist climate activism.* And more recently, idiot parents have sanctioned their primary age children's involvement in the BLM movement – and we can expect more of suchlike copycatting spilling into school life. It could be argued that primary age children are too young to spontaneously engage in such advocacy, and this is true; however, the tacit encouragement of teachers who embrace such values and the direct encouragement of certain tweet-hungry parents, added to MSM complicity, will ensure that the children will get full exposure to each new cancel culture campaign and will be increasingly activated to this end.

A template of indignant, self-righteous behaviour has been proffered to the well-meaning idiot-dupe, the resentful who need to be breaking things to feel any self-worth and those who judge their

---

* Imagine being a scold at 16! How pitiful is the exploitation of this girl.

power by their ability to offend. And for the race warriors, perpetual racial outrage has been legitimised. All this will come to school.

Eventually, some attention-seeking parent/child combination, or video postings by activist teachers, will become viral, and then the subject of counter-action and, as the frequency of such incidences increases, a commonplace within our schools – which will become the cultural battlefield it has already been decided they are to be. The chaos is a consequence of the intent by those in control, not an accidental side-effect; this shows things are going exactly as planned.

Can't

Ye cannae say that.

While cant is everywhere, 'can't' can't be spoken.

Can't is a bad word in this age of goodthink and is not allowed; whether a child can or cannot do something is irrelevant to this way of thinking. If a child actually can't do something, then we'll just pretend they can. Just like in magic land, where everything you want to happen, happens.

Some imagine that this development of excessive positivism as a positive thing, but paradox again, excessive positivism transmitted to children whose grasp of reality is incomplete sets them up for failure, deceit and delusion, and often all three. A positive can-do approach to life (and school challenges) has to be built upon, personalised to child and circumstance and tempered. Sometimes one can't do something and sometimes that's ok, failure has to be permitted a full part in this process. The can-do attitude is a consequence of this realism of effort and expectation.

This endless focus by teachers in constant encouragement and optimism is an aspect of the rod with which we break our children's spirits which chaining them to the treadmill.

There's nothing wrong with being positive with children, but there's something wrong in making it an imperative.

Carrot and Stick

Where there used to be two forces in instructional partnership, now there's only one. They knew well how this would go bad, even hundreds of years ago:

Whasoever o ye pupils wha rede weel tae the dominie and thusly profiteth thereof, sa sall they be judgit as favoured and rewardit wi carrots in abundance proper tae their vertue.

Whasoever o ye pupils wha requitit the stick tae profiteth, alack for him. For henceforth shall he be judgit as favoured by the dark dominie and thuly brocht tae correctioun in the fullness o time by strokes in abundance proper tae their lack o vertue. Treuly, I tell ye, there maun be muckle greetin and gnashin o teeth.

from *The Most Excellent Theorie in Judicious Instruction of Godlie Knawledge and Common Vertue for Younge Gentillmen Scholars.*

[Revised Editioun, Edinburgh, 1591. available fra packmen and bra bukebooths naciounwide. Priced thrie merks scots]

Carry on Excellence

The original fun-loving productions with Sid, Kenneth, Barbara and Hattie et al, in which a sex obsessed, local government education head of service introduces 'gender studies' to primary pupils as part of a plan to import and sell naughty Dutch videos at the UN Sex Swap Week school fair. But things go awry when the videos are accidently delivered to a local mosque for Ramadan and a dirty-minded HM School Inspector has all the school toilet signs changed to TRANSGENDER ONLY. Much hilarity follows with head-chopping results. Luckily, a visiting niqab dancing troop provides the perfect cover for the staff to escape amid the flying underwear.

Released in Scotland at the Glasgay Festival retitled as *Excellence Right up the Khyber.*

The Scottish Education Department released a follow-up entitled *Excellence in the Jungle* in which representatives of the Scottish educational establishment journey to the Dark Continent in search of enhanced diversity. But things don't go as planned when they get captured by a cannibal transgender tribe. While machetes chop the kebabs, much hilarity and sex changing ensures, with the odd tire barbeque and spear chucked in. Will the gang be able to keep their election promise of delivering one million extra multi-culturalists to Scottish classrooms by Rosh Hashanah?

Released to primary schools across Scotland as part of the Pan-sexual and Cross-gender History Month.

CCTV

Reality stars and teenage girls excepted, no one likes being filmed all the time. This accounts for the resistance to the suggestion that full CCTV coverage in school is the way of the future, bringing security and protection, somehow. In real life, as we know, this will have no impact on school playground crime (boys chasing girls, big girls being mean to an infant ginger-haired orphan, etc.), children being naughty in class, or parents behaving badly; nor prevent genuinely serious outrages. Although in the aftermath the CCTV recordings would make interesting viewing at news time and will provide further evidence of the need for more security (and the necessary funding) in school and at home. And this leads us to the important point about CCTV in schools; the symbiotic relationship between the CCTV and the creation of the type of society which needs and accepts such. The issue is not security, but surveillance. And we are already among the world's most surveilled societies, with scant evidence of the benison of the all-seeing eyes; but much to be concerned about the ultimate use of such power. However, staff, parents and children are daily so inured to this linkage that the introduction of the next stage of surveillance will be accepted hardly with recognition, far less resistance. And any such encountered would be neutralised by the coda 'for the children'; which it is, obviously, although not in the way one thinks this means.

It is claimed that the coming 'Classroom Live' video stream will provide protection for the teacher against malicious claims by pupils and parents, as well as enable the latter to better sue the former when such claims are sufficiently suggestable by video evidence. Pupils' school life will be well immersed in this paranoid reality of surveillance and fear of denouncement. So, then, well prepared for a future life!

Sell your shares in energy renewables and space tourism, the killing is to be made in school surveillance and embedded pupil security solutions. Ethical Investors Monthly. June 2018.

TWITTERFLASH: I regret to inform you that the head teacher has been summarily removed from her post after CCTV evidence examined by our justice security team revealed that she was not celebrating PRIDE with proper enthusiasm. Be aware; we see and always prosecute. (Message from *Classurveillance @ Don't worry, we're watching*)

Celebrate

Whenever you hear something being 'celebrated' in schools, it is invariably something not worth celebrating; false achievements, no achievements, participants as champions, revisionist-inspired 'girls did it first' femiganda and ethnic others' 'you're just amazing being yourself' awards.

Check this example of down the memory hole; April 23rd 2016, 400th anniversary of the Bard's death. At the school assembly, not a single reference to him. Children instead watch a video of Barney the Purple Dinosaur who's your friend and mine. Celebrate this, ye apostates!

Shakespeare, ooz dat dude?

Dat be dead White dude wat rap in crazy English to puts dem bitches in dey place for dickin. He be da man!

Yoos rong. Dat be Capin Kirk.

EMERGENCY ADDENDUM: Woops, almost forgot; diversity, that's certainly worth celebrating. And tolerance, and same sex marriage, tackling poverty, empowering un-empowered women who have been denied their voice, speaking 25 different languages in your school, respecting rights (or not), accordingly.

Challenge

This is what everyone agrees children need and should be built into their lessons. However, such challenge is, as demanded, the classroom equivalent of a woman asking if her bum looks big. The challenge should be such that it is easily achievable, as in blowing bubbles level of difficulty, while disingenuously capable of upbigging for reporting purposes. Those teacher-idiots who foolishly actually do, academically or otherwise, challenge a child, will find the script switched, doubly up-bigged and a challenge too far. For them!

Challenging children; either very, very gently or don't!

Chaos

The big wheel of history turns and chaos once again gets the opportunity to teach sanity a lesson.

Charity

One would almost think that a major purpose of our schools is to promote an iron-cast obligation on the part of us Westerners to be always thinking and acting for those limitless others requiring our patrimony. Perhaps it is!

When not motivated by Christian piety or self-discovered compassion, nor properly located at hearth and home, but instead obliged by diktat, our schools' very many foreign charity initiatives are in fact not charity at all, but political manipulation on the one hand and self-regard on the other. Rather than teaching compassion, as is claimed, children learn counterfeit compassion through virtue signalling. The charity 'gifts' themselves, unwitting propitiation to those who caused the need for such charity; who then inwardly smile at our moral grandstanding, knowing that thusly do we prove their mastery over our worldview and behaviour. They delight in the feedback loop that schools have developed between parent and pupil, each unknowingly reinforcing in familial competition the true end point of this project.

For them, demonic mission is achieved with our children's future locked into this self-ruinous mindset – the so-called purity spiral – where we compete to outdo each other in ever more ruinous public acts of charity and self-effacement. Only Whites exhibit this excessive altruistic concern for the plight of others outside their kin or ethnic groups; and it is this inherited moral kindness that has been turned against ourselves, with our schools the hothouse of this fever and female teachers the janissaries. We thought we were raising the enlightened child of the 21st century and doing our part in setting the history record straight, but were negligent in thinking through the good intentions to their final effect.

Leaving aside the well-explored inefficiency and corruption of such, especially global, charities, and the various societal disruptions and unintended consequences that arrive with the charity organisations in those other lands as the ugly, and never mentioned, backdrop to such charity; let us consider the essential nature of the Act of Charity, as it is mandated in our schools: Here we have an act of Western power that corrupts on either side of the outstretched hands. A truth sarcastically recognized as such by the ingrate recipients – enough is never enough! Our ancestral fathers knew the truth of this; that continually mitigating the plight of an unknown other only serves to make them HATE YOU. What, think ye, are foreign recipients of our largely sacrifice-free largesse to make of such gifts following on from our sometimes literal physical destruction of their world, Western interference in the organic development of their own society and constant global images of Western degeneracy and racist apologising.

As Captain Willard mused out loud: *We cut them in half with a machine gun and then give them a Band Aid. It was a lie, and the more I saw of them, the more I hated lies.*

You will be made to care when you go out to eat, when you play games, when you watch TV, when you take a drink of water and, especially, when you enjoy yourself. No aspect of your life will be left undisturbed by the thought of charity. Schools lead the way in strapping this mindlock into place.

Awake ye parents and intelligent pupils; masked as charity this moral grandstanding is not social justice, nor compassion, but planted mental destruction of our children.

Charity begins at home; *Ah, so that's what it means.* Charity does not scale up and so keep out of other people's lives. Know this: White charity has only ever had one child, and his name is Black resentment.

Cheatyness

It has been observed by the foolish brave that certain groups are more prone to cheating and gaming the system than others, and that representatives of such groups are thoroughly embedded within our school system. Cheating is their default attitude to interaction with ethnic others; ethnic others, for them, being us. They scarcely need it, but extra justification is provided by our constant beating of the racist drum and self-apology for cultural excellence.

Perhaps the infamous, but necessary solution, adopted in certain countries of sitting exams in underwear might have to be introduced here too. A certain demograph, at least, would welcome this with pleasure and posted videos.

Whites did not evolve to live among large groups of cheaters and liars. In former times such were harshly dealt with, now we celebrate them instead.

Children

Our pride and joy, as it pertains to school.

Loved by us, but hated by them. Thusly, the target of a multi-generational plan of diabolic wickedness to weaponise pupils against, in order; themselves, us parents and their society. Education is the key that opens the gates to their ruination and our demise, as per the plan.

The forces behind the dysfunction in our schools are generally invisible, preferring to achieve their goal through the use of the usual sock puppets within our education system. However, they are revealed by tracing backwards from any discivic idea to their (admittedly luxurious) pit in which they wallow in naked envy of us for our beauty, creativeness and kindness.

Hatred of this intensity usually results in irrational outbursts of rage against the target, but in this particular case the animating power is as intelligent as it is malevolent. And patient! Our children are to be psychologically weakened by subversive ideas, drugged, fattened, spiritually abandoned, rewired crazy by technology and then let loose on their society, our society, to complete the mission. Their ruin is a dish to be served cold. And we will be witnesses at this darkly lit banquet. Truly, the greatest of punishments is destroying someone through their children.

Who cannot see this happening in front of their eyes?

Children's University

If a child naively thought that they could do children's things in the summer hols, then think again. Two birds with the one stone; more pressure on our children 'to achieve' and false achievement celebrated.

Actually, this university is a delusional summer school puffed up by wordy verbiage, as is SOP nowadays. This done without (apparently?) considering the endemic effect on real childhood experiences and achievements by conflating them with phony ones, like the C U. Children even get a 'graduation certificate' on completion of their 'degree'! Everybody graduates, of course, except they don't really. But the inversion, devaluing and degrading of language is real, as is the child's loss of valuable playing time.

There is a time and a place for everything, but it seems that every time and place is to be seized as an opportunity to impose 'good ideas' on our children. Everything is about achievement, it seems; it's as if children are preparing their C.V. at 8 years old.

C.f. *FFS!* and *Here we go again!*

Child Soldiers

There isn't a child alive the professional justice activists won't try to turn into a soldier for their cause. This is how they see your children, as cannon fodder.

Meanwhile, in Africa, they take this concept more literally.

Child Trauma Toolkit for Educators

Containing: pliers, eye patch, 24 x tray of Epipens, pepper spray, Gameboy 4, spare paper underwear, kebab spillage pack, amputation consent form, holy water, jumbo bag of chocolate buttons.

Chill-out Booth

A little secluded booth kept outside the class for various shades of dis and mis functional children to enjoy playing with some toys, a Gameboy or just doing nothing, if this is what they want. Has proven very popular with various forms of duckers and divers too, especially if permitted to bring a friend to help them 'cope' with the loneliness.

Of course, addressing a problem like this creates more problems, but by that time the psychologist who recommended it has left. But don't worry, that this ridiculous idea will result in deserved damage to their career as educational experts or their top salaries; it won't!

To be fair, it does provide some early training for a life in telesales.

Chips

These are bad for your children.

Radio ID tags are now used on cattle and, sub-dermally, becoming more common for dogs. They have been tested 'successfully' on senior citizens; Alzheimer patients – it's ok, though, as they've forgotten it was done! Children will be next under the guise of security. Then various state services and banking will require chipping. That's a plan; No, seriously, it is an actual plan. The school's role is crucial in enabling this by legitimising this digital world and the Satanic organisations that promote it.

Via nano-technology, widespread digital tag use and aerial surveillance drones, all pretence of privacy will leave the life of our children. And their imagination. They will be tracked like the cattle they have become, eavesdropped as the norm and punished as required.

O, brave new world that hath such creatures in it!

There is another type of chip which, in moderate doses, has much to recommend it; freshly cut, deep fried in dripping, lashed with vinegar and vigorously salted. Hungry yet?

Good chip, bad chip, we've mixed them up.

Chocolate

Needs no introduction in the life of a child you would think, as its precursor role in establishing metabolic disease and eventually, through its associated role in creating various corporal and psychological health issues, lifelong pharma dependence is well-established. Rightly seen as a gateway drug to injected insulin. And more dangerous than when Dougie took a chocolate biscuit to school and a big boy from P4 stole it and ran away.

However, chocolate has recently been further weaponised in the war against our children's sanity. Now they can't even eat some chocolate without racial guilt.

AN AFRICAN FARMER ONLY GETS 62P A DAY FOR HIS COCOBEANS! (poster on P3 class door)

WTF does that even mean? And why are our children to be daily reminded of this? I know that you know!

Christianity

Considered from the primary pupil's viewpoint our culture's religion is arguably a spent force in their school life. However, there is one consideration, invisible and paradoxical, where its impact is very powerful which justifies its inclusion here. This being that while great reverence is rightly shown to the religions of others, principally Hinduism, Judaism and Islam and the new religion of Multiculturalism, with riots, lawsuits, stabbings and loss of employment invariably following disrespect; in contrast, any form of disrespect shown to Christianity is perfectly acceptable. And, as you know, it is extremely common. Gentile atheists ranging from intellectual philosophers to anger-filled vulgarians fulfil this role.

Much of this shown disrespect is casual, sometimes unintended, and arguably therefore a consequence of the diminished social position of religion in our secular age. But some of it isn't; this being sourced to the media and entertainment world, especially the TV/movie industry, and having high production values; which translates as powerful propaganda. That these anti-Christian activities are almost exclusively Jewish productions is not an accident. And one is forced to consider the mentality behind, and intent of, an historically alien group being so willing to deride the host's religion and religious figures, in often gratuitously vulgar ways. This same group also gives a platform to calls for the desecration, and even complete destruction, of Christianity's scared art and public monuments. In defence, this has been presented as sometimes just a big joke and other times as artistic licence, or a defence of free speech, but it's not. All institutions decay, but foreign groups unashamedly accelerating this process is a hostile act of great arrogance, or more properly, chutzpah. The reader knows the same treatment returned in kind would not be tolerated, indeed, would bring the severest of sanctions in any of these other religion's home countries.

This proposition leads us to our children in primary school. As our ancient institutions, habits, laws, monuments, public building, art in all its variety, connect to our Christian heritage, and as the latter is mocked and lessened, so are all the former by association. Children don't need to understand this as an adult would, they just see their, however putative, religion ignored and disrespected in contrast to everyone else's and draw the only conclusion possible; a conclusion which supports a wider mission to undermine their place in their own world. The world is full of symbols, these symbols have socially significant meanings beyond the apparent and intended ones; when you attack Christianity or Jesus or an ancient saint or openly celebrate the physical destruction of its buildings, you attack the heart of a people's identity. Children understand the emotional and symbolic significance of this, before they understand the facts of it. Unlike with denying, rationalising adults, children don't need the full message spelt out; they get it right away.

This is akin to salting the fields before the planting. Why would someone want to do this?

Church

Easter (Passover) and Christmas (Chanukkah) being the only guaranteed points of contact between the school and the church proper, it is important that the true modern message is maximised; guilt for our sins against the rest of the world and a collection predicated on this. Nothing numinous spoils this prostration, God's presence is as a sort of reparations tribunal judge. And so we have a sermon as if written by Madonna (the so named billionaire idiot screecher and African baby snatcher), emphasising how much 'we' can still do for poverty, sexism, female equality, race relations, midwives in Africa, thirsty jungle denizens, non-swimming female Madagascans, and the like. The whole thing with the feel of a low grade production of Jesus Christ Superstar.

In a subtle little epiphany created for their future (perhaps), the little boys are cast in the role of Jesus before the Sanhedrin, but without the opportunity to reply to the slanders to their sex.

Claret

As in, complimentary crate of;

Please accept this complementary crate of claret with my gratitude.
Head teacher ☺

The above, received from school management, is not even believable in a fantastic dream. I can confirm this as a fact as I awoke from the dream in question when this event occurred, thinking that even dreamland is going too far into the fantastic.

Classics

The literary canon that was the foundation and grace of high culture now finds itself whipped from the college precincts as a leper. The ability to read, understand and appreciate such works is not easily acquired, and possibly never if not built on during early schooling. The crucial first step has been largely achieved in employing teachers that have little interest in such works. The next, currently underway, is the great replacement of the classics with works of decidedly inferior literary merit and clear politico-social agenda. This is my judgement. Others, wickedly motivated, argue that broken family porn, LGBTQ+ self-discovery, racial persecution and Holocaust narratives are a more appropriate literary landscape for the modern young master, miss and mx+.

The classics don't stand alone, they are part of a larger thing which scaffolds our life as the lucky recipients of a magnificent tradition of creativity and scholarship.

As FM Nicola rightly complained to the Scotch Times reporter:
Our primary pupils scarcely know Burns or Shakespeare, far less the classics. My government will correct this.

Classicists who greeted the FM's statement with unbounded enthusiasm, imagining Thucydides or Horace on every schoolchild's lips, soon found themselves contemplating hemlock, when she claimed to be misunderstood. It was not deservedly dead white supporters of slavery she was referring to, but in fact, gay and lezzie classics.

Cleaners

Representing by their quiet efficient industry and an excellent template for the lower-middle level IQ cohort of pupils, although (as the Lord gives as he takes) the upper level of decency.

Thusly, invariably the best people in the school. And just as invariably left off from any self congratulating list of future careers referred to. See, poem *The Rescuing Pie*.

NB. Cleaners are not to be confused with scrubbers.

Clicker

A little hand-held device which makes a loud, sharp clicking noise and can do so repeatedly at great speed with little to no fatigue to the operator, but much (*click, click, click, click, click, click, click, cl...!*) to the surrounding listeners. This device, a form of fidget toy, is given to ADHD boys to distract them from fidgeting. Its great power of distraction is best demonstrated during quiet moments in class and assemblies, especially if there are a few operating in unison. Many teachers exposed to this device feel that they too are developing ADHD as a result; so it does work!

What sort of nutcase would think of this as a solution to distracted kids? The answer is obvious, the well-named education psychology services. *Click!* Works best with Ritalin. *Click, click!* I once saw a child keeping both hands busy with two clickers; very funny for a few seconds.

Clubs

Ref: lunchtime and school-time clubs.

That is, then, those which school management wishes to promote to their credit. As can be guessed these clubs follow all the fashionable social and justice concerns. e.g., the anti-bully club, save the world, friendship meeting, the vegan group, animal welfare, etc., etc. Leaving aside any debate as to the value of such promoted activity, or more properly, the hidden damage they do, we note that such clubs are completely feminine. That is to say, they reflect the concerns of females and do so in a female way, i.e., talking about problems with themselves in the central role. This phenomenon is, of course, independent of the merits of any club's particular interest, which is not of itself necessarily gendered.

This leads finally to the point of this entry; as most little boys prefer to be doing things, rather than talking about them, they self exclude. Thusly, unknowingly, training themselves to respond in same fashion in their adult lives to the colonisation of public fora by females, or otherwise by feminine sensibilities. The feminine nature of such clubs, combined with the absence of male-oriented equivalents, brings a tacit message to all children about how the world is – and it's a girls' world. And this has consequences for how little boys come to understand their future place in the world. This effect is like a quiet, almost invisible, part of this general war on boys – now easily seen to continue (and be triumphantly celebrated as such!) all the way up to adulthood. White adulthood, obviously!

To correct this, future schools will offer such lunchtime/school-time clubs oriented towards boys interests.* These would include; runic stone carving, metal working, camouflage and field craft, gang hut building, construction of fortifications, archery (English warbow), lager lovers (low alcohol brewing and distilling), radio controlled combat drones, destroyer robot programming and a swordsmanship club, offering falchion, claymore and cutlass to the usual foil. This latter club could help resolve disputes and a *schläger schmiss* beats a tattoo × 100 for cool factor – just ask any boy!

Cluster Meeting

This is where policies are cluster moderated and rafts of initiatives are ring fenced for passionate commitment to target enhancement.

Large get-togethers with tea and buns of girl (and girl like, except me) teachers reinforcing educational orthodoxy and identifying apostates. Politburo meetings (under Stalin) demonstrated a more honest sharing of opinions. Bring your class First Aid kit as a precaution and check your back on leaving for daggers. Better described as a cluster f..k meeting.

This is what cluster bombs were made for.

Collective Memory

Our education system is like a person with Alzheimer's. All the failed pedagogies, technologies, productivity initiatives, governmental targets, political promises, IT resources, social justice ambitions that come in the front door with fanfare, leave at the servant's rear with

---

* Girls would be welcome, but on receipt of any girly behaviour; attempting to alter the rules, complaining about not fair, crying, etc., would result in immediate expulsion. As would be the case for the boys too.

a whimper, and are forgotten as quickly as if they had been huckled through the corridor to the exit.

The present eye praises the present object.

The repeat cycles appear to be about half a generation, just enough time for the memory of the previous introductions and failure to be forgotten as a result of natural wastage, bureaucratic stupidity, regular stupidity and the innocent ignorance of the incoming teacher cohort. Comes the situation where no one remembers anything about previous systems and practices, thusly allowing the cycle of failure and waste to continue.

However, this state of affairs is not entirely due to stupidity. With so much money to be regularly plundered from the public purse, mendacity and cowardice also play their allotted roles with the usual suspects. Hat check to school management and Heads of Service!

Comfort

Comfort, security and safety are all prerequisites for class learning, however, these can so easily segue to indulgence, ingratitude and laziness that wisdom is called for in their application to avoid unthinkingly over-applying them or, even worse, believing that more of a good thing is even better. There has to be a hard edge to any enterprise that sometimes has to be approached and even touched; failure and discomfort looming ahead serves a purpose.

And comfort brings no value in life, even at six years old.

Common Sense

Unless applied secretly, often draws the severest of penalties. Now so rare as to be almost a super power. There is no place in our schools now for practical, achievable and consequential thinking. And so, chummed up with its pals, wisdom and honesty, common sense takes the road to the wilderness. (see my movie, *Three for Oblivion*)

Question from the conference floor: ...*but all these covenants and agendas supersede common sense!*

Government Education Dolly: *What's your point?*

Compassion

An essential school goal which, allegedly, can now be taught. And feeds the need of people to feel they are the virtuous actors in the great drama of life, especially as lived on screen.

Compassion is what you pretend to have when the person you pretend to care about is far away and different from you, but other Whites who could pretend to have even more compassion are watching you and they too could tweet about their greater compassion than yours. At their animal level, our children understand this public falseness. There is NOTHING to admire in this disingenuous and showy compassion; and we all know this.

Computer

It is almost impossible to believe that at one time, and not so long ago, all learning took place without this device. And arguably was better for it. Comparisons fail in contemplating the hyperbolic claims of the benefits to education delivered by the countless trillions spent on this technology.

A computer is, of course, only as good as what's put in it. It is the perfect garbage-in garbage-out machine, and almost all human input is now garbage.

Complaints

It seems that in enabling the school system to more easily address genuine complaints, we have only succeeded in empowering idiot-parents and perennial malcontents; and genuine complaints, typically pursued in a sensible and discrete manner, are, paradoxically, actually less likely to get a fair hearing in proportion to their reasonableness.

Along the way, complaints have too often lost all connection to common sense and trust. For example, your boy child comes home with his jacket dirty – you naturally email a complaint about his teacher somehow being responsible. Your five year old girl child complains about getting cold and wet during a past playtime (she cannot remember when) because the teacher allegedly stopped her wearing her jacket, even though it was lashing with sleet – you naturally accept this as a fact and phone up a complaint against the teacher. A child with certain psychological problems complains that their teacher never allows them to play with other children; indeed, apparently instructs other children so – you naturally do not bother asking the teacher about this, but formally complain directly to council headquarters.

A robust defence of common sense and the teachers involved could, I believe, resolve this problem. Such a thing will never happen because the system is actually against the teacher and their pupils. And in realising this, you come to see the complaints procedures as a sort of sacrifice of teachers to deflect blame from the true source of the complaint. This is, of course, what a sacrifice is!

Conformity

The natural state of the feminine mind is to repeat and promote whatever is being instructed by those with power, this being directly management and more generally the mainstream media. In the almost exclusively female primary schools, then, this becomes a crushing power to conformity which brooks no dissent. Thusly, there can be no escape from the negative consequences of this while schools are structured as they are. What need for the secret police when each teacher is their own secret police officer?

The thought is all we care about, Winston, said O'Brien, the school's feared QIO, or Quality Improvement Officer.

Consequences

Ref: of bad behaviour;

At last, proper consequences for naughty pupils: *No Mozart for you!*

Otherwise, none, excepting extra concessions and privileges – here we have the classic example of getting what you reward.

Consider

There's a lot of considering expected of our primary age children now. Could one then also expect that the spirit of Socrates and his Academy is behind all this philosophising? Here's the answer;

One school posited this challenge to P5s: Consider ways to fight intolerance and racism in the school yard and classroom.

Idea; Black to White and White to Black Facepaint Day.

The bullwhip cracked like a pistol shot. *How do you like being Black now?*, said the Whited-up Black child to the Blacked-up racist White as he whuppt his ass.

NB. This being 2015, when such face swap was still acceptable.

Consultants

The con is the important part.

Modus Operandi of:

1. Make a problem or 'discover' one.

2. Proffer solution to get ticket on educational gravy train.

3. Pretend to solve the problem at max cost.

4. Make the problem worse.

5. Profit.

6. Return to 1 and repeat.

Conversations

1. Pupil
This human-type interaction between teacher and pupil is now frowned on, especially where the child might just want to privately share something with you, or you with them. Such conversations

need not connect with learning as such; these were often the richest moments in school, on both sides of the conversation.

Another type of conversation also almost extinct, is where a teacher has a wee quiet word with a child, discretely imparting a concern for them to consider, or should circumstances require, immediately action as a direct instruction. This being an art form too human for our bureaucratic age, we now timetable this formerly genuine to a formal interview of a few minutes duration, styled as a review, and thus neutralising the value to the child. Children understand this instinctively, and the conversation becomes a stilted thing. Thus a simple thing, formerly powered by concern and wisdom, becomes a box-ticking nothing. Such conversations prepare our children for more of the same in their working future, especially in the knowledge economy.

2. Teacher

Conversations also come in one basic adult flavour; excessive. Countless hours wasted because of female insistence on 'keeping the conversation going'. This is particularly the case with issues we apparently need to have a conversation about. In actuality, these are things we need to NOT have a conversation about; but try telling that to a woman.

I have been recently implementing a class project to draw attention to the issue of male beastliness and their over-representation in primary schools. It is time we had a whole staff conversation about this.

[Male teacher, thinking of Captain Oates, 'I am just going outside and may be some time.']

Cost

Viz. The true cost

In the world of Scottish education no spreadsheet of costs and benefits is required as there are infinite resources, these being magically conjured by the wish. So no hard choices need be made. All pupils will leave school as compassionate global citizens and professors of celebratory justice.

True cost economics tells a different tale, with cash and carry costs the least of our problems. Anxiety, depression, faux compassion, inflated egos, identity complications and inchoate antagonisms (to name just a few) are a legacy of public education; what are their costs? You be the judge. Future society will be the jury.

Continuous Professional Development (CPD)

Check out some of the latest exciting courses on offer. Career enhancing badges issued on completion;

PREVENT: To keep individuals from becoming involved in or supporting terrorism – mandatory training.

SAFETY: Bomb Threat and Suspicious Items – mandatory training for school management.

SUSTAINABILITY: Incorporating global awareness into the primary curriculum.

CHILD PROTECTION: Identification and Effective Responses to Child Sexual Exploitation.

CHILD PROTECTION: Suicide awareness in the primary school setting.

SUPPORT: Coming Out; supporting the transitioning child in the primary class.

SUPPORT: Emotion Talks – a tool for listening to children and young people experiencing addiction issues.

SUPPORT: Equalities Trans-Training for Schools' Equalities Coordinators.

The debates that follow on from such courses are like watching a competition between treachery and insanity – and it is always a draw! That so many CPD courses are total junk does not automatically mean that they can be just ignored. Even with nonsense pedagogic courses never afterwards utilised, one still wastes precious time marginalising their effect, or pretending to have incorporated them into routines.

The most lethal CPDs are those with a potentially slight future utility, as they hang about one's practice like Banquo's ghost, phantasmagorical, unwelcome but not ignorable. They reappear to remind you of what you've <u>not</u> done as your annual review comes up, and with it the question: *Tell me about a useful CPD that you have introduced into your practice?* And at such a moment, Solzhenitsyn's injunction to never let the lie enter through you, flees the nest along with your integrity.

NB. tbf, CPD does enhance careers, just not for the teachers.

CPD Coaches

Good God! why should they mock poor fellows thus?

Come in three basic forms, the good, the bad and the ugly. The good and the bad can speak for themselves. The ugly propagate and enforce teacher fidelity to the ideology and practices advocated by our enemies. These party apparatchiks waste millions of taxpayers' shekels and thousands of hours of teachers' time. Their main effect is to stupefy and demoralise the teacher. However, give credit where it is due, from the viewpoint of 'the agenda' these have been among the most successful fifth columnists in history, perhaps only equalled by the [censored] opening the doors of [censored] to the [censored] in the [censored].

Step aside, ye Bolsheviks, there's a new kommissar in town.

This business model thrives on endless churn. And for the churners this is their salad days.

Credit

Ref: given where it is due.

This is hardly ever given to teachers in schools within their lifespan. And so with me, a typically too late correction to Mrs M, Miss B, Miss G and Mr B.

Further to this, I would like to acknowledgement the debt this work owes to Mr W S. I have extensively plundered his writing for material and metaphor, as well as direct quotes. I believe that he approves of this, but just in case and as a mark of respect, I would like to apologise if he feels that this has not been done sufficiently well to reflect the credit due.

Crypsis

This is the word of our time.

Here meaning a hidden intent, under the guise of something acceptable, to introduce something not acceptable. Who would have thought that this concept would become the apt and perfect description for what is happening to, and in, primary schools.

DALE, P5 (to his parents): *Of course, you don't see it. You're not meant to. But do you understand, that's the question?*

Culture

The root of our being, whose best expression humanises and ennobles the organic recipients, the native us.

The excellence of our culture leads, alas but inevitably, to envy for those whose natural culture cannot be relativised to equality, try as they might. Thus, those excluded, self-excluded or otherwise of felt inferior legacy, stew to bubbling rage which will in time find an outlet; this is why some come to hate. While we, true to our inherited good manners, apologise for our insensitivity in being so good.

A nation lives by its myths and heroes. Many nations have survived defeat and invasion, even political and economic collapse. None has survived the corruption of its picture of itself. High and popular culture are not in competition here, both serve the same purpose. In our age, however, our high culture finds ever less champions in the face of the political attack against its alleged racism and elitism, and our common culture now belongs to someone else who does not love us. It is not an accident that there are so few respectful references to our cultural legacy or uplifting national themes in our entertainment world, for those that produce it have no affinity for it, or any true personal connection to it. Likewise, it is no accident that there is a relentless media pressure to force upon us the abstract globalist ideologies behind multiculturalism, as well as social and sexual degeneracy.

We do not have to study Nietzsche to realise this. Just turn on your television.

NB. Asserting the superiority of our native culture is not an attack on other peoples' cultures. They may consider their own culture superior if they wish and by whatever metric they choose. Indeed, I encourage them to do so.

Culture Wars

Not Greeks vs Latin literature, Romanesque vs Gothic cathedrals or the best Wagner (Richard vs the X Factor winner), but an attempt to subvert the glories of our ancestors and replace them, in the apparent interest of inclusion and diversity, with the values of Sodom and Gomorrah.

Our native culture evolved over ages and, expressing best our aesthetic, political and moral sensibility, acted as a kind of social immune system protecting us from dangerous foreign ideas. Global digital entertainment culture, in contrast, acts as a kind of AIDS-like virus to our native culture, damaging and replacing it with poptrash, reality garbage and subversion. Not only are we who own and need the protection of our native high culture rendered ignorant of what we have lost, the subversion has turned us against it. What you don't successfully defend, you don't keep. Schools will be the killing fields for the coming battle, the skirmishing has started. The situation does not look bright. However, we still have Wagner and Shakespeare, so all is not lost.

Curriculum

Formerly, the knowledge to be studied and acquired.

The former curriculum's scope was limited; the child's political understanding and its family life were not within its purview. Traditional values were represented, not preached; these did not include 'tolerance'. A child's sex and its attendant behaviours were not subject to proselytising. Not being the object of official interferences, the pedagogic practice was simple and consistent.

Currently, the opposite of formerly. But check daily for the latest updates.

Future Curriculum@Luvtolerance™ will be further streamlined to only include the 3 core topics; sex awareness, climate change and the Holocaust.

Curriculum for Excellence

Scotland's modestly titled national curriculum which daily invites, and receives, correction from the Fates. And often from the pupils too! At gigantic public cost and teacher heartache, this replaced the previous fairly benign and moderately useless curriculum to introduce, with great fanfare appropriate to its name, NOTHING new that was useful. But lots new that wasn't!

It massively complicated the creation of the curriculum by introducing all sorts of rubrics and targets and social ambitions which will never be realised – also at great public cost. Its main achievement was to introduce the cancer of social justice, virtue signalling and global political activism into primary teaching. An arrival which conveniently, and tragically for pupils welfare and education and pupils, coincided with the majority of new teachers being on-board with these ambitions, and thusly 'willing accomplices' to the changes they wished to effect.

see, Endless Revolution

Curriculum of Hate

In this world turned upside-down, the content of this curriculum is gradually taking shape; it would include noticing truths about certain cohorts, honest appraisals and deserved censure. It would involve putting manliness, femininity, loyal marriage and devoted parenthood back on a pedestal. Celebrating matriarchy and pride in one's national culture would represent the zenith. Those who promote the curriculum of hate have already been identified by those who promote the curriculum of love. All that the love group are waiting on is the demographic shift that will allow them to destroy the haters. Love trumps hate, you see.

D

Daily Mile

It would be churlish to mock the one good idea for decades, except to see it as an idea out of whack with the 'body positive' times and full to bloating with all the absurdity of the age. Everyone knows that exercise is good for you and that children should do it more, so why not marry this idea to their parents. And keep the school off the children's broad and flabby backs. And the tubster youngster, what message to him as he hechs and pechs his way around half the course to come last? Is the teacher now a track coach? And what does the over-beefy teacher represent in this diorama, should they be training for fitness too? What other habit judgements on pupils should the school not feign to withhold?

What is unsaid; the daily mile will run out of steam soon enough and will quietly disappear, to be only requested as an excuse to avoid work on a nice day. Another good idea from education experts usurping the role of the parent, carrying a lifestyle judgement, becomes a scam for some pupils to just hang about and chat, with weaklings complaining of sore legs or too tired after 100 yards. With any exhortation on the part of the teacher liable to complaint from the weakling's parents. And in the end, the joy of speed, of outdoor challenge and of perseverance, that should be at the heart of such an undertaking, is forgotten. Adults just say things. There's your learning outcome.

Dark Continent

That place to which all our powers of self-deception are bent and where the recipients of our benison fully repay the gift by sending to our safe European home guilt-assuaging future (witch) doctors and (human rights) lawyers.

The Dee Cee is also a source of much needed cultural enrichment, currently in our schools confined to FGM and so-called 'white-biting', but soon enough (see Sweden) to be extended to tribal warfare, tribal lawfare and tribal bomb making habits, as a part of the school curriculum. Indeed, in some tribally advanced Swedish schools the enrichment has reached such a level that labasha has been incorporated into the search for White apostates. Apparently, this method guarantees 100% success, regardless of the outcome.

NB. Like the 'Scottish Play' in a theatre context, the Dark Continent can never be mentioned in a school context without the usual caveat of proclaiming that which it denies. And so, we hereby all celebrate the great Dee Cee achievements; the invention of (almost) upright walking, banging sticks on tree trunks and the rock hammer.

Death

Referencing ways for a teacher to die early:

In primary schools (as recorded); fall down stairs, fall out window, drowning in sink, broken glass (carotid artery or wrist cut), dehydration, physical exertion, abnormal marking stress, baited by cruel children, manual lifting, insulin spike after eating parent gift of Scotch tablet, dropped brick on head, thrown brick at head, twilight CPD, angry parent, angry dog, misdirected drone strike, employment at Sandwood Primary (Glasgow), inspection panic, mystery troll attack, SEEMIS* logon issue, Power Point presentation

* an ersatz suicide machine under the guise of an IT-based, national marking scheme.

failure, unfinished marking apoplexy, back-stabbing management, witchdoctor hex, poisoned tea bag, unlucky punch (see Sandwood Primary), just happened (no reason recorded), running with scissors, secret Santa 'funny' gift stress, wrong video posted on Youtube, seemed like the best thing to do.

C.f. ways for a teacher to die early; Male version:

As per regular Grim Reaper, but also including: jealous female colleague hex, disappointed female colleague rumour spreading, female colleague random back-stabbing, angry (menses) female colleague ambush, alcohol poisoning at Christmas party, deaved to death by a scolding teacher-wife, staffroom gossip overdose, single mum's transference* attack, suddenly swooned and dropped down dead, and finally just had enough of it all!

Deep Thinking

It's just like thinking, except deeper!

This phrase has recently been turning up a lot in educational circles. Used by shallow thinkers, naturally, it means the exact opposite of whatever is being claimed. Thusly, do idiot promotors of educational nonsense conveniently identify themselves to you.

The actual level of deep thinking involved in, say, spending millions on some new idea no one wants or needs, and that does not work anyway, is as follows:

Monkey sees banana

Monkey wants banana

---

* remind her of currently jailed boyfriend.

Monkey steals banana

Monkey shows deep thinking.

Defeat

Every defeat can become the father of a subsequent victory, this is why it is crucial for children to be allowed their failures. And these to be honestly identified as such without censure or excuse; advise as appropriate then move on, allow the child to respond as they can.

Defenceless

Referencing feminist teachers and female pupils:

Minds scrambled with the relentless babble of popnews from their portable brainwashers, denied the wisdom of great literature, and unable to understand evidence or discern intent behind the inversion of the cross held before them every day, I note with sadness the headline on a staffroom copy of Cosmo (aka Sheol) hammering home the lie to which they have no defence or defenders.

Single Woman are Happy Women; How having a baby can be the worst thing to do.

(Guess the ethnicity of the person who wrote the article, the editor and magazine owners?)

Our White females have had their minds hacked and been turned into the enemy of themselves. We ask, is it right to hate those who have conspired to make them confused, then dissatisfied, then crazy, and always unhappy?

Our beautiful girl children have no chance against this global Moloch. And yet, their beauty and fertility may be the least of their future loss.

Degeneracy, Promoting of

The brainwashed becomes brainwasher in turn.

One might be reassured that the curriculum obligations regarding sexual identity and alternative lifestyles and family structures only require these topics to be discussed, and not promoted as such. However, in practice this distinction will not necessarily exist because many teachers are fully on-board with the whole radical social agenda. Thus, not requiring teachers to actually promote subversion and degeneracy, but just discuss it, is like not requiring orcs to invade your country; they will do it anyway because it's what they want to do and there's nothing stopping them. Many young teachers, fresh off the Globohomo assembly line, regard it as a duty to be crusaders for the cause, and to recruit your child too. Our teachers have been turned into the enemy of themselves, and pass the curse in turn to our children. There is no need to oblige it.

Delivering

A word much in favour among the educational Sanhedrin. Refers, alas, not to sandwiches or a parcel, both of which are welcome deliveries, but 'ideas', i.e. delivering enhanced outcomes for poverty, delivering increased attainment with diversity, etc. The word is chosen with psychological deliberation, as it subliminally links to positive associations of something free and valuable being handed over, and with the grammar logic suggesting that the delivery has been, or is being, accomplished.

In fact, the only delivery actually accomplished is chaos. This following honesty has a nice ring to it:

DEPARTMENT OF EDUCATION; DELIVERING CHAOS WITH EVERY WORD.

Always delivering, but never delivered.

Delivering excellence would be best achieved by pupils delivering milk and rolls each morning to the local community. All the experts agree that this would be an excellent way of delivering the Curriculum of Excellence.

Depression Starter Pack

The children's version contains an i phone, high sugar drinks, carbohydrate as principle source of calories, computer games and 20 hours plus TV per week synergistically combined with minus 20 hours outdoor exercise. Add drugs as required.

Devil's Bargain

Requires fresh victims and these have to be virgin blood.

All the empowering talk, the 'you can be anything you want to be' lies, the 'you go girl' encouragement and the social justice activism foisted on our children is a devil's bargain that forfeits all their future life by not building for its second half. By this meaning that due cognisance has NOT been given to the role of children and family and community in what, at the time, must seem like a remote future; and with these crucial anchors of future self-worth (and not least blood survival) exchanged for career or political goals. Such a bargain is easily and unwisely advocated by too many young women teachers who themselves have still to find the lonely truth waiting for them for the same bargain that they don't even know they've made.

Diet

Kids are so over-sugared, sugar level up, sugar level down – no wonder they don't act right.

Too many (Most?) kids are on a diet of 80% simple junk carbs, this appalling situation reinforced by the erroneous propaganda of the food pyramid, with its claims that GM budget flour products and sugar bomb GM fruits and juice cartons are good for you.

Pupils' diets are too often stage one of metabolic disease, with all the related problems of insulin response, inflammation and auto-immune disorders, and their crucial impact on serotonin levels. All this food malware is driving the downstream effects on general intelligence, interest level and the spectrum behaviours. But don't worry, for if your kid is sufficiently dysfunctional they will eventually get a diagnosis, and in turn perhaps an adult school slave, but certainly some pills to fix everything – or not fix anything, as the case may be.

Of course, in real life, adults often don't have the time to cook a proper meal for their children, although amazingly these too busy parents find that same time for twitting to pals and working towards the 30% of their lives that they spend watching the tele. It's just a question of priorities. Perhaps they don't notice that their child looks like a human/potato hybrid?

Direct Instruction

Like sunlight, running and fresh air in the life of kids, this too is due a comeback. Gimmicks are torn off and pedagogy is stripped down to its underpants when direct instruction is paired with the unburdened teacher, and the only necessary technology in the blackboard; it works like a charm on kids tired to death of tech this, that and the next thing.

For those teachers brainwashed to progressive ideas involving so-called discovery learning and so-called collaborative group learning and so-called choice based curricula, there's nothing can be done to help them. Failure will dog their days and bad dreams their nights.

Disciplina

Roman soldiers worshipped this goddess; they knew their success in arms came from their devotion to her and her to them.

Centurion Lucius Annaeus recommends a little corner shrine in each class to be used as required by lacking pupils. *Disciplina* certainly whips the arse of *Indulgentia,* and not in a nice way.

Discipline

Discipline is life changing. A child must be encouraged to find it: Centurion Lucius Annaeus

The force exercised by the pupil which attracted praise and simultaneously held back the punishing hand. In former times this was not a matter of choice for the pupil, but only of method for the teacher. For those, admittedly few, pupils whose insolence or poor choices led to the need for discipline, sarcasm was always popular as an *hors d'oeuvre* to the selection of belt, cane or paddle.

Nowadays, the coin has flipped and discipline is an extinct force in the pupil's school day, but very potent in the teacher's. The threat of this; sometimes from pupils, often from parents in the form of Sauron-like threats of sacking, tweet mobs or an actual kicking (Sandwood Primary, Glasgow), and always from school management. Occasionally, the 'wider school community' is involved in the form of car tyres let down.

If one has knowledge of many schools across cultures and socio-economic class it is obvious that the biggest factor in success is pupil discipline. Where there is strict discipline the children have a chance to learn. Where there is poor discipline, even the best of teachers still struggle; the school becomes a day asylum; and sometimes a day lunatic asylum. This is a simple and eternal truth that stands alone. Our modern schools have lost sight of the truth that discipline is the father of the hero, and not their enemy!

Discovery

Isn't it great when kids discover something by themselves and are compelled by curiosity to explore it further? The key factor is that the discovery is by themselves. Alas, like other nice thoughts in school it has been force-fed steroids and became a bully. Thereby, killing the wonder that gave rise to it in the first place.

We note that this gift for wonder is not evenly distributed. Ask not for whom the bell curve tolls; it tolls for thee!

Discovery Learning

A progressive pedagogy in which children are expected to 'construct' their own knowledge by collectively determining what they want to know and how they should acquire this knowledge; with the teacher acting as a mentor. Realistically, very few children are equal to this methodology when employed as described; thus accounting for the popularity of this method among head teachers and other bandwagon hopheads. What one discovers using this approach is that the children don't know what they should have been doing and haven't learned anything. Any success enjoyed by this method comes from the direct support of the teacher, which short-circuits the whole point of the exercise. This should not be a surprise. The phrase 'stupid beyond belief' could have been coined for this method, although it competes for the appellation with many other equally stupid pedagogies.

Discreet

An understanding of when to be discreet is a great advantage in life and one that schools should be encouraging in pupils. Naturally, therefore, school does the opposite and by recommending 'sharing concerns', 'confronting intolerance' and 'tell an adult' we are not only creating a race of mental weaklings, but encouraging tell-tales and justifying back-stabbers. This augurs well for the future police state.

In actuality, children should form a natural tribe against teachers, and loyalty to this tribe should not be cheaply betrayed. By encouraging reporting of the most trivial of incidents, schools are by extension also encouraging a future race of informers. For the little girls this has a certain tragic utility in giving them early practice is using and manipulating the authorities to crush opponents, and especially males. For little boys, the tragedy is the damage to their developing sense of honour, setting some on the road to absolute scoundrelry as represented in such so-called professions as journalist or lawyer.

Of course, why even bother discussing this in an institution staffed by females; point taken!

Discriminate

Our Future School™ discriminates on the basis of race, colour, national origin, sex, sexual orientation, body decoration, health practices, fitness, age, disability, dress code and general appearance in admission to its programmes, services, or activities, in access to them, in treatment of individuals and in any aspect of their operations. The lack of English language skills shall be a barrier to admission or participation. We also discriminate in hiring and employment practices following the trend outlined previously. This notice is provided as required by the law to prevent unwelcome groups from wasting our time.

Discrimination

Only if Whites are doing it. Or men. If both categories are met, then by definition whatever is being done is discrimination, even if it's not! It would be sexist and racist and discriminatory to disagree.

Disingenuous Concern

The most obnoxious emotion there is. And this is what we promote to our children with our charities and action weeks, along with approval of their virtue signalling. False compassion teaches our children to lie to themselves and imperil their soul. It is integrity killing.

In addition, when everyone is lying like this, what would otherwise be a moral lapse becomes a necessary behaviour and a valued skill. We see where this is leading us; lying and falseness begets more of the same. Thusly, by our apparently well-intended concern we corrupt our children. A start to correcting this situation could be achieved by the simple expedient of banning all activities involving global mega charities.

Dispute

If the dispute involves parents who are unreasonable, stupid or otherwise badly motivated the teacher must expect no useful, if any, support from management, HQ or their union, if it is the EIS. Ditto for a dispute directly involving management, such an occurrence instructively reveals the full sham of the 'respected professional status.'

Should the disputant be a man, he will find that his colleagues and supporters are former and erstwhile respectively. The Jezebels, Salomes and Dalilahs of the female staff in such situations align themselves according to the only principle females respect, that of power and orthodoxy. And too, sabotaging a man brings its own personal benefits. ☺

Should a dispute be between a male teacher and a female teacher, the power the man is going up against is so huge that he has already lost before it has even begun. His future interests would best be served by resigning and performing a citizen's arrest on himself.

Diversity

This is a good thing because it obviously is and one is not allowed to say otherwise. If one notes that it is only the Western media and elites that promote diversity and anti-racism, and that the rest of the world looks after its own – indeed, is hostile to diversity as a source of division and permanent strife – then one is in need of a training course or a sacking, the latter should you have queried out loud near an i phone.

Correct thinking is best accomplished via a 'diversity training' course. O, the magnificent irony to be enjoyed, divine providence gifting this to the intelligent, of a training that achieves the exact opposite of its stated goals; reinforcing prejudice by requiring people to process one another as members of categories, rather than as individuals. There is nothing like course attendees being collectively indicted as race bigots in the *welcome phase* of the training to make you query the whole project; enter the training as a rainbow, come out as triple K! As we add more big diversity, so we add more competing norms, and take away more of the national cohesion that makes us a real country and not an international depot for discarded goods. Everything, it seems, has to be subordinate to the goal of having more diversity and the (apparent) concomitant struggle against racial discrimination. This totalitarian worldview is a mandated policy and by design permeates every aspect of your child's life in school; you should be worried for its openly stated goal is the end of whiteness. This means what it says.

Diversity is our strength is so manifestly untrue that they need marketing, laws and the police to make sure we pretend to believe it. Luckily, diversity destroys diversity. This is as axiomatic as it is meticulously unmentioned. One just has to wait it out.

As President Obama noted: *Diversity is something you do to your enemies.*

Diversity is *our* strength and *your* punishment. It would be racist to disagree.

Diversity Points

We already see this applied in institutions of (formerly) higher learning. It seems 'equal' was not enough; and so now, a higher grade for lower work.

And now, coming to a school near you. A quota system to take earned benefits from your child, dear Reader, and give them to someone else's child who is currently playing a computer game. They will not be grateful for this largesse.

Dog Whistle

Medieval cathedrals, Shakespeare, Mozart, Greek mythology, ballet, space exploration, Dostoyevsky, science, Formula 1, folk dance, the Dutch masters, weightlifting, model boat building, lace making, collecting stamps, choirs, wherever excellence shows its pale face.

Okay, I see what they are doing now!

Invented by Whites, even a dog whistle is a 'dog whistle'.

Drag Queen

Your future teacher; and why not?

Then, since the heavens have shaped my body so

Let hell make crooked my mind to answer it.

Like everything subversive, it starts with nothing, then a little insignificant something and before you can say, *Hey, what's going on here?*, it's too late! Now drag queens are a 'movement', presented as a part of the post-modern liberation from culturally imposed shackles of gender identity, and so required their place in the new school curriculum of tolerance. Think of the DQs as the scouts of a Sodomic Army and the media fanfared, nursery DQ story time as their marcher camps. With much wailing and gnashing of teeth these 'inclusive readings' will be rejected this time around, but they will have fulfilled their allotted role in the plan; the future societal boundaries expanded, children exposed ever earlier to sexuality and fetishes, 'intolerant' resistance identified, necessary propaganda disseminated more forcefully and, crucially, the new tolerance and inclusive laws tabled.

The new laws tabled, this is the important part for your child's life in school. This is the means whereby the reading of a story to infants will come to look like a part of an atrocity exhibition,

Drama

In a bureaucracy staffed by women, some have claimed their rules-bound personalities, meddlesome proclivities and general solipsism lead to an increased risk of drama, even over the littlest of things, and this this contributes to the ongoing dysfunction. Although this is true, no sensible man would claim such a thing and expect to avoid a starring role in the latest show. And, as I wish to avoid huff and tears, neither do I.

Dream

GT: *I had me a dream last night; that the children in my class were obedient, polite, diligent and respectful.*

MLK jnr: **Keep on dreaming, Bro. This side of judgement that could only true in dreamland.**

Dress Code

Down with yoga pants, as these are too often accompanied by an unhealthy thickness in the ankle, leg, A-zone, P-zone and centre section (or sections). No pupil should be exposed to their teacher's substantial, practically barenaked rumpa and crackatoa on them bending over or, worse, the forever horror of knowing that they are wearing a red thong and –alas, it can get worse – have a tattoo'd [censored] just above the coccyx.

Let us agree that the experiment in letting female teachers dress as they wish has not produced the daily fashion parade of togged *Milano* elegance we supposed, but permanent dress-down day from TK Maxx.

It is time to return to a dress code. White or cream blouses and pleated, hipped, mid-length flowing skirts (for effective twirling) with discreet metalwork accoutrements are recommended in the confident expectation that such ladylike attire will encourage ladylike behaviour. This code could be enforced by the school jannie doubling as sartorial enforcement officer and holding a supply of burqas for any miscreants.

NB. Obviously, at certain schools (e.g., Sandwood Primary), a stab-proof vest, combat gloves, safety helmet and Batwoman utility belt will be needed to complete the ensemble. These need not be necessary in infant classes.

Driven

1. by motor vehicle: How most children journey to and from school. This commonplace partly explains why so many children cannot walk properly, far less route march. It also provides an ironic counterpoint to the various saving the planet initiatives. In the interests of fairness it has to be noted that the cost of petrol is balanced by less wear on one's segs if wearing tackety boots, rubber if commando soled or skin if jungle shod.

2. to madness: A common fate for teachers. Achieved through the whips of management or the scorns of pupils. All that is needed is a little time, hence the phrase: *The whips and scorns of time.*

Duty of Disclosure

Under the guise of pupil protection, promoting tolerance and preventing discrimination, the disaffected, the schemers and the jealous now have carte blanche to secretly report on colleagues, while pretending that they are doing their duty. With Wisdom permanently retired, Revenge gets a free pass to sow discord, risk free. O happy day for those who would bear false witness with delight, for they shall enjoy promotion. One can only hope that women teachers don't hear of this new rule.

The following conversation, secretly recorded, illustrates Duty of Disclosure in action:

Hello, Council Educational Tolerance Unit. How can I help you?

I want to complain about a man, under Duty of Disclosure.

What did he do?

He was being a man. Explaining things, fixing stuff, he's balding too.

This sounds like a serious case of sexist micro-aggression. Balding too, you say. Did he look at you?

Yes, I think so.

He seems like a beast. You've definitely got a case. I'm sure we can take his job away, just for starters.

That's what I was hoping for. I've never liked him.

Well, you did the right thing in disclosing him. We've too many men in primary teaching anyway. Another one down, Ha ha!

Oh, by the way, there's a Jew hiding in the loft at Prinsengracht 263.

E

Earning

This is just like learning except missing an L. Given the incentive that money provides, it should not be surprising that earning actually results in more learning.

There is no reason why children from middle primary upwards could not have earning real money, or some other usable credit, incorporated into the school day. This would involve proper necessary work, properly executed and properly paid, and not an extension of pupil sales of cupcakes or clothes-peg fridge magnets, etc., at the school fair. As such this would provide a real-world example of concentration to a useful end. Given the nature of modern jobs, many young children are equally usefully employable as their adult equivalences. Why not, mines are less dangerous than they used to be.

Earphones

Encouraging public disengagement; imagine taking and collecting your kid from school and doing so wearing earphones, so that you don't miss your favourite tunes. You might ask, isn't this insensitive to your kid who might want to talk to you, or disrespectful to other parents, as it indicates your unavailability in what is otherwise a social setting. What sort of social signal and behavioural template does this demonstrate to children? And the answer, presumably, would be; It's their favourite tunes, ffs, and that's what favourite means! Life is all about getting your priorities right; # 1. Favourite tunes.

That's commitment to the pop matrix. Truly, awesomely sad!

Ebola

Tokaloshe laugh and say: *Big fun, black juju come. Prepare your potions, Whitey.*

Ladies, you asked for it; you want Africa, now you get it good!

Admittedly not a welcome enrichment from Africa, but like chimp-outs, it's coming anyway. It would be racist to question any aspect of this near future scenario, just like it would be sexist to just accept that bio-hazard suits are blue.

When Ebola runs out of traction and goes into the viral pit stop for an update to Version 2.0, thanks to diversity, we can have another pandemic flown in from sweatier zones as a replacement. Interesting diseases from tropical climes are yet another strength of diversity, and all we have to give in return is the cost of treatment.

Educationalists

A whole class of admin drones disguised as experts and doing busy-work, justifying their existence, complicating the simple and breaking things. Then blaming others for it, before coming up with 'solutions' to the problems that they have created; integrity level zero. And so it goes in a circle of nonsense, the dog chasing its tail.

And, as we see every month, their assignment is also to post a huge amount of contradictory theories, reports, claims, and accounts of history, so that you can't remember which way is up. Part of this last assignment is redefining words out from under you, so that you feel like you are standing on quicksand. Just when you think you have a grip on some term, they throw out its old meaning and create a new one that is just the opposite. This isn't an accident and it isn't a sign of progress. It is the purposeful denial of firm ground, so that you have no position from which to attack them or question them. Them? Yes, them.

There is no honour in this occupation. A useless class which produce nothing of value, but produce plenty of no value.

Educational Psychologists

In lieu of common sense we have ed psych. There is NOTHING in their advice and written reports that could not be better found in Aesop's Fables or any Shakespeare play, or talking to your granny. The very best only tell you what you already know; but too many others run scared of parents and bend to their desire for a therapy solution, and are then complicit in the proscription of Ritalin and Adderall, or worse unrealistic and potentially negative recommendations. Of course, to be implemented by the teacher who will also take full responsibility for their failure.

The schoolboy's triple whammy; ed psych, IT and pharma.

Education Department

Our various enemies, the multiplying villainies of nature, do swarm upon this place. The debilitating cost to Western societies of their presence is incalculable. We await our Cromwell:

I command ye therefore, upon the peril of your lives, to depart immediately out of this place.

Edu-speak

Basically, a form of lies.

A special language spoken by educational managers, academics, HM. Inspectors, consultants, and bureaucrats consisting of randomly arranged progressive clichés regarding the need for more inclusion, diversity, attainment, standards, accountability productivity and sexualisation of school life, issued as a prepared statement in which they are always cast by themselves as visionary champions calling out for reform. The order in which the lies are presented may be switched to especially focus on a preferred crisis or create a sense of wide expertise and concern, but the content is always the same – fluff.

However, one would be mistaken in conflating empty content with empty message. For it is by Edu-speak that the agenda is set, parents distracted from the true source of dysfunction in the system and teachers frustrated. These wholly owned subsidiary creatures listed above are the means whereby educational nonsense enters school life. They obfuscate the public to easier achieve their subversive goals. They love not our children. Their end intent is evil. When they speak they lie; this is their natural language, for there is no truth in them – just like their true father.

For an example of award winning Edu-speak check out GTCS CEO: *To improve inclusion and attainment in primary schools we must have more teachers from diverse sexual, racial, religious and refugee backgrounds. Young learners deserve the opportunity to collaboratively construct meaningful social knowledge and curricular forms with strong, resourceful minority leadership. This*

is why I am proud to call for improved funding to the Wakandan
refugee to Scottish teacher programme. Diversity is our educational
strength too.

Egalitarianism

Always betraying itself and toxic to the common good.

The prevailing philosophy and operating sentiment of our age, and to
the service of which our primary schools are dedicated. So powerful
is this philosophy's grip on our world view, that where this stance
is contrary to social and psychological reality, we bend our will to
denial. This denial is at the heart of our pedagogic practice; we see
it daily doing subtle harms to those it is supposedly intended to
benefit, as well as, more obviously, those more academically able
children it is secretly intended to impede. With a fantasy goal of
equality that will never be achieved, allied to a hidden resentment
against any distinction, egalitarianism is a destroyer doctrine.

Arguably it is a sentiment that should be considered in an
ethnostate, but a doomsday philosophy in our multi-ethnic state and
otherwise divided to itself. Forever pitting unequals against each
other, feeding the rivalry and selfishness it is supposed to cure. The
real social rot is what it does to integrity.

It is not possible to disarm this bomb in a liberal democracy, but
don't worry, times a ticking ever faster.

EIS

The Educational Institute of Scotland; supporting equality,
challenging racism and sexism, stopping violence against women,
supporting asylum seekers and refugees.

This is the main teachers union in Scotland and its stated purpose.

Rather than focusing on protecting the interests of teachers, the EIS pushes their members into fake international politics and divisive social justice issues. Energies diverted thusly, their incompetence in respect to protecting teachers is near council HR levels. It's almost as if their real purpose is to serve the agenda. Hmm!

Electric Scooter

This idea was first suggested by a male pupil in a discussion regarding playground improvements, who then had to fend off accusations that boys would just use them to chase girls. This fun-filled image of screaming girls and whooping boys, perhaps with lassoes too, had to be put aside when another use was suggested; a better way to complete the daily mile for those pupils who don't like running. A genius level idea, even as it crushingly defeats the purpose of the daily mile. For my part, I would swap a whiteboard update for the cost equivalent of a dozen class-based electric scooters and a couple of quad bikes; some tasks would surely get done quicker.

Given the trend in childhood obesity, such scooters (with beefed-up frames) may become a commonplace in school. This is a powerful response to those gainsayers who claim that ever improving technology is not always a good thing.

Eloi, Eloi, lama sabachthani?

That feeling, every single day.

Emergency

A kid claimed to lose his inhaler on a trip. Then claimed a panic attack, which manifested itself as the need to avoid doing what he didn't want to do anyway. Of course, teacher's fault, and teacher blamed and censured for failing to ensure that said kid brought his inhaler. This teacher failure could have caused a medical emergency, and: *How would that look for the school?*

Later discovered that said kid didn't have an inhaler, didn't need one and never has; but 'forgot' this crucial aspect of his own medical history. Of course, apologies followed and teacher's reputation restored. (But only in dreamland).

Empathy

'...encouraging empathy should be embedded in the curriculum.'

(Certain exclusions apply; native culture, males, traditional families).

God has so engineered this attribute so as to be available in harmony with social need and personal well-being. Thusly, we are equipped with a finite stock of this molecule to prevent us being taken a 'len of', as we say in Scotland for a kind-hearted mug, and thus undermining our own patrimony and posterity. Once empathy is used up, not only is it gone for good, but the self-protection needed by its opposite attribute, indifference, kicks into play. And so, empathy fatigue by P5:

This empathy thing, I've noticed that is always us that are supposed to have it and always us that give it. But not them. Why is that?
(Irene P5 at the Global Caring Workshop)

Our advocates for values have not considered this aspect when promoting appeals again and again and again to children's empathy. And not just the children, us in Scotland have dished empathy out by the gigamole, and still more is demanded; this is the exhausted background to similar operant conditioning of our children. Of course, even when expressed, the empathy is an illusion. Actually, what is being activated is social approval. That darkest and most volatile of social forces. And toxic to a child's development when solicited thusly.

Starving are you? Your first instinct is to feel sorry for them, probably your second instinct too, but then,...*Let them eat cake!*

Employment

Schools should not employ a teacher who does not read. By 'read' I mean proper books, not Cosmopolitan, Love Island updates or tweets from besties. Elitist and exclusionary? Absolutely!

Empowerment

This type of power is only available to colourful, special people and females (of whatever sex). Once acquired, allegedly by a sprinkle of fairy dust, this power allows the recipient to be simultaneously victim and conqueror; able to crush a male's spirit by relentless tongue lashing of the victimhood mantra. In Scottish primary schools there are always empowerment officers on duty, these may be adults or children, but regardless, a baited male or traitor-female crosses them at their peril. Indeed, even a stubborn donkey that chances a wrong-think sexist remark (*Ee-aaw!*) risks leaving the fray as a bipod. This is the truth of empowerment, its goal is actually disempowerment; of whom, I'm sure you know. If not, you can check in the mirror.

Even if one accepted that empowerment is a good thing, specifically, what is it that is to be achieved and how is this to be effected in class? Advocates could not answer this question because the whole thing is a scam.

Everywhere empowerment is present, it always stands in opposition to civility.

Endless Revolution

Attendant with the nature of having so many topics politicised and racialised, a sort of endless revolution is introduced to schools. This creates more discord, more misery and, ironically, more calls for even more change to fix the new problems which are always blamed, not on the changes which caused them, but – as per radical guidelines – on insufficient zeal and funding for the previous changes. *Plus ça change!*

Pupil and teacher anxiety and neurosis are a consequence of this endless social challenge and change.

The curious thing about this situation is that it is well-known that it is the familiar – custom, tradition and habit – that reduces stress and conflict. And that complying with those brings our pupils personal and social happiness. But such manifestations of the apparent privilege that the familiar brings are nothing compared to imparting to our pupils the 'correct' attitude to the really important things in preparing for the future.

Enemies

1. central government **2.** local government **3.** Department of Education **4.** HM Inspectors of Schools **5.** GTCS **6.** mainstream media **7.** university departments of education **8.** colleges of education **9.** educational consultants **10.** CPD **11.** activist pressure groups **12.** rubbish pupils **13.** rubbish parents **14.** governing bodies **15.** exam boards **16.** admin and record keeping **17.** unrealistic targets **18.** reduced budgets **19.** increased workload **20.** whole country going to pot.

Energy

The educational establishment makes much of their investment in developing teacher skill, knowledge and competence; however, no cognisance is taken of the need for this essential ingredient in teaching to be recharged. It is taken for granted that the teacher will bring Energy Max to every lesson. How this capacity is built and sustained is the teacher's problem.

English

Changing into something else, even as we speak. But not like Latin becoming Italian, more like 1984's Newspeak, where each day we become less and less able to express a complex idea or want to. The idea that can't be expressed, can't be thought. You know that there are those who would welcome this development as a necessary condition of us becoming the helots they desire. This is why books and literacy are so important to have and why IT-based learning is so necessary to NOT have.

Enigma

The school Pharisees try to trap Scotch Jesus, but he flips their script with a clever conundrum and has them reeling at the thought of their racial apostasy being exposed.

One day, as Scotch Jesus was encouraging his class to feel pride in their ancestors' technical and artistic genius by teaching them about the development of the European cathedral while gently listening to some Bach religious music, the chief diversity teachers and department anti-racist scribes, together with the school Babylonian lifestyle advisers, came up to Him. 'Tell us by what authority you are doing these things,' they said. 'Who gave you this authority?'

'Let me ask you a question first,' he replied. 'Half the diversity – is it still twice too much; or is twice the diversity, half of what it should be?'

They deliberated among themselves, but found that their brains addled by repetitive tweeting could not reach a conclusion, and so said, 'If we answer wrongly all the pupils will stone us, and we will become infamous as racists and lose our high salaried jobs.' So they answered that they did not know. And Jesus replied, 'Neither will I tell you by what authority I am doing these things.' And the pupils were amazed, never before had they heard such wisdom.

NB. With thanks (and apologies, if required) to Luke, the evangelist and saint. See, Luke 20:1–8.

Entropy

Things fall apart. The centre cannot hold. The bubble bursts. The games a bogey.

Entropy always wins.

Epictetus

Appropriately introduced, much profit could be obtained by studying the ancient philosophers, even as infants. Epictetus recommends himself by his entire Stoic advice being reduced to a level equally intelligible and beneficial to adult and child; Persist, Resist.

Equal

As God noted: *You are all made equal, then you are born.*

True; Women are equal to men. All men are pigs.

Equality

In primary school practice this basically involves taking rights and interests from little boys and forcing them on little girls. Then presenting this action in terms of unjust privileges won back in a righteous war.

The type of equality is not equality at all, but the public face of resentment and revenge.

Equality Coordinating Officers

More commonly known as Koordinierungsbeauftragte für Schulgleichheit (KfS):

Only recently introduced (although not yet issued sidearms) and yet already they are having an impact. Prior to the new KfS 'visiting' our school 'for a chat' the head teacher recommended we spontaneously enrol in an online Global Citizenship Course, as it would be sure to impress our new lady master. In the future, of course, this offizier will be able to insist on teachers enrolling in such courses, or sending them to special camps, constructed on the European model, to achieve the same end, but with better concentration.

Equity

Equity means equal outcomes.

With a presumption whose height overleaps the heavens, our Scottish scheemie sages in the gossip box at Holyrood demand the same educational outcome for children spread over three standard deviations. The application of excellence makes this easily achievable ☻ – which is why we have a Curriculum for Excellence. ☺ The means to achieve equity will be vigorously imposed (i.e., unequal treatment, preferential judgement and competition handicaps), even though we know that they will not, indeed cannot, be successful.

In our hearts, we know the whole equity thing is based on the denial of certain racial and cultural realities. Those who promote this within our schools as a justice issue are actually arguing against a fundamental principle of our society – that people should be judged as individuals and treated equally. In their opinion, though, it is not so much a case that some pupils should be treated *more* equally, but that some other pupils should be treated *less* equally. Born of hate and hubris, equity is a destroyer's philosophy in the school context.

At meetings concerning such stuff, I don't know whether to laugh or cry, but I keep a straight face and don't meet anyone's eyes. – Komrade Minister of Skottish Edukation. (Later shot as a classroom traitor, after freely admitting to having doubts about the guaranteed success of the equity programme – and to poisoning working-class water supplies.)

Essential Knowledge

As defined by our local authority Education Department Information Governance Unit:

Fraud, bribery, grievances, ICT acceptable use policy, corporate health and safety, whistle blowing, stress, customer complaints.

Eugenic/Dysgenic Incentives

By policies and strategies that legitimise and support dysfunctional individuals, our primary schools are well-embedded in that great societal loop that causes the dysgenic families we see overwhelming us. Whatever you incentivise, you get more of. Individual teachers that try to put a spike in this process, however done and motivated to do so, will find themselves cast out from history's spinning wheel, for the great age of dysgenic ruin is on us.

One might think that this problem would be simply fixable, for, as there is no operating space between eugenic and dysgenic, if you're not doing one you're doing the other. And so just shift the balance to promote good families or not promote bad ones. Alas, in our democratic age, with so much public funded effort and employment linked to our dysgenic families, and eugenic practices still linked to discredited national breeding stock ambitions of the last century, the prospects of us correcting this phenomena are zero.

Fear naught, Mama Nature has the solution in hand. She fears no tweets or Facebook dislikes. Hold her beer while she clears and levels the table!

Evil

Inefficiency, waste and absurdity in their myriad forms are to be expected in every institution, and are no more than expressions of institutional evolution wedded to human frailties. This is bad, but not evil. What makes something evil is the conscious intention to undermine social norms, transfer blame to innocent actors, to destroy from the inside. For why; because those so motivated hate you. For why; as the externalisation of their own self-hatred. For why; their souls cry out in confusion. For why; grace has passed the by. For why; they do not deserve it. For why; they chose to serve the other. For why; because they're evil.

This evil in education is usually achieved by use of zombies; dimly gas-lit teacher proxies, self-righteous Twitter fiends, the flotsam and jetsam that wash around public funding, bureaucratic placemen, unwitting child innocents taught to parrot destructive shibboleths.

Often in life one has to choose between stupid and evil, in education the choice is pre-made, you get both.

Example

As the teacher is one by default; it is always best, should your obligation exceed your interest or capacity, to be a good example of a bad example, rather than vice- versa, as is more commonly found. See me for example.

Excellence

Claims for this should always be paired with humility, but never are.

Recognising that good is not good enough, our nation's shekel-powered sages invented excellence. And by deeming this the new baseline standard for teachers in Scotland, success and happiness ensued. For those few Jurassic-era teachers still stuck in the rut of merely trying their best, the public purse was not spared in developing an extensive selection of corrective courses. Genius meets simplicity, who would have thought that public education in Scotland could be transposed by the introduction of a mere word. Some smart-asses have claimed that our excellence is a delusion achieved by a fusion of subliminal psychology and voodoo, and that in fact we have come full circle back to rubbish. Such wrongthinkers are currently reconsidering their position while domiciled in a special camp to help them concentrate on the undeniable improvement brought about by excellence. After all, even the curriculum is excellent now, as can be readily ascertained from its name; *What say ye to this fact, ye cynics and apostates?*

This challenge always shuts them up!

Excellence is not applied to multi-million pound scams like Growth Mindset and SEAL; when these fail to deliver excellence, this is the fault of the teacher.

See also, Tired of Lies.

Existential Crisis

aka; the everyday life of a teacher

Daily jousts with stupidity, fraud, ingrates, respectively from ideas, false claims and pupils.

You wonder if you're doing any good, but your conscience already knows the answer.

Experience

This is the best teacher; but only for people with intelligence and humility. All the others just keep repeating the same mistakes.

One would think that experience would, of all places, be respected in a school. However, as it implicitly carries a threat to incompetent management, it always flirts with resentment and marginalisation. Either way, it is trumped by credentials, croneyism and virtue signalling.

Experts

Our children's education is developed, delivered and implemented within a system dominated by gullible people who are manipulated by subversive and half-wit experts. Chief among those gulled are the politicians who, thinking they are addressing real needs, are actually fronting institutional interests they are hardly aware of. The entire process of fixing our education system from seed planted to shekel harvest home involves expert opinion. And it is only at the implementation stage, when the teachers are given empty envelopes containing their instructions, that the experts disappear – along with the money! Unable to implement as required leads us back to where we were before. Luckily, another expert has a mate who's an expert on that very topic. It'll cost, but the kiddies are worth it.

In an educational context the word expert should be spelt, f.r.a.u.d.

F

Facecrime

The unintentional exposure by facial expression of one's sceptical attitude to some new policy initiative, IT update or productivity improvement. This is a very hard thing to control, even when one is aware of the likelihood of it occurring. And it is always spotted by female colleagues, whose natural inbuilt Voight-Kampf test is always searching for hive mind deviants (via retinal diameter) with a view to their later exposure and destruction.

Even immature females (only of the XX female-female variety) have this faculty at a mature operational level. For example, at a recent Soviet-style, justice cheer assembly, I noticed Meggin (7 years) in a glance had ascertained my true level of belief in the party line. Her sly smile to me charmingly indicated that my secret was safe with her – for the moment.

Once an HT, on seeing my pain of disdain at a policy initiative workshop, apparently misread it (or double bluff?) as actual pain and asked if I was feeling alright. Thinking quickly, I was able to say that I felt a headache coming on. This was to be true. As it still is!

Don't look in their eyes, they can read your mind.

Facts

Ref: part of a knowledge-based pedagogy.

Actually teaching literacy and maths to children, as opposed to talking about teaching it, confirms the common sense belief that a secure knowledge of basic facts forms the bedrock upon which other skills can be built; and that the automatic recall of facts frees up working memory for higher order tasks. However, facts have fallen out of favour in current pedagogic practice, partly because pupils have to learn them and then be tested to confirm retention. And the crucial words here are 'learned' and 'tested'; strategies which do not find favour in our easy-going, just look things up and then forget them, age. Also, acquiring and recalling facts is a function of intelligence and the clear display of this by the more intelligent pupil falls foul of prevailing egalitarian ideologies. Facts can be prejudiced, you see!

Unable to ban facts, because they are, after all, still facts, the solution has been to misrepresent a fact and knowledge based pedagogy as consisting of unnecessary information which impede comprehension, or sometimes even as pointless lists devoid of meaning. This argument is advanced in in order to sell the new pedagogy; 'sell' here meaning for money. This new pedagogy focusses on the process of acquiring both a 'proper context' and a' learning strategy' as a precondition to developing understanding; this, the so-called 'active learning'. 'Understanding' being the learning goal here, rather than knowledge and operational skill; although it is, of course, impossible to understand exactly what understanding means anyway, when it is shorn of knowledge and operational skill.

In real life, children cannot create the desired understanding in the absence of facts. The important fact here, however, is that a fact and knowledge based pedagogy not only actually works, but is preferred by pupils. However, that it is NOT in need of replacement is irrelevant in the selling of the new ideas and associated materials. Shekel collectors gotta collect!

The active learning process reverses horse and cart and wastes effort; but don't worry about this causing slipping standards, they've got even more products on hand to fix this. The true thing about facts is that they are real things to have in your mind and their relationship to context becomes clear when they are applied to a problem. Whereas, understanding context and learning processes (whatever this actually means) was always a nothing sort of thing without facts. The attacks against the fact and knowledge based pedagogy were based on false distinctions, and basically a lie dressed in educational psycho-babble.

Little boys in particular are attracted to such list learning, as a part of their wider interest in a topic. This is natural to their nature. And so, they are disproportionally affected by the teaching emphasis on learning processes and discussion. Facts were always a more contingent thing for females, as you will find out if you question them on this! Hidden deep in the female reptile mind, an unconscious awareness of this sex bias, may be a part reason for hating on facts.

Facts don't deaden the mind, but help structure it. It is incoherence that kills learning. Mastery is built on facts sorting themselves into context and system. Learning facts is a triumph over laziness.

Good old facts, please come back!

Tommy, tell the class the list of English monarchs, with dates, starting with Alfred the Great?

Yes, Miss. Shall I list his Wessex king predecessors too?

Failure

Failure is actually one of the good guys. It's time it was given more respect, and even a little loving too

Poor old failure, that moment when reality meets fantasy and converts to an engine of positive change or acceptance, has been given a bad rep in the modern school. Its crucial role in learning, both academic and social, has been binned in favour of constant success and praise. This done by those who have no understanding of the source of motivation and the nature of true achievement. Much failure must be banked before competence is reached, this is why failure must be accorded respect; to deny failure its place in the scheme of things, as we do, is to encourage real failure.

Failure is how children realistically rank themselves and their potential. It is a source of their self-motivation. It is the character forming balance to the child's natural solipsism and conceit. This is especially true for boys, who having no natural female recourse to stepping aside for the men to take over when it all goes wrong, must acquire a realistic sense of competence.

For the teacher, of course, failure is less a part of learning, and more a part of being sacked.

False World

The sum total of all the dyscivic, value-laden, disempowering, over-protected, over-explained, dishonestly rewarding, tolerating, disingenuous concern, rights respecting, policy dense, over-regulated, counter intuitive and anti-human school environment we create for our pupils.

Fatherless

The saddest children. Little boys with no hero-dad to share and connect, little girls with disastrous mum's boyfriend templates held out as examples of male relationships. The family community broken, single mothers a danger to themselves, truth tellers punished. Luckily, I avoid this by having no opinion on this phenomenon, as you have just witnessed.

Female

Preferred sex for employment. Empowerment or victimisation as required, often both simultaneously.

Soon to come in many forms, including male.

See, stupid ideas, talking up a storm, drama and tears, secret plots, good at lying, wonderful creatures, God's best gift, Satan's best weapon, bits and bobs.

Female Leaders

Arguably the most salient aspect of our current dysfunction throughout the Western world is the role of women leaders at every level of our institutions creating a gynocracy. These are not the wise matriarchs you would wish for, because such women are typically childless and have reached their position of authority by accepting the poisoned chalice offered by our feministic times. However, in avoiding (or rejecting) motherhood and replacing it with political power, something life-affirming dies in the psyche to be replaced by unfulfilled and misdirected impulses of the sort that having children tames to maturity. No admonishing hand from a male ever restraining their worst impulses and ever, of inherited necessity, plotting against female colleagues, such leaders end up living the lives of dowager queens. In general, they are incapable of accepting criticism – even should they appear to do so. Much of the primary school ethos can be properly understood by this framing.

This is why dowagers lived the lives they did, and were feared and rejected.

NB. An honourable exception is made for Marie de Guise. If only Scotland had another such woman and queen!

Female Social Aggression

Males, with their occasional predilection for direct confrontation and physical violence, don't have the neural wiring to deal with female social aggression, and especially its relentless, merciless and surreptitious nature. In the arena of mental manipulation, which is the default arena for confrontation in primary school, female power vastly exceeds the male; it's not a fair fight. And it is never one on one, as females always group bully a male. It is for this reason that men seek company of their own kind, and not for the denying of female rights, far less hatred. This male requirement also applies to boys. Socially and legally denied a natural male response to such female social aggression makes the consequence of it far worse for male mental health than its reverse. Pleading for male time and man caves, of course attracts the claims of misogyny and cavemanitis; although the reverse, that females need time and space and organisation away from males, which is equally true, draws understanding and approval from those same femi-tyrants. And, indeed, from men too, who are almost universally happy for women to have their girls' night out, muffin mornings, stitch and bitch clubs and pamper spa weekends – if such men are married, they greet such women-alone time with joy.

Feminism

As with all forms of misery, never unhappy alone.

Feminism attacks the foundations of the society that made it possible and ironically depends on its forbearance as it continues in its mission – it is no accident that it is only a feature of Western societies. Has always been a self-deceiving hate machine dedicated to churning out Big Lies about the sexes and about their roles in society, with the too obvious and expressly stated purpose of handicapping boys and men, and bestowing favouritism in myriad forms on girls and women – to their ruin. To the extent that it operates over and above genuine – although now, historic – female complaints regarding access, it is an intel project; Operation: All Men are Pigs. As it is manifested in the media and as an organised political movement, it is totally controlled by the usual tribal infiltrators – as an examination of fundings sources and leading personnel reveal. It is a, perhaps *the*, crucial element in the unravelling of Western societies. If men and woman can be separated from each other by distrust and legal complaint, then our future is bleak.

After helping to encourage the revolution, Feminism found itself able to capitalise on the unhappiness which resulted. Indeed, the survival of the movement depends on a continuing supply of resentful women who believe their rights are being violated and that this is the proper way to consider the relations between the sexes.

Today we encounter a situation where the maenads of this religion, and the progressive world view to which it belongs, dominate in careers dedicated to children. They may believe that they stand for Rights, but really their demand is for privilege; and the end effect of this assignment is the promotion of neuroticism, depression and genetic extinction. This is an especially powerful force in primary schools which cannot be gainsaid or ignored. The recurring patterns that we see in schools, the obsession with sex and gender, and claims of injustice directed against males, the self-loathing pressure everywhere, are founded on this sexual frustration and wrong-headed anger, at last given an audience that dare not answer back – themselves!.

Little girls are led down a path to the Feminist temple precincts where they are taught to celebrate the dyscivic thoughts and actions of this religion. Eventually, as young women, they are abandoned by their barren banshee mentors to the confusion and despair which follows this manufactured indignation. Some never find the route back to home and family.

This force for evil is particularly tragic for little girls when it is used as the justification for celebrating precocious sexuality as demonstrated daily by teeny celebrities given space and airtime for Feminist fluffy nothings and faux indignations, while complaining in a half-naked state about male sexual objectifying of the female body. It is a tall hurdle to jump, but some way must be found from within the female community of rejecting the idea that feminism in any way protects or cares for women as people; thousands march in faux outrage over naughty words, and zero for the ruination of little girls in their own country. This tells you everything you need to know.

Nature's three lovely daughters, Beauty, Grace and Wit have been replaced by Resentment, Complaint and Confusion. Solace is found by knowing that nothing lasts forever and the justice the Feminists pray for they will receive. Too often childless, or single-childed (possibly by un-orthodox methods), the hormonal anger powering the Feminist worldview will devour itself. And that once their work is done, these useful idiots of dystopia, these wretched wrecks wrecking others' lives, will enjoy their well-deserved desserts. Barren and hated, the world says: *Bye, bye. Don't come back too soon!*

This is a mighty foe for Western men to contend with, as it takes the disarming form of that which we love best.

Fertility

What should be celebrated in partnership with femininity.

The power and the glory contained in little girls. Mighty Aphrodite bends the worship and will of every man to this end. As it should be. The false futures promoted for females when fertility is not even respected leads to their and our ruin. Girls' education and female self-esteem inversely correlate to lifetime fertility. We have already seen the effect of this on intelligent White women, setting themselves firmly on the path to extinction by abandoning having children, or squeezing one out just before the gate closes for good. And, of course, the opposite effect on their genetic opposites. Hence, the downward trend of European intelligence. No one told these strong, independent women that peak and best fertility occurs while they are pursuing the all-important career at 20. And that 30 and 40 come around quicker than you think.*

And then, too late, the bad choice realised with the barren future beckoning; 9pm, house lights out, chocolate, ice cream, warm bed, knees up under the blanket, cat as companion, TV glow; *Love Island?* – possibly, but not this one.

---

* How many at 45 have not caught up with themselves and still see 25 in the mirror?

First Day

Ref: Mr Duncan's first day at a new school.

7.17 am. Teacher stands before the secure entrance gate. Crows circle overhead, crying. The thought occurs:

The raven himself is hoarse that croaks the fatal entrance of Duncan under my battlements.

Fitbit

Who would have thought that the time would come when children would require a digitally delivered instruction to tell them to walk or run, with a view not to escape the school bully or PC Murdoch, but further deposits of adipose tissue?

Further preparing our children for the life of surveillance.

Thirty to Forty Group, take your places, please. Right, let's see which one of us can touch his toes. Right over from the hips, Brothers and Sisters, please. 6079 Smith W. Yes, you. Bend over. You're not trying, watch me...

Fitness Week

What is said, what is unsaid; so, what is unsaid in the introduction and implementation of this programme? What hidden judgements are handed down to the millions of lardies blocking our school corridors, like fatbergs in drains, as the head teacher introduces Fitness Week while unwittingly (one assumes) mocking the same with ten extra kilos on her arse and ankles shaped like boiled hams stuffed into her brand-new trainers? What do children make of this perfect example of adult irony?

Fitness Week for the fitness weak – another improvement of the digital age.

Folios of Learning

Collected evidence of a child's learning across various topic areas. Brimming with excellence and happy photos that have been claimed by cynics, although not me obviously, to be the educational equivalent of a budget holiday brochure. This would suggest, although not by me obviously, that the better the evidence looks, the less evidence it actually is of learning. But who could believe such a thing? Obviously, not you.

Fool

With no one able to say to the HT or Head of Service what we all silently think, dissent festers and turns up in complaining volumes. This is why every school needs a fool, patterned after the medieval model, to say without fear or embarrassment the truth. What a service such a servant performs! The deputy head would be ideal for such a role; well, actually, …

Foolish Notions

In an institution in which these abound as foundational of much of our pedagogy and practice, it seems evident that our foolish notions have not been chosen wisely. However, this is just to consider the proximate cause of things. Once the spell is broken and the hidden world is seen for what it is, then we see that we have misunderstood the intent behind the ultimate power that shapes the form of our future. And that the nonsense herein identified, is not nonsense at all. It is wicked. It well serves its ultimate cause.

All the decision-making that seems incomprehensible, becomes intelligible once you understand who's sticking it to whom. Whom is us and who is them.

Forget

...?

Forgotten

It doesn't matter how good you are, you can easily be replaced and then forgotten. Keep this in mind when you are being treated like shit. Although he didn't know it, Boethius was writing for the modern primary teacher. Take note of his fate, it is yours too.

Four Horsemen of the Apocalypse

1. Google, Amazon, Facebook and Apple are well-established in schools, promoting their wares, sponsoring 'research', spreading 'values', rewiring our children to their end.

These giants of our destruction with their footsoldiers in the form of Instagram, Twitter, Playstation, Whorebox, etc are welcomed to feed on our pupils by complicit education leaders and their useful-idiot addicted and addled teacher drones.

The Apple logo, an apple with Eve's bite out of it; the idea inspired beyond the realm of logic for those who can see to see its meaning.

2. There is a female version of the above targeted specifically at young girls. Their mission is to fill the children's heads with popworld garbage and feminist hatred, all the better that they may be led to depression, despair and death. Emma, Lily, Taylor and Ariana; the four My Little Ponies of the Apocalypse. It would be wonderful to be able to someday say: *Thank goodness, children are no longer being exposed to the dreck pedalled by these fluffy-brained, squeaking fembots.*

Fourteen

Ayont, and quit this place.

Without a high IQ, by 14 years old school education has reached its limit, and at this age and stage of your life you should be out of school and doing something useful that earns money. Those that want to can stay on, providing they've got a reason and the cognitive firepower to back it up. However, as the general level of intelligence declines, we should be adjusting school leaving age downwards to give the less brainy children an opportunity of usefully employing ages 14–18. My mum and dad left school at 14 and this did not harm them. Nor were my grannies rendered deficient by leaving school at 12, indeed, the exact opposite.

This strategy is not insulting to the less intelligent, less academically gifted, or those whose interests lie elsewhere. Such children know themselves well in advance of leaving age. It does them no good to pretend that they have a potential for a certain sort of future, when they have not. Indeed, forcing them (for such it is), to stay on past their threshold of tolerance for school-life does them harm, and often others who are forced to accommodate the disruptive power of unwilling teenagers. This Quit at Fourteen strategy is thus realising, not denying, options.

A very large proportion of jobs, particularly service and support, could easily be done by 14 year olds – as they were in former times. Indeed, many of those jobs could be done just as well by even younger children, and to their pleasure and development.

By providing employment for our now school-free teens, this would have the added benefit of reducing the sad need for military-age males from broken countries (perhaps broken by us while wearing our NATO mask) to come here seeking employment or welfare or revenge – the first two categories now being filled with our own young people.

Middle primary should be preparing children for this possible meeting with reality, rather than indulging them in fanciful, if not dishonest, dreams of reaching for the stars.

Frauds

In educational circles can be identified by being at least one degree removed from pupils and the classroom, and at least one degree nearer the public funds.

This gang of freebooters and parasites is responsible for the double educational crisis of none of this and too much of that, namely money and stupid ideas.

Standard solution recommended; sword and flame. Will accept next best offer!

Freespace™

According to experts, this space-time anomaly – typically lasting 10–15 minutes – just appears out of a wormhole into the primary classroom and radiates calm, thus allowing the teacher to lead the class in the value-added activities (Just *whenever you find ten or fifteen minutes…!*) which they previously could never find the time for.

Thanks to the discovery of Freespace, teachers can easily catch up on admin chores, locating hidden resources, creating fantastic lessons, responding to complaints, learning Somali, etc. All the hundreds of extra unpaid hours devoted each year to such are now, thanks to Freespace, to be more wisely spent on TV and quaffing wine.

One CPD expert running a Freespace workshop suggested using the last 10–15 minutes of the school day to activate calmness by having the class meditate to whale sounds.

Teacher attendee to fellow attendee: *The last fifteen minutes of my day feels like I'm the captain of a depth charged and sinking submarine, roaring instructions to an infant crew that's half panicked, half catatonic.*

Fellow attendee to teacher attendee: *Me too! And I've got a P7. But don't worry anymore. Freespace will ensure that we will have all the time in the world. The job will become a doddle. These peaceful whale sounds seem like a good idea. They should have a special workshop about it.**

---

* They do.

Free Speech

In education, the issue of this being denied is easily fixed; If we don't want to have our free speech silenced, we should stop talking about subjects which anger the censors.

Friendship Seat

aka, The Loser's Bench. (this, as I was informed, is the pupil's own designation)

Here we have a playground bench so designated that those who have no one to play with and are feeling lonely can sit and identify themselves to all the happier and busier children. The idea is that they either meet like-minded sad cases, enjoy a sympathy session from the school's mini Mother Theresa, or popular children invite them to join their game – which latter, obviously, never happens. Adult observers may occasionally force a Friendship Seat orphan into other children's games, thusly adding resentment to their loser's portfolio.

This popular idea illustrates the low level of child knowledge and basic wisdom in primary schools. Whereas, in the past, such children had at least the comfort of anonymity, this is now removed, as the entire school can see their loserdom. This initiative does not help the genuinely sad and lonely (and perhaps unpopular, and perhaps deservedly so!), nor does it help neophyte victimarians who are testing the sympathy route to attention. It does, however, dovetail nicely with the whole 'safe space', 'poor me', excluded by prejudice or bullying, mental health crisis, victim mindset. It encourages the vulnerability habit it seeks to address, that there is a place where one finds security and concern; sometimes there is, but it is absolutely not the friendship bench.

Like many feminine ideas, this one talks up what is usually a nothing into a something, which is worse than the nothing which caused the problem. Children sometimes say they feel sad and lonely, sometimes they are; help them to robustness. Keep them away from the Friendship Seat.

Full-blown

Ref: to racism.

This occurs after 10% and by 20% of any community's native population being ethnically replaced. By this upper level, disruptive concessions, system-gaming for advantage, lowered standards and various other factional issues have reached undeniable levels. Or more properly, publicly undeniable levels. We are now at the 'racist percentage' and witness a diminished capacity for the altruism that characterised earlier, more innocent days. Full-blown becomes the accusation, regardless of how one thinks or expresses concern. The ruinous intent finally exposed, inevitably leads the accused to embrace the accusation. The final ending is always the same.

NB. The emerging from the chrysalis as a full-blown racist only applies to Whites. The others were all along. However, their form of racism is termed pride, anti-racism, reparations and making the school system fair. So that's ok, then.

Fun

School is no laughing matter, and this word is here by mistake.

Funding

The government cashathon always coughs up the shekels for school-based social engineering projects and for their attached party kommisars. e.g., equity monitors and racial prejudice advisors. Likewise, CPD reinforcing the above projects never lack the proven love of a cash transfusion.

Also favoured by public gelt are cash-hungry teaching fads, unwanted and unloved resources, endless IT updates and anything that generates paperwork for busy bureaucrats. But funding for books, trips, or teachers? GTF or find your own funding! And anything that promotes native pride has as much chance of funding as a Palestinian appeal at a kibbutz.

Basically, a sexual focus and advancing societal dysfunction is the way to go for obtaining educational funding; £20 million here for LGBT+ inclusion, £30 million there for race awareness workshops, £10 million for refugee children skateboard training, another £20 million for school equity enforcement officers. Pretty soon it adds up to real money! The system falls over itself to give your money to such projects; we should be worried about this.

Good to know: When you read of extra funding being kindly allocated to education, these scams are what is meant.

Futility

High IQ teachers tend to leave the profession early when they recognise the futility of state education and realise the impossibility of reversing away from the errors when the entire institution is established for self-protection from such correction. Like anything else the government attempts, public education serves only the administrative class.

Future School

Looking like an out-take from Total Recall; swarthy quasimodos, seven year olds with unnaturally thick ankles and pie-eating faces, pale faced porkers, the double melanised, Australopithecines (apparently), tattooed teachers with facial studs, Whites identifying as Blacks, drag queens shrieking in the corridor are now the least of problems, hadjiis and hijabies, posted terror attack plan, corridor speech code enforcers, lawyers on speed dial. School runs on Asian time, or jungle time if the clock gets broken by a chucked spear or random bullet. School orchestra replaced by African tree trunk drumming. Burns' Week replaced with study of the great Wakandan poets, once they are discovered. Curriculum goes full tilt Europansexual, one degree removed from porn – or sometimes not – but still good prep for future life. FGM celebrated as native tradition during assembly – well, it is now! Intolerance severely punished, so tolerance abounds. Universal open toilet with security cameras relayed to management and hacked by perverts, or perhaps sold to them in a value for value deal. Reading is elitist – because good parents read to their children, which gives them an unfair advantage in life, as well as making lazy parents who don't, feel bad. Reading is also, except for a certain child's diary, anti-Semitic. So is Santa and this is why he is banned, but dynamite vests and dildo balloons are given out for Purim. So win – win.

Justice with excellence at last achieved. *Scoff now, ye scoffers!*

G

GAD (General Anxiety Disorder)

We are all anxious, some more than others; however, as a condition to be formally attended to, this is another modern invention whose antecedents are all around us. And whose prognosis is just more of the same throughout life, probably with lots of pills.

At least some of this pessimistic outcome can surely be first traced to the exaggerated feminine indulgence with which such pupils are treated. This support and concern almost begs the weakly constituted child to require more of the same. Which they do, and so their condition is reinforced. This is not to endorse harshness to a sensitive child, but if one desires to encourage robustness in their approach to life, then a robust response must be utilised.

As the infamous delinquent, Billy the Kid, noted in his comments on rearing a sensitive child:

You ain't doing no kid a favour if you let them be namby-pamby, too afeart to try. Sometimes you've got to make them bite the bullet. They'll thank you later. That's what ma maw did wi me. And I recommend Colt's revolvers.

Cold water swims and all-weather route marches will definitely help such children, especially whiners. As you know, no one really cares all that much; it's best to learn this in a small way early on, to avoid learning it in a big way later on.

Gaming

As social trust is increasingly replaced by the law, and those who never cared for either seek and obtain advantage, more and more others are compelled to enter the game with whatever hand they hold. In the school context 'hand they hold' can refer to some supposed disadvantage their child suffers in school. Unfortunately, many contemporary conditions, such as dyslexia, ADHD, ODD, spectrum behaviour, allergies, phobias, gender dysphoria, to list just a few, are very prone to gaming. And so, this is happening. Single mums are especially active in this respect, as it garners sympathy attention for themselves, in addition to providing tweeting topics. Children pick up on this social contagion and the whole thing becomes self-perpetuating, as it now is.

In real school life, the advantages accrued to the genuine or gaming complainant are always less than hoped or needed, and the disadvantages of gaming the system come later, but are always greater than feared and possibly deserved.

Gaming is an ineluctable feature of the social systems we have put in place within our schools, and although already absurd and dysfunctional, it has a generation to run before this train to Bedlam Station meets the buffers. By that time everybody will be spectrum, and when everyone is spectrum then perhaps being normal will be the crazy condition that garners credit.

Gateway

Our schools are a gateway to the world of learning and socialisation.

This approximate truism comes with caveats regarding the actual meaning and content of learning and socialisation. And it is here that the thinking adult becomes worried that the gateway leads to a microcosm of the police state and that schoolworld is in fact a preparation of our children for a future dystopia crudely disguised by high sounding principles.

From the moment a child passes the gateway they will be exposed to a steady stream of tolerance policies that censure certain behaviours while hypocritically exonerating others, overreaching anti-bullying initiatives, the demeaning of native culture, the creation and celebration of various victims, diagnosis and therapy with the gaming thereof for advantage, party kommissars disguised as school officers tasked with ensuring proper faith and targets met, drugged-up boys, politically correct mindsets that teach young people to censor themselves and little girls to censor those around them, surveillance systems, targets, targets and targets, and the computer addiction daily endorsed by their teachers with an end point of total IT dependency, and all of which too often ends in an adult life sterilised by porn (male version) and social media deviancy (female version). Just like in Civvy Street!

The gateway is rapidly becoming a one-way only passage; perhaps portal would be a better word for our children's induction into this future world.

Gay Children's Literature

or perhaps more properly, children's gay literature.

This is all about love and acceptance, and so makes no reference to the not so gay nature of Gay sexuality (except that it is a good thing, obviously); the enormous rate of STDs, the over-representation in sex crimes, drug use, related health problems (anal fissures, anal leakage, hepatitis) and early death. As depicted, such literature is 'all about love and depicting gay characters positively, thus freely giving children (apparently) the necessary knowledge and 'option of choosing this lifestyle' without prejudice. To this end the government funds an Xmas (to avoid offence) gift book furthering gay tolerance; this year's was *Buttplugs for Christmas.* As a fan of colourful interior arrangements, I really enjoyed last year's offering, *The Boys A-Z of Soft Furnishing.*

Indeed, progressive book publishing is a major part of the globalist propaganda effort; *Dads' Sleepover, My First LGBTQ+ Wordbook, Kipper's Bangkok Surprise, Noddy's Coming Out, Wonky Willi and The Fudge Packing Factory.*

Gay Station

A quite corner where a child who is a bit confused after the workshops, videos and gaysemblies, about what it takes to be gay and if it involves more homework, can drop in and privately discuss the issues with the funded in-house pride coordinator. This will be a person experienced in handling confused children and thus able to set them straight, so to speak.

Genders

Gender politics plant confusion where there had existed the one certainty.

Formerly considered an essential, immutable characteristic of individual premortal, mortal, and eternal identity and made in two forms for reasons only known to God. This arrangement was evidently lacking in justice and progress, and has been made 'fit for purpose' by those who know how to do such things. Where we had a measly two, we now have 68 genders and counting. Where formerly a child could wake up in the morning to the unjust certainty that they were either a boy or girl, as they were when they went to bed the night before, now they can choose by the mood and the wardrobe to match. Schools are on-board with the mission and we have seen terrific progress there at the cost of some friction over the ladies bathroom. The confusion is a consequence of old world thinking which will be purged by Globohomo Inc's whole school pogrom enacted with its partner organisations in the EU and UN.

Girls will be boys and boys will be girls
It's a mixed up, muddled up, shook up world, except for Lola
La la la la Lola.

What happens when you tell White kids that being White is racist and worthless, even evil, and that the curse is doubled if they are males? One obvious conclusion is more psychosis, more neurosis, more anxiety, more depression; but perhaps, as a desperate escape for the especially vulnerable, finding another identity that is less persecuted, and indeed, apparently – and at last! – finds approval. For such as those, this might seem like a solution.

Can it be entirely coincidental that the total demonization of whiteness happened at the same time as the equally total celebration of queerness in all its rainbow colours? Check Sweden for how that has worked out – with transgenderism too perfectly mapping the Swedish curriculum's focus on racism, white-ism, sexism and 'intolerance'. For some boys, becoming a girl, may have seemed to offer a respite to the cacophony. If only we could find out where all the shekels sloshing around the gender dystopian project were coming from, then perhaps we could begin to straighten this problem out. Thinking like Sherlock, one must deduce that this shady group must have a certain appetite for misanthropy, perhaps only matched by hubris. Forms suggest themselves, but curiously dissolve to airy nothings on reviewing legal codes

General Knowledge

Why bother wasting time acquiring this when it interferes with screen time, and anyway you can just ask Siri? This strong query actually put to me, although by an older than primary age child.

In the primary school context, familiarity with a topic is the most important variable in reading comprehension and, therefore, as a general principle, general knowledge is the most important variable for general reading ability. A case of the more you bring, the more you get back. Given that reading comprehension is the crucial catalyst that enables progress in all other tasks that require reading – which is almost all of them – then it stands to reason that we educators should be doing everything possible to increase general knowledge. This further strengthening the argument for a facts and knowledge (content based) curriculum as opposed to the 'thinking skills' approach.

Imagine having instant access to a wide and deep body of general knowledge; what an asset! Should you wish this, then all you need to do is learn it!

Gifted Kid

The less academically able child is betrayed by bombast and his opposite by silence. There was a time, allegedly, when gifted kids were identified for special treatment, but realistically this was never more than noisy nothings. This is because at the deep levels whose undercurrents propel public policy in state schools, the egalitarian creed is hostile to superiority as it is a tacit affront to their beliefs. In one sense, the gifted child represents the timeless enemy in the great struggle against privilege – however acquired and manifested. Of course, no one need be directly hostile to gifted kids, nor necessarily want to be; this situation is simply the emotional and intellectual backdrop to the presence of such children. This situation can best be understood as the mirror image of the time, some generations past now, when academic excellence was personally identified and gifted children were feted, perhaps as dux. We celebrate different things now.

If a kid is gifted nowadays they represent everything our nouveau Jacobins hate and thusly they have to be educationally levelled. Our schools are experts at this. As our school's Director of Public Safety said to a gifted kid: *Gifted are you. Well, you can just GTF!*

NB. If your child is academically gifted, they could probably do, and with pleasure, two curriculum years for every one school year in a state school. Of course, it may well be that the loss of properly paced academic progress is the least of their losses.

GIRFEC

'Getting it right for every child.'

This brilliant acronym is the education warrior's version of the Marine Corps' mantra of 'No wounded left behind.' Some educational colonels, safely ensconced in a chateau far from the classroom front lines, may imagine their goodthink has delivered success. Others know better that the slogan in reality makes us hypocrites and betrayers, as well as setting up class teachers as the fall guy for the failure. GIRFEC is gerfukt.

The whole point of this is deceit. The GIRFEC moniker fools you into believing that something is being done, because it has a name. In actuality that's all it's got! But in order to discover the truth of this, you first have to get past the gate-keeping lie provided by the name.

The Fermat's Theorem of educational science; how is a single 25 minutes per week group lesson for the struggling child GIRFEC?

Girls

The company of the finer representatives is probably the best reason to be alive and the cornerstone of natural order. There can be found a little trinity of transcendence; beautiful, good, pure. And if one can add the interlocking trinity of intelligent, kindly and light-hearted in the same personage, then one is blessed just to be near. Alas, current social attitude and school practice attempts to remove the angelic stamp by denying their higher soul and purpose. The physically and spiritually ugly resentfully lash out at the beautiful, no matter how innocent, and their media frames this as a justified moral reprimand. In this attempt to remove her dignity, a beautiful little girl can become an outcast to herself; and her natural feminine gifts denied – pending her rescuing cavalier swordsman – thus risk atrophy.

For the philosophers among the readers, please refer to James Brown and let his feet do the talking about the role of girls in making things work:

It's a man's world, but he ain't nothing, nothing, without a woman or a girl. Aaoo…ooowwww!

Girls' Education

As an aspect of Women's Rights, girls' education is one of the most important weapons in the battle to reduce Western fertility, as it inversely correlates with motherhood and thus positively with extinction. It is the very definition of a false flag.

Of course, when activists proselytise about girls' education, they actually mean their concept of education, aka Feminist propaganda, and the right to acquire debt while collecting a joke qualification. The Taliban and Boko Haram were founded mainly to stop us from doing the same to their people; credit where it is due!

Girrlll Power

Is responsible for the wealth of all nations. And it's about time girls were shown some respect, and some shopping vouchers thrown in. It is crucial that young girls are made aware of this power before it's too late. As Hendrix prophetically noted:

She's walking through the clouds
With a circus mind that's running wild
Butterflies and zebras, and moonbeams and fairy tales
That's all she ever thinks about, riding with the wind

Can it be made any plainer?

Girls, don't let White men deny you your voice and choice. Enough of their chains and Western civilisation, now is the time to break free and do stuff.

Glass Ceiling

A literal limitation arranged by the patriarchy to prevent women being all they can be; a school example would be to keep women head teachers at just 92% of all HTs, and men stealing nearly 4% of primary teaching positions. Men secretly build this ceiling while women are shopping or having a manicure. Of course, women can't see this barrier and only discover its presence when they bump their head off it when changing a lightbulb – or rather, attempting to.

cf. the somewhat related idea of a glass wall, which invisibly protects women from peer level criticism or competition from men. Obviously, women can't see this either.

Then you realise that in most professions the glass ceiling protects women from themselves, and society from female complaining and their meddlesome proclivities.

O, for goodness' sake! Now what's she complaining about? I see poor Adam's getting henpecked again, something about the patriarchy and needing to discover herself. No wonder he's looking so worn out recently. I'm beginning to have my doubts about this Eve project. I wonder if sending Michael and his flaming sword can get her to shut up? Probably not, he'll end up with a tongue lashing and a court order. Oh, I know, ...I'll put in place a kind of invisible barrier to stop her rising above herself and messing everything up. If I don't she'll be up here deaving my ears next!

Global Citizen

The avowed end point of our children's education, and which is stated with the assumption of one's approval; as if one could not willingly travel the world, effectively interact with other nationals or make cross-culture friendships without embracing this mindset. But even asking the simple question of what exactly global citizen means, what its implications are for us natives and why is it a good thing in and of itself, is to reveal the emptiness of the idea and the intent behind it. In short, what deficiency among us does this actually address?

This being, to disarm us from a rational preference for our own welfare and to prime our minds for more of the same globalist, anti-White rhetoric.

The phrase is a bully and a threat whose real purpose is to lock your child's mind into believing that they are being forward-thinking and virtuous, thus disarmed from a rational preference for their own welfare they willingly surrender their patrimony. The global citizen too, thus uncoupled from native-based reality, is easily persuaded by similar empty rhetoric –from always the same source – of the need to bomb and murder people in other countries. And we wonder why they hate us! In all of history, every high sounding universalist ambition turns out to be a con.

The global citizen really wants to take your rooted self-confidence and pride in your own nation, then your wealth, then your land, then your life. It's just the old universal brotherhood scam for the budget air travel age.

Globalism

We all know, as our media constantly tells us, that us Y-Ts should care about the world on behalf of all the global others and show limitless respect for those whose putative level of development is inferior; and that the various correctives required are best delivered via shekels taken from our patrimony and converted to military ordinance, and then having the recently-bombed foreigners come here to celebrate our inclusiveness. All this makes perfect sense to believers and they rightly enjoy the full collaboration of our schools in this project.

What exactly is supposed to happen to their (i.e., our) native culture and welfare is not considered, and critical questions on this topic are considered as an expression of racism. This one world, big happy café is an idea to which lady teachers are especially susceptible, as it allows them to simultaneously show how kind they are with public funds, how superior their inclusive thinking is in comparison to non-believers, and lowers the price of imported shoes and handbags. And, of course, barren female teachers can secretly void their angst by celebrating the replacement of the kids that you had and they didn't, by the kids who will replace and eventually destroy yours. (see the childless woman's angry soul)

Sometimes in life what you are told that you are doing, what you think that you are doing and what you are actually doing are not the same. To see this of course you need to have some understanding of consequences – before the hindsight:

We thought we were raising the enlightened child of the 21st century. We thought we were doing our part in setting the history record straight. We did not realise that in dedicating our child to the global future we were sacrificing to it global chaos. Why didn't men stop us?

THE MOTHERS' GROUP
OF
THE GLOBALLY SACRIFICED CHILDREN

So tell us again about how happy we are
on our journey to global citizen
that wonderful future café where
we share recipes, laughter and love
before the machetes arrives and
the fat lady finally sings.

God

Is not in school. Where there is no God, there you will find the devil.

Golden Age

There was no golden age of teaching. But comparisons can still be made in costs and outcomes; and however these are defined and measured, the past environment seemed better than the current. I contend that this is true mainly because the class in past times was a more realistic environment in terms of goals and outcomes, and could thusly be more honest. The deceit of our false and dishonest targets and expectations, allied to defective pedagogy makes a liar of teachers. And in this grey fog of confusion, the past in comparison is a sunlit golden age of integrity.

Good Ideas

Arriving daily, travelling salesmen with a suitcase full of good ideas always find a warm welcome from education chiefs who invariably buy one on impulse and then pass it to teachers, but never with evidence of need, or effectiveness, or cost, or admin workload, of how to be implemented, or cognisance of possible undesirable consequences, or memory of the previous good ideas' fate. It's almost as if the system is institutional barmy and the froth rises to the top.

No new ideas are necessary, few are useful, less are efficient and almost none are realistically sustainable.

As Laurel said to Hardy: *You know, Ollie, I've got a good idea. No new ideas!*

Good Intentions

The road to hell is paved with good intentions; following countless examples encountered in life, and especially in teaching, I now know the timeless wisdom of this warning.

Good Schools

This has two meanings, one literal, to which no more need be said.

The other meaning is part of the gigantic lie to which this entry defines.

Like everyone else on your half of the curve, you don't want your kid to go to school with the other more enriching, but also more delinquent, half. This desire for progeny safety and success runs afoul of the levelling narrative of our school religion to such an extent that directly (and surely unwittingly) expressing this preference for a non ESL (English as a Second Language) or non-biting classroom will result in social shaming, harassment, and perhaps unemployment. Parents thus exposed, would find that privately expressed support from the like-minded, would result in no actual support when the tweet bombs start flying. As always, the first truth-speaker finds that they have been staked out as decoy to divert attention from everyone else's apostasy. Thus parents negotiate this moral minefield by parroting the usual platitudes about diversity, while doing everything they can to subsidize a life far away from it. The most common camouflage for these revealed preferences is called Good Schools.

Thusly subterfuge and virtue signalling knowingly front a falsehood. Like the canny opossum, the 'just looking for a good school' parent protect themselves by playing dead – brain dead! And the gigantic lie bandwagon rolls on.

Goodthink

This is the prevailing official attitude to mission and pedagogy within the state school system. There is no possibility of opposing the shibboleths that are ruining our children's education. Everyone knows the topics which cannot be even referred to. However, Goodthink is more insidious than simple loss of forum, as there is another degree of recursion involved; you are only good if you think the right thoughts. The party wants to own the thought and it must be an approved one, or else Badthink. And Badthink equals loss of career. Deserved loss of career, of course!

Fortunately their operant conditioning at teacher college has worked well and most teachers not only know what to say, they also know what to believe. Their Newspeak education has removed from their vocabulary the ability to think the bad thought and put in its place a lack of interest in doing so. They would race to have themselves chipped and barcoded if it came with an Amazon discount!

Grace

In all its distinct, although related, senses this is ever present in the presence of children, but hardly ever brought to mind, far less referred to. This is a little tragedy, for the full uplifting power of this paraclete depends on it being recognised and embraced. The child and their teacher, sometimes stressed beyond measure, would then find comfort in each other's company instead of the isolation of persecution.

To know that an ineffable love is manifest, even in the classroom, would be such a source for good. That we may get teachers to whom such awareness is nature, must be the earnest prayer of those who wish well for our children.

Graceful

Graceful: a lovely sounding adjective, and a quality full of gift-having and gift-giving.

For the teacher observer, it is most wonderful to observe this in action in a little girl – invariably its highest expression – where deftness of movement takes on a balletic quality and unintentionally displays the innocent equivalent to the high style of a lady. This perfection of poise carries over to stillness, with no loss of marvel and power. The same gracefulness in little boys translates to a miniature musketeer. Properly considered, the graceful is the means whereby the numinous enters our life; a small sort of golden moment by which beauty suddenly and naturally reveals itself in the otherwise mundane life of school.

The expression of such gracefulness is not only a delight to the grateful observer, but a positive power to the holder. Alas, although this is a natural attribute of young children, it seems to be fighting against cultural trends. For it does seem that modern sofa-bound habits, and slovenly templates displayed in screen life, have conspired to deny and even denigrate this quality to those who need it most. And parents and teachers, themselves victims of a lamentable lack of instruction in this regard, pass the same habits of movement, posture and expression to their children, as can be seen at handing over time daily – it is as if *EastEnders* has come to the playground!

As adults we need to fight back against this trend, in order to properly empower our children, lest they turn into sofa-boys and tank-girls. Grace and charm are not signs of feminine weakness, but of essence. Nor is a soldierly bearing in little boys evidence of an unwholesomely masculine home life, but rather of boyness encouraged. Luckily, though, where degeneracy has taken from nature, correct instruction can return it. As we note:

Marie de Guise Academy in Leith, having abolished tolerance, is replacing it with daily gracefulness. The girls practise walking, sitting and various charming gestures of assent; the boys marching and standing to attention in silence. It seems to be working, as press reports confirm the Venetian ambassador's words in his attempt to purchase the children for the Doge:

Che ragazze affascinanti avete in Scozia. E i tuoi ragazzi scozzesi sono così dignitosi. Vorrei che avessimo questi bambini a Venezia.

Grammar

as in, the correct form.

At last, identified as a form of White privilege. Having no intrinsic value, once it loses its unearned merit, it can be seen as no better than any other grunt based communication system. To be fair, bad grammar nicely matches poor literacy and numeracy – so our schools are at least providing an education that is consistent across topics.

English grammar in particular, associated as it is with imperialism and slavery, has now been explicitly identified as racist. Translated into Edu-speak: English grammar transcribes imperialist tropes to minority language constructs and oppresses by the expectation that minority pupils should be competent in the syntax and morphology of the English written word and speech patterns; this itself is yet another expression of internalised racial constructs.

And so, we now have calls to incorporate 'critical grammar' into our pedagogy.

NB. If anyone understands what any of this means, please get in touch immediately with your local secure psychiatric care unit.

Graph, The Intelligence

see intelligence and IQ entries

Plot the graph from *The Ring's* Wagner to *Britain's Got Talent's* Wagner; it's not going upwards!

TBF to the latter day Wagner, he does a good rendition of The Sash. Ask Celtic manager Neil Lennon about this.

Growth Mindset

aka. Doctor Dweck's dreck

One of education's top charlatans, Prof Dweck, took a simple well-established banality (teacher attitude impacts on the pupil; *who'd have thunk it!)* and by means of smoke and mirrors tricked the visitors to her tribal tent that she was selling an educational elixir of such potency that after one session children are improved. The Growth Mindset is properly named, check her bank account.

Although this fluff has no positive impact on children, it is worrying that such obvious charlatanry finds ready acceptance among teachers. This is something of the budget-priced knock-off Gucci handbag about this idea, which explains completely its irresistible appeal to female teachers.

By numinous agency, warnings are sent to those able to appreciate them; it's not an accident that Dweck's name is an almost homophone to what she sells us. And that she has been given a face to match.

At assembly, a six year old demonstrated their full appreciation of the Growth Mindset: *A detective penguin was looking for a jewel thief, but couldn't find him. So then he used the Growth Mindset to find the thief. And then he battered him and put him in jail.*

Doctor Dweck; if ever a name came with a built-in warning, this was it!

GTCS

GTCS: General Teaching Council for Scotland. Formerly a simple creature keeping a box file list of qualified teachers, but lately suffering from such an excess of excellence that it has become, through its various self-serving councils to simpleton-government ministers, a blight. GT should mean Gravy Train. Its various initiatives to 'maintain standards', 'bring the profession up to date' and 'equip it with the globalist values of tomorrow, today' are a perfect example of FFS by mission over-reach. Without question, the GTCS has been a driver of the technocratic hellscape into which the teaching profession has descended. All the fixes are bureaucratic, all involve themselves as service managers, all operate beyond their native ability, all further embed the problems, and all will fail as teachers are not equal to their schemes.

Here is everything you need to know about the legitimacy of this cabal:

GTC SCOTLAND COUNCIL ELECTION 2019–2020

% BALLOT RETURN FIGURES
Primary: 7.2%
Secondary: 6.89%

Guilt

Inducing this is a major feature of our children's education and is an important prop (arguably the most important!) in the creation of the White Zombie Army that will deliver the futureworld@ diversityFU.

This guilt is achieved by good-lies and the hyper-stimulation of Y-Ts generally open-minded and generous nature, partnered with the suppression of tribal, or any other self-surviving instincts, with shaming as Badthink.

In terms of resources to achieve this goal, primary schools are embarrassingly wealthy.

see Holocaust (holocost), anti-racism, Feminism, poverty targets, global citizen, etc.

H

Handouts

The use of is a major component of modern teaching practice. Indeed, as most of the lesson is on the handout, much time is saved by not having to learn anything. This permits the timely ticking of boxes and almost enables the pupils to keep up with the pace of the curriculum. Although such use also prevents children learning layout skills and practicing penmanship, these antique scholarly habits also slow down the completion of curriculum goals and in any case are believed to be unnecessary for the life online, so win – win! All the time saved by handouts can be used to cram in more time-saving activities, making a learning double strike; although without any learning as such.

Don't worry about such parent handouts never being read at home, for they usually don't get that far. Typically being left on the desk, accidently stashed behind the storage boxes or ensconced (forever) in a school bag.

This has been a great boost to the British gluestick industry and I suppose someone will be happy at all the printing of paper and subsequent (?) recycling; just don't mention it to Greta T.

Happy

A happy teacher leads to a happy school. Focusing on making the teacher's life simpler *ipso facto* brings about the child-centred view that is being sought. However, as we see, none of the initiatives for improvement make the teacher's life simpler, and again and again we see the paradox at the heart of every attempt to tackle complex problems bureaucratically, or by diktat.

Happiness

Exceptions excepted and accepted, this has been totally smashed in primary schools. Smashing happiness, achievement unlocked.

Harry Potter

It is perhaps the last publishing and child reading phenomenon of our age. The way that the characters, actors and target audience grew up with each other gave these books a power like no other.

However, as time passes this phenomena with its anachronistic obsession with boarding school life and magic and evil starts to seem strange. The contemporary and should-be familiar setting of the story is discordant with all the sorcery goings on and the evil backdrop. And the Potter enthusiasts, always seeming a little too enthusiastic for their own good, cult-like even. It's almost as if *they* had been put under a spell. And us adults swept along in the mania, so delighted that someone got children to read, that we never considered anything beyond this. Like, for example, that the psychic impact on post-Christian, and thus spiritually unanchored, childish minds of such a world of evil wizardry, is an order of magnitude greater in apparent authenticity than witchy folk tales, not least because of their brilliant movie renditions. These stories that define the Potter generation are not at all like their Blyton-esque equivalents of an earlier age. Blyton's stories leave no negative psychic residue, the same could not be claimed for the Potter series. One can, of course, easily overstate this claim, but just as easily understate it. Perhaps this Potter phenomenon explains the recent presence and apparent appetite for black magic/Satanic imagery in youth popular culture, and especially music videos. And anything that feeds this morbid nihilism is to be feared and resisted.

Obviously, Rowling has talent. After the talent, and treasure chests filled to overflowing with geld, comes the hubris: JKR revealing herself as the Bono of literature. And it is in the revealing of this aspect of her nature that also gives one pause.

Unlike, say, Enid Blyton, whose social opinions were invisible and irrelevant to her readers, JK's are highly visible. Intentionally so! And many of her fans are inevitably fated to become followers of her pronouncements and thusly led into her digital world of opinion, conflict and abuse – and doing so while still children. Here they will find in real form all the dark arts described in JK's novels; pontificating, real hatreds, secret enemies, implacable opinions and plots to destroy lives. This doesn't have to be sought out, it is part and parcel of her life as a sorceress-author. And, by extension, the lives of her young fans who follow this.

It is my contention that this association of JK's young fans and the social media world is not appropriate, far less uplifting. These crazy disputes, in addition to all the other junk content of Twitter and the like, provide a damaging template of how adults conduct themselves. Who would want their child being exposed to this?

JK, of course, did not invent social media and is entitled to her opinions, but I wonder if she has overlooked the responsibility that should come with being an author of children's books. This should have entailed maintaining a certain distance between this problematic digital world and her young readers. There are ways she could have done this. She chose not to. And I wonder, then, if in that mystery realm where lives and souls are traded, this was the deal she made.

The sorcery seems to have a meaning beyond the plots, a metaphor for something unwholesome that connects all the parts of this mania together. The inspiration inspired to what end, think it if ye dare!

NB. Too, I don't like that Rowling has not acknowledged what is surely a direct debt to Ursula Le Guin's *Wizard of Earthsea*. Again revealing of something more than nothing.

Hate

One cannot look at this ongoing disaster of the Scottish primary school, and have some forward view about how it must end, without coming to hate those responsible. Hamlet speaks to my passion:

What would he do// Had he the motive and the cue for passion
That I have? He would drown the stage with tears
And cleave the general ear with horrid speech,// Make mad the
guilty and appal the free,
Confound the ignorant and amaze indeed// The very faculties of eyes
and ears.

Hate has been given a bad rep recently. Without hate, how would you know that you loved? All this talk of hate and haters and hate speech, is designed to disarm you from embracing the thing that would give you power to resist. If you love your own, how could you not hate what is being done to them. And then speculate as to the source of the powers which effect this? *Ay, there's the rub!*

Healthy Life

There was a time, probably when the North Sea was Doggerland, when this was a simple thing to achieve for our children; take care of them, fresh air and running, don't interfere overmuch in their own daily adventures and shout them in for their dinner. A little good advice, *Keep away from the hyenas, I heard them over at the lake last night*, tied up nicely the parental care package. And all the parts of a healthy life interlocked to achieve the result without any other active measures required. But since that happy time of guaranteed fresh air, the daily mile target easily achieved and organic meat for dinner, promoting the healthy life has been on and off problematic.

Even for the aware and motivated parent, living (as opposed to promoting) the healthy life for your child has never been easier and harder at the same time. So many of the right choices have the wrong consequences; organic blueberries flown from Peru, dance class involving two car trips, security bought at the price of melding with the Borg. So many choices where personal benefits and social costs have to be squared. Choosing for your kid's healthy life can often become something of an ethical issue, in addition to the formidable practical ones.

Whereas, for the idiot parent, it has never been easier. The responsibility has been shifted onto the teacher's plate, leaving the said parent free for their life of TV and carry-outs, while their wobbling, sleep-deprived, weakling offspring are sustained by mock food and diabetes syrup. The endless mantra of healthy choices, promoted by our schools, has segued to a dirge lamenting those children tragically lost to the healthy life. After a while, no one listens.

But should any of this be the responsibility of the school? In legitimising the promotion of health by our schools, we do the same for every other lifestyle choice and attitude the school may wish (or be compelled) to promote. Has no one considered the consequences of taking away the responsibility for a child's welfare, in whatever domain, from the parent? In the taking, something is surrendered. In that triangle between parent, child and school, a responsibility surrendered, an influence acquired, and adult double standards illustrated daily in staffroom snack choices and arse-straining lycra beyond what's decent.

Head of Service

The local big chief in our public school system. Him very well paid.

Remove from your mind any notion of leadership within the educational community. Imagine instead a filing clerk promoted by their own filing error into a post an order of magnitude above their ability – of course, being an order of magnitude below the necessary ability level, they don't realise this! Still, they can't believe their luck getting all this money for doing even less than they did as a filing clerk, and so they determine not to chance it by doing anything like work that would expose their incompetence. Fortunately, as public employees there are many boxes to be ticked and this allows them to duck and dive until the pension is safe and then they cut and run. Ha ha, now beyond sanction or reproach – no, they really are! The fools at the top don't suffer for their mistakes, when your child can suffer for them. So they think.

Referenced in Deuteronomy:

The LORD will lay his judgement on the Heads of Service and send them back in ships to Egypt in chains. There they will offer themselves for sale to their enemies as male and female slaves, but no one will buy them. And there will be much gnashing of teeth and wailing to heaven, but the LORD will ignore their pleas. 'We didnae know what we were doing,' they will cry. **'Weel, ye ken noo!'**, *the LORD will answer.*

See also under Imposter Anxiety and World's Stupidest Advice.

Head Teacher

Formerly a role to which was attached much authority, respect and social standing, and now it is not.

Very well paid, though, and suitable for someone who likes money, admin tasks, self-congratulation, using globalist clichés, ticking boxes, talking on the phone, following orders and who is not inclined to be at all reflective regarding the actual route and destination of the 'learning journey'. A highly functional airhead, basically. Very suitable for a female of whatever sex.

One hears of people wondering (although, not me obviously!) to what extent this loss of status coincides with the near total female-isation (good thing obviously!) of this position, with the female management style now the norm; nice shoes, the emphasis on solutions involving conversations, the dramatic emotional switch, the inability to concede error, blame transfer, the gullibility to nice sounding ideas, plot-counterplot mindset, social preening, hive mind, the time of the month x factor and the absence of loyalty to staff.

As a head teacher you will be ridiculed and hated; you should find your self-value in that.

PARENT: *You're the worst head teacher this school has ever had, and that's saying something!*

HEAD TEACHER: **Well, thank you for that distinction. It's appreciated and now fuck off, I'm having an early lunch.**

Helicopter

Ref: Sandwood Primary Primary, among certain others.

At the day's end, while readying pupils for departure – and the playground parent confrontation – in the mind's eye, this flight of fancy; 30th April 1975, Saigon, Roof of the US Embassy, the whump-whump of a helicopter, red signal flares. Teacher's best getaway!

Hill To Die On

Where we plant our banner and, in respect to our ancestors and with concern for our progeny, we refuse to yield any more, regardless of the consequences. This is, of course, a figure of speech, but its ending is always literal.

What should that be, think ye, with respect to our children's education?

History

Our shared past with its wonderfully rich history is psychologically like a home. It provides context to our understanding of ourselves, it shapes our character via revered templates, and is a secure and familiar space against the cacophony of the rest of the world. It is not merely a chauvinistic and triumphant celebration as enemies might claim, for our nation's history is complex and often ugly, and as such when properly taught, it introduces the same complexity and subtlety into our self-understanding; this in turn can lead to realism and balance in viewing the world and our place in it. It is very apparent that we are well able to be critical of ourselves when reviewing our past; this is to our credit. And in considering this point we note that the celebration of our history then, cannot be, and in our case is not anyway, demeaning of other peoples.

However, this adult and mature worldview needs the security of our own history well-founded and well-respected before it can consider and assimilate that of others. This process should take place in school, but alas, our children are increasingly denied the proper and prideful introduction to their own past, in apparent deference to the sensitivity of others from less happier lands, who would, so the argument goes, feel excluded by our celebration of our own history.

It is difficult to know how true this attribution is, as the claim comes from mischief makers, but it has the potential to become true, as all lies can, just by being repeated enough. And it has a powerful evil ally (or evil Svengali) in the media, and especially the BBC, which regards as its job the destruction of our nation's well-being by undermining our historical legacy as erstwhile Brits and ethnic Scots. Compromising our children's well-being in the future is not a consequence of presenting alternative histories, or setting the record straight, or journalistic misunderstanding over content, but is the intent.

This self-depreciating – self-defecating, even! – mindset has led us to denial and fabrication of historical falsehoods to satisfy the inclusion madness, e.g., The media witch of the moment, Prof Mary Beard, drinking deeply from the poisoned chalice of media attention by incanting straight-forward lies to pander to this crowd regarding negroes in Roman Britain. Similar egregious anachronisms are now legion. Our children cannot know the false history being delivered to them, the pride denied, nor the intent behind it. Although something of the sense of this might be intuited by the mob's destruction of public monuments as allegedly foundational to White supremacy.[*] Here we see in angry action the attempt to uncouple our children from their anchoring past, in order to better lead them to their unanchored future as native Whites.

History has never mattered more. The steady weight of tradition makes people a people. The need for it can never be removed, except at the cost of dissolution and destruction. In denying the need to know and celebrate ourselves, multiculturalism's legacy will be a people with no known past and no cultural centre. And a people without a past, is a people without a future – as Rome is our witness.

---

[*] One must note the curious nature of this putative supremacy which is not even able to protect its own public monuments from desecration by ingrate outgroups, and whose default response to such insults is the strong apology.

Hive Mind

Referencing the female instinct to group think and to ruthlessly and collectively enforce the prevailing mindset. This is their role in society, and it is in their social policing of social mores that men are prevented from having to continually punish or kill rule-breakers. All goes well with the hive mind until it becomes infected with some or other planted mania; like, for example, the pathological altruism and social justice obsessions that are presently running riot.

For the hive mind, approval is everything. Those who incur its disapproval are not long for this school. This analogy has great explanatory powers with respect to many, otherwise inexplicable, behaviours we observe in school. Of course, female teachers are generally not aware of their hive tendencies, and most male teachers cannot conceive of its power, so alien it is to their mindset. Those males who enjoy some understanding of this force, nevertheless enjoy no benefit from the insight.

The solitary bee does not survive long. He is also very lonely *en route* to his oblivion.

Holocaust, The

aka. holocost

The top trump card in the game. The foundation and keystone whereby our children are primed for guilt, and arguably the ultimate expression of the new purpose of our children's education. That there is no connection whatsoever between us here and the Holocaust is irrelevant, all European Gentiles will be farmed for shekels, as we see with 4th and 5th generation Holocaust 'survivors' carrying on the family business. Currently in school and the media just a week's worth of force-fed guilt –although, stretched out in class by the approved use of Holocaust children's literature – but soon to be via legislation and diktat so much more, e.g., 'Never Again' Holocaust Education Act. Give credit where it's due, in its integration and layered defence, this is a plan worthy of von Manstein. Although inspired and overseen by a power much more ancient!

Fly your scheme for self-aggrandisement under the flag of principle, claim a universal legitimacy to distract attention and appear O so moral using other tribes as dupes (as if you give a shit about them). It works for a while. Eventually, though, in some future, there will be a cost to this pressure; one cannot oblige millions to explore this topic, but only within parameters that the tribe want to set. Someone will see the pattern not very well hidden, discern an interest previously denied, notice double standards brazenly celebrated and think, *Hmm...?* They will lose their job, of course, but this is the price of entry to this ride. And this will keep on happening until...

What was a tragedy of staggering proportions within similar tragedies in that whirling madness of the war becomes weaponised against innocent others as scapegoats and marks for better leverage, or as we know them, our children. However, the tenacious diligence and cunning in putting together this multi-generational plan only temporarily hides its irrationality, genome-deep hatred and ultimate stupidity, as will be evident on exposure and collapse. As a people, it seems Jews psychologically need a collective enemy as a focus for their energies and mission. The actual Nazis are long gone, but Jewish media and political power has no problem conjuring others to be scapegoated in their stead. The others are now us. There's a name for this eventually self-destroying arrogance.

And so the big wheel will come full circle. Yet again punished, the lesson not learned, YHWH shakes his head.

This week on Twinkl: Auschwitz colouring-in sheets.

Home

It all starts in the home. If you have broken homes, you have broken individuals, and a broken society. Which, of course, we have. The broken educational system is a cause and a consequence. Every day we stare at the sad results of failed fathers and mothers, but this is never referred to.

Every social intervention in school designed to address the broken children of broken families is actually trying to recreate the things that parents do in the shared family environment of a normal happy home. It is this simple.

HR

Human resource departments. aka, other things that cannot legally be written.

Often one has to deal with this witch's brew in the course of some issue involving education. And, in its combination of comedy and tragedy, this is always an experience almost Shakespearean in its revealing of the true nature of modern life.

The technological revolution has allowed the managerial state to grow into something inconceivably massive and, too often, inconceivably useless. HR is the epitome of this trend. The ultimate end of our civilizational trajectory, the HR department in local government service. Surely diabolically inspired, its whole point is to give women (of all genders) a career path for their meddlesome proclivities. This make-job alternative to honest work in a harem, combines all the plotting wiles of the eternally jealous courtesan with their languid habits. Gossip bureaucratised, time bends back on itself as tasks are undertaken, layer upon layer of meaninglessness at cosmic level, stupidity concentrated by tremendous forces of female narcissism, self-regard inflated by gaseous titles as empty as the heads of the 'consultants' or 'senior managers', as such photocopiers are called. Contacting HR is not an experience to be undertaken lightly. Pity the men employed there, hopefully they are eunuchs.

Just another time-sink for prideful and incompetent busyworkers, and a major impediment to any sort of rational progress in education. Perhaps, HR departments in other organisations are different: I recommend checking with HR about that.

Hubris

In a presumption inflating the wrong sort of confidence among P2 innocents, the following on the classroom door:

IN THIS CLASS ARE FUTURE ARCHITECTS, TEACHERS, ARCHAEOLOGISTS, ACTORS, GEOGRAPHERS, AUTHORS, ASTRONAUTS, SURGEONS, ENVIRONMENTALISTS, OYLMPIAN ATHLETES, DESIGNERS, EXPLORERS, AIRLINE PILOTS, MUSICIANS, RESPECTED SCIENTISTS*

but no hairdressers, cleaners, check-out operators, bin men, plumbers, bar maids, policemen, cabin crew, shop assistants, white van drivers, ffs is no one going to work in a chip shop?

and thus inviting future correction from Fate who delivers the hubris-adjusted careers;

EQUALITY OFFICERS, BARISTAS, SELF-EMPLOYED PIZZA DELIVERY CYCLISTS, TELESALES CONSULTANTS, FREELANCE GAMES TESTERS, DELIVERERS OF CHINESE RESTUARANT MENUS, INSTAGRAM FASHION INFLUENCERS, CUBICLE FARM DATA INPUTERS, AIRPORT SECURITY, SUPERMARKET SHELF MONKEYS, HIGH STREET CHARITY CHUGGERS.

---

* We are pleased to notice that only 'respected scientists' were noted. Presumably, they would work for the UN on climate research or puberty blocker drugs.

And equally loved alternative lifestyle achievers, sex industry workers (and activists), enterers of competitions, recovering junkies, post-graduate students, pill popping dependents, suicide bombers, internetists, basement dwellers (virtual and literal), gangsters, cam whores, Only Fans 'performers', TV addicts, various hooring hairies, and assorted kept women, purse-dipping men and tattooed unemployables. And primary school teachers.

Human Trafficking

Prior to the government stamping out this practice in Scottish schools, thousands of children were sold each year by teaching staff to human traffickers. Parents were usually fobbed off with a claim that their child had joined a travelling circus or were finishing off their maths and would be along later. In Bonnybridge Primary, the teachers used the old alien abduction trope. Actual aliens who really had abducted some Bonnybridge pupils quickly returned them on discovering what the teachers already knew; in addition to their poorly copied transcription codes making them unsuitable for slave cloning. Humorously, the aliens compensated the abductees with rice paper and sherbet flying saucers, at least that's what they told me on getting caught eating them in class.

Hopefully, our regular pupil conversations about slavery and human trafficking, added to the school's vigorous 'No tolerance within these walls' statement, will banish such disgraceful and uniquely Scottish behaviour to the past.

NB. Obviously, where such policies may clash with the respected tribal traditions of new Scots, then multicultural inclusion takes precedence. Obviously.

Humour

Casse toi!. Go somewhere else to be humorous, and take Laughter and that French eegyt, Joie de Sens, with you.

Humour is not generally welcome in our primary schools, and is especially frowned upon if exhibited by teachers. Of course, children, being starved of adult humour and light-heartedness in school, love having a humorous teacher. This is usually a man, because, as everyone knows, while women are good fun, they usually are not funny in their adult form. This observed truth providing another reason to (secretly) deal a blow to the hapless male teacher. [Secret male teacher info: no one thinks that you're funny, but if you are actually humorous then you will be hated too.]

The complaints, then, come from the usual suspects, idiot parents, trouble-making colleagues and cowardly management.

Hypocrisy

This is a universal feature of human life, but is particularly prevalent in teaching now as the focus shifts from teaching subjects (how do you be a hypocrite in the teaching of maths, for example?) to advocating attitudes, condemning wrong-think and promoting lifestyles. The potential pitfalls for a teacher are limitless, virtually every time they open their mouth they risk being a hypocrite. Thusly, the breach of trust occasioned by a knowing hypocrisy contains an ethical fall from grace for the teacher.

There are costs to the teacher of this situation which are seldom mentioned, as they are invisible. Nevertheless, these are real forces in one's internal life; diminished in self-regard, loss of innocence, constant awareness of risk, doublethink needed to square the circle, the risk to their moral well-being, and a loss of favour before God.

Even hypocrisy has a price.

I

ICT

Self-destruction always comes with a smiling face bearing advantages. The gifts of connection and convenience have a cost, that much is obvious. But the ever increasing use as the only knowledge resource, and the means of delivery of the same, worries the thinking parent. It's not only the developmental effects of continual screen time on our children and the effective removal of alternative sources of information, but the trivialisation of one's world by celebrity advocate-whores selling popnews and assorted effluent, all of which lead to the legitimisation of the Borg and its hive mind that brooks no dissent. How will it end?

DRUMCHAPEL WOMAN DISCOVERS THIS ONE TRICK THAT IS DRIVING PROCTOLOGISTS MAD

All that technology to deliver porn for the boys and to trick women to click on ads.

People have been diverted into spending thousands of hours effectively talking to themselves, while not getting things done, learning anything useful or having to question stupid beliefs. Creating thusly a race who need constant validation of the kind that only a combined echo chamber and mirror could give them – the i phone life!

For all the billions spent, and our minds twisted beyond recognition in a generation, in what way has our children's education been genuinely improved by IT at all?

The soul's ruination may come to be the least problem, as HAL said: *I'm sorry, Dave, I can't let you do that.*

Identification Guide

Field guide to immature humans

Boy 1969: bruised limbs, possibly black eye, kicked shins, scrapped knees and scuffed shoes. Outdoors in all weather, typically moving quickly. In arboreal environment, found perched or swinging. Can climb over wall. Generates occasional income from returning lemonade and beer bottles. Life in analogue, much purpose found. Innocent.

Boy 2019: skin pallid and undamaged, excess subcutaneous fat, indoors in all weather, no monkey skills. Cannot climb over wall. Typically found slouched, quickly fatigued, acedia often observed. Loaded with spending cash. Automated life with concomitant loss of purpose. Perplexed.

Girl 1969: skirted, underskirted, charged with wardship of infant sibling, terrific simultaneous four-limbed coordination, often laughing, typically kind-hearted, uncomplaining and willing, gracefully feline in movement, but capable of burst of speed equal to male. Never heard of 'Rights', but aware of responsibilities. Saves money. Innocent.

Girl 2019: unskirted, excess subcutaneous fat, indoors in all weather, bold in manner, much unwarranted vocalisation, perfect finger dexterity with cellphone, sullen, stress precursors evident. Proactive in asserting 'Rights'. Digital presence and future. Can pole dance. Spends money. Sexualised.

Identity Issues

According to the critical theory, which is the real source and force behind our curriculum ambitions, race and sex are social constructs by which racist White men oppress everyone else. Accepting this, we can solve the identity problems by allowing anyone to identify as black or white, male or female or whatever, regardless of the colour of their skin or background, and chose an orientation that meets the moment.

And so; start the day as White male to enjoy that colour privilege and the patriarchy bonus vouchers, then switch to female for access to the nicer toilet, convert to Black to access some affirmative action gibs and perhaps escape police interest – or a shooting. Stay Black, but switch to female for some theatrical complaints to avoid doing schoolwork. Stay as girl, but switch to Asian to get someone into tolerance trouble for racial facial expressions and then back to boy at home to avoid doing the dishes. Quickly switch to girly tears if mum is not accepting of 'your body, your choice'.

Problem solved and everybody happy.

Imagine

John Lennon's *realistic future vision* of ending poverty and war and religion metastasised into Utopian public policies which inform our schools via Jacobin propaganda terror. This dirge has become a sort of unofficial anthem of the progressive mindset. It was once played at a school assembly I attended as a preamble and justification for the 3rd World charity strong-arming that was the assembly's purpose. More to the point would be the 9mm Bruvvas' hit, *Hand over the dough, Ho!*

You may say I'm a dreamer (No, you're an idiot.)

but I'm not the only one. (That's true, but alas!)

Impertinence

Formerly ruthlessly crushed to encourage *les autres*, now welcomed as a virtue

Pre brave new world, this contagion was a rare visitor to the classroom, as the slightest sign of infection resulted in a very bitter one pill cure. Impertinence is even less tolerated nowadays, but the coin has flipped, and teachers must ensure by word, gesture and expression that they display no disapproval of any pupil on pain of a (social media) whipping, followed by a contrite apology or expulsion. In contrast, the most intractable of pupil villains are free to express their disdain in fashion best suited to their style. Plans are afoot to reintroduce corporal punishment as a solution, a visit to the head's office for a caning should wipe the stupid grin off of an impertinent teacher's face.

Impossible Dream

Referencing, The

Fancying themselves in the same light as earlier Scots who achieved world renown for their contributions to mankind, your Napiers, Bells, Flemings and the like, our educational establishment reach to the same heavens of invention, but for different stars. Science and engineering being frankly a bit too pale and too masculine, they go for the harder option (although, not for them) of world peace and equality. Alas, the humanity, the hubris, the humbug, the humbling:

1. The impossible dream is not going to be achieved.

2. It is a waste of precious resources.

3. The devastating costs and social dangers which go with these attempts to achieve the impossible should be taken into account.

And in response, the impossible dreamers chant: *No free speech to Nazis!*

Imposter Anxiety Fraud

A permanent feature of the teacher's internal landscape. It's the secret motivation behind the question; How can I make my job more complicated in order to boost my insecurity about its perceived lack of value and my own actual felt lack of value? You can't.

Impressed

Usually prefixed with not. But sometimes not, although alas in our jaundiced age such honestly intended praise can seem like sarcasm.

Formerly applied to snarky pupils and smart alecs, now only applied to teachers, e.g., Tonia (P4) to her teacher (me): *You think you're clever, but nobody's impressed with you!*

Inclusion

This is the means whereby a parasite enters a desirable system and disables its defences. Tolerance is what gives it time to destroy its host.

In educational circles, inclusion it is among the highest values and a stated end purpose of our schools. It is also the perfect example of the thoughtlessness that accompanies social justice dreams when they find political power.

Although ideologically motivated, this idea, whereby special needs pupils should be taught in mainstream schools, had a kindly sensibility which led the dubious to confuse its simple appeal with its actual appeal to simpletons. No serious debate regarding the rightness or feasibility of this idea took place, inclusion was just forced on schools. Our teaching Cassandras saw where this was going, but who listens to them anyway! As the disasters and betrayals unfolded, the promised funding disappeared and the government supporters of this plan, only ever interested in their virtue being broadcast, and instead seeing their stupidity exposed, backed away from it, as if it was never anything to do with them in the first place, and left the problem with the teachers. Such problems being an increased planning and management load, often compromised pace of learning, sometimes physical disruption, possibly lowered all round standards and unrealistic expectations. Often the disruption of special needs pupils to their classmates can be significant; and this has to be borne in silence.

Except by their physical presence, children whose special needs mark them out as different are, honestly, not really included, usually because they cannot be or will not be; and so, in a cruel polarity, their disadvantage is emphasised to them even more, the which will likely be felt as an additional psychological burden. The same to their regular classmates, who are obliged to chaperone, aid, ignore or avoid a special needs child, and who may witness the reluctance of the responsible adults to successfully manage or exclude such children, should this be an issue. Often the class management of such a child is dependent on the direct support of classmates, typically the girls. This is an unfair burden on such children, although to their credit many shoulder it with continual good grace. In contra, we note that of course some special needs children may benefit from inclusion and it could be argued that, if they are properly supported, this may have a neutral effect on the rest of the class. However, even if they are properly supported; eventually they won't be.

All this is part of the world of denial in which teachers and pupils live; to call the truth on this agenda is to invite attack as a hater of the disabled and disadvantaged. As a fact, of course, special needs children are equally worthy and occupy the same range of agreeableness as anyone else. Looking back from 100 years into the future, as I can, I note that inclusion has been a Trojan horse that has compromised education by lowering standards of behaviour and otherwise altering school ambience. In truth, inclusion was an alternative and surreptitious way of achieving equalist goals of levelling society. One where the true haters and misfits that promote this agenda don't feel quite so bad about themselves.

Inclusive Language

Coming soon to your child's school is a mandated list of appropriate terms for everything. This is the next stage beyond the 'my chosen pronoun' issue and it involves taking the fight for inclusion to the entire English language – other European languages will also enjoy this reboot. Apparently, use of this new language (or Inc-speak) will prevent certain previously excluded groups from feeling excluded – these groups include all Africans, Asians, Australopithecines, various other sexuals, vegetarians, very fat people, small people, couch potatoes, hard of hearing, etc. In common with the wider agenda, this process is mainly concerned with race and sex. Children will have to learn these new terms in order to speed up the flush to deserved oblivion of the old hate language of English. In order to usher in this world of love more quickly, special language officers will be stationed in school with full sanction powers against pupils and their presumably apostate parents.

For example; a blacklist will become a darkly shaded list, a big black pudding will become a coloured pudding of size, homosexuals to bestsexuals, a transitioning person to functionally alternative gender, less able to equally able in a different way, etc. Expect much use of hyphenated names, e.g., -replica or -'proxy'. Symbols will also be popular, e.g., +performer.

Whimsy has overwhelmed this entry yet again, but this clownworld is no laughing matter. It's all to avoid offence, apparently. But really, the point of this project is to destroy the language and the identity that comes with it, with the useful side-effect of identifying resisters for further processing. These will be identified by female teachers who would generally enjoy this role.

In the inclusive future, one will not escape the consequence of mixing up a person with 'inoperative sex growth-hormone imbalance syndrome' with 'not right in the head'. The authorities will probably construct special camps after the old German pattern to help such anti-inclusionists to better concentrate on their inclusive language. An appropriately inclusive name for such concentration camps will be found.

INKLUSION MACHT FREI would be a good motto for such camps. Perhaps it could be placed over the entrance gate.

Inclusion Progress Report

RAINBOW SPECTRUM LESBIAN MEMORIAL PRIMARY SCHOOL

HT YEARLY REPORT 2030

SECTION C. Inclusion: Redefining progress

We are proud to report on significant success in our goal of total inclusion. P5 has now passed the 50% mark for SEN (Special educational needs) pupils: 3 Autists, 2 Asperger's, 1 Global Delay, I Down's Syndrome, 1 VRD (violent resistance disorder), 1 wheelchair cerebral palsy, 1 walking hemiplegia with VRD, 3 ADHDs, 1 transgender, 2 gender fluids, 2 EALs, 2 dyslexia, 1 dysbraxia, I deaf, I vision impaired, 2 awaiting diagnosis, I undefined, 2 dafties and one half monkey/half biscuit (as identified). I am also pleased to report that two pupils have recently joined us who speak no English, this will be a rewarding challenge to their excited classmates. The remainder of the class is, as yet, defined as cis-abnormal (formerly 'normal') and while this is somewhat behind government inclusion targets, we can be optimistic that the weekly visits from the trans-conversion coordinator and the Gaylife assemblies will boost the figures. The class is very excited to be at the forefront of inclusion. I am sure that their parents concur, some tweets from parent Munchauseners notwithstanding. Well done, P5!

Incoming Legislation

Misgender hate speech, compulsory safe sex ed, school tolerance indicator standard, diversity equity targets, historical female injustice equalisation, historical racial injustice equalisation, historical sexual injustice equalisation, in-house gender conversion counsellor, notification of non-discrimination, anti-slavery policy review, removal of male privilege in classroom settings.

Funded in-house designated investigator of above

Infantilised

It may be surprising to learn that many infants (and particularly little girls) turn up quite adultised in their obviously smaller and more charming way. However, the school emphasis on adult intercession in all child disputes and of encouraging fragile responses (recognising the hurt) to events, soon begins to compromise the development of maturity. This process is unwitting on the part of the teacher and other facilitators, but not on the part of the instigators of this trend. For why; an adult-sized and adult-aged, but otherwise immature, person presents no threat to the system. Whereas, an actual adult is independent in thought and action, and is responsible for defending themselves and advancing their interests. And, this type of adult is not required in the future-world. Infantilising is about creating compliance. The infantilised adult is a puppet in someone else's play.

The teacher-puppet-meister is a puppet in turn to the puppet-führer. At puppet-führer level we close in on who is behind what is going on.

Informer

Typically about 10% of primary teaching staff are professional informers. A female head teacher, of course, sees through the disinterested claims of 'concern' to the jealous, or just plain spiteful, heart underneath; but, nevertheless, she disingenuously accepts this secret intelligence, as if also concerned, as it provides a doubled supply of ammunition that can be used as required against both the target and targeter. The only limitation operating on the informer is the knowledge that a counter-intel operation may be mounted after a double or triple agent informs the target; the female teacher is well aware of such spy networks and is accordingly wary. This limitation of action does not apply where the target for disinfo or destruction is a male teacher, he will be completely oblivious to plots against his name and welfare.

Where a male teacher is concerned, typically 50% of the female staff are informers. The safest advice for a male is to assume that all your colleagues will rat you out, because of the patriarchy, or because you are too aggressive/wimpy, whatever, etc. Being careful is of little use to the male teacher, as the informer will just make things up. The female head teachers will know this, of course, but will still be happy to receive a little dirty intel. Where the head teacher is a male, excepting his dark arts level is truly Satanic, he too will be completely outplayed from day one.

Informers come as double, triple or even quadruple agents and some are just free-spirit, freelance demons that alter their level of betrayal according to the phases of the moon. It is not unusual to find such fickle informers occupying a charming skinsuit; why this should be has baffled scientists.

Ingrate

A category of pupil who must always be appeased. In the past such persons were instantly banished to their own hard-scrabble land where their unfortunate, but deserving, example provided a necessary warning to potential apprentices to remodel their attitude. Being a teacher nowadays, however, is more than a bit like being a slave to a thankless master. You may beg for some recognition from the rude and ungrateful, but resist the 'home truth' urge or face the hardest of ironies.

Insolence

The kissing cousin to impertinence, the attitude that underlies the action, *that* look.

To permit insolence from one is to court it from all; this is the supreme truth in teaching.

Picking up on my admiration for the educational policies of Catherine the Great, Empress of Russia, Tarra (P3) disseminated it in advice to a classmate regarding a lippy teacher (me): *Crush the insolent and deprive them of a platform, lest you earn a reputation for timidity.*

Alas, our pupil overlords in our new school world have well heeded this lesson.

Instinct/intuition

Intuition is when instinct speaks to you. With respect to children, intuition is not always right, but hardly ever wrong. It is a friend to experience. Naturally, it is accorded no respect from educational frauds and firebrands. But when the latest instruction comes along and one senses something not right about it, then to whom should one listen? Educational experts and their freebooting hird, or that quiet voice of intuition?

When Dokter Dweck turned up trying to sell her Growth Mindset spells, my intuition sensed a tribal trickster at work. As if by instinct, I immediately ordered her whipped from the palace. Later events proved me right, she was a total charlatan. And so you see why, with regard to education, I always advise the children's governesses to follow their intuitions. Catherine, Empress of Russia.

Insulin

Insulin resistance is the bodily equivalent of the 'values' curriculum's assault on our children's minds. This phenomenon is working its way down the age range, and is soon to be coming to a school near you. Sweeties, pizza, juices and biscuits, so much garbage coated in sugar, it's no surprise that sugar brims the bloodstream. Thus porker at 11, obese at 21, diabetic at 31. Eat your way to pharma dependence, a personal tragedy, but good for business.

This outcome is not an accident.

Intelligence

Intelligence in humans is synonymous with planning, focus and working memory

The least egalitarian of attributes, and therefore an enemy of progressive future thinkers as the owners of the said quality keep spoiling the fantasy upon which their levelling plans are based.

It is not permitted to think of this topic with reference to pupils, parents or school management. This is because there is obviously no such thing as intelligence, except where it might be credited to minorities, lowered by incompetent teachers or by the previous government's policies. Inadvertently assuming that intelligence may be a limiting factor in a pupil's school life is a gulag crime; although the direct expression of 'thicko' or 'idiot' is permitted if the recipient is a teacher.

Apparently half the population is below average and, as noted by a recent government minister, this is not acceptable. Again, teachers to blame. As the First Nippie Sweetie asked: *WTF is going on in schools if only half the pupils can reach average?*

Alas, in the real world, there is strong scientific evidence and your own eyes that there is such a thing and that, apart from early nutrition, nothing increases what you are born with. Hence, the total failure of various Head Start and Catch-Up programmes. However, while you cannot make someone more intelligent, you can help them to become less intelligent. To avoid this please accept this advice; turn off your device.

Internet

Defenders claim it is like all the world's libraries in one place. True, but a library well stocked with popfluff garbage and nude books, where everyone is screaming for attention or fighting, when they are not shopping or trolling.

The low sensitivity to organic stimuli witnessed among pupils is an aspect of uninterrupted videogames and surfing. Of course, by P7 this would be vice games and porn surfing for the boys, and sexual exhibitionism and shopping for the girls.

Intersectionality

That happy confluence of the victims of White patriarchy where their poisoned streams meet, mix and rush together to their safe haven.

This is an idea whose time has come to the primary school and it is knocking on the classroom doors, demanding admittance and safe spaces.

The intersectionalists definitely need more safe spaces and the patriarchy (represented in school by the jannie and some toxic P7 boys) definitely need more zweihänders. We just need to bring these two together. Now everyone is happy!

Intolerance

That most masculine of virtues. Our society is predicated on it and equally our demise is predicated on its antonym. It was never the bad guy it was knocked up to be. And is well due a welcome comeback.

Hey, Tolerant Father of the Year; go teach your boys to be Crusaders and your girls how to use a whip!

i pads

The portable form of mental stress incubator

An enstupidation device invented to distract with pointless geegaws while reinforcing the Borg. An electronic version of smarties, colourful and attractive to innocents, and with a neural equivalent nutritional level. Works by snaring with instantly accessible games and infant beeps and buzzes, and then addicts.

So what if kids can make a stupid little video which are as stupid as the ones teachers make as 'evidence! Let's put this i pad skill into context; idiot tarts have no problem making knock me up videos for income or pishing in the street instagrams, and thugs filming themselves slapping up random people for Youtube LOLs

i phone

An even more portable form of the above. And a godsend for the dramaturgical aspects of a girl's life and a teacher's too, should she be of that sex and/or so identifying.

Now one's ongoing descent into trivia and enstupidation can be tracked. Also great for transmitting infection as the screen is dirtier than a Bangladeshi toilet on ladies day.

Narcissus reaches out to touch that lovely image again and again and again. Were we always like this, stupid and vain, but just waiting on the technology?

i means intelligent, even the name takes the piss!

IQ

This is widely recognised as a weapon wielded by Y-t supremacists and their phrenology loving pals to batter down the educational achievements of ethnic others with alleged intelligence levels in the banana range. Paradoxically, it is celebrated when IQ is claimed to underlie the ability of certain urban jungle denizens to run fast, this being an intelligent adaptive strategy to avoid blame for street robberies. Can't get arrested if you don't get caught; clever, thus, high IQ.

And too, when such scores are 'corrected' to prove that Y-t is not so smart after all, as rap star Thuggee noted: *If wyties are so smart, how come they're getting replaced in their own land?*

Those educationalists and political activists who deny the existence of IQ, except as a racist construct, are probably correct. It does not exist in their case.

Oh, by the way, good news. Your IQ test came back negative.

Irony

To save teacher time for enhancing diversity and tackling poverty, our educational policy experts have built irony and absurdity into our strategic vision. There is no need to mock policy; it does it itself. Like many others, I'm tiring of this force, but still it returns to its home in my head.

Irony used to mainly apply to pupils who finally received, typically by numinous agency, the correction they deserved. As such it could be universally enjoyed. But now, as schools are responsible for everything in the world, from healthy choices for pupils to Ethiopians lacking goats, this universal power is getting stretched thin. There is no pleasure any more to be enjoyed in such a relentless presence infecting the school day from forward plan to twilight teacher's workshop. Some forms of irony have became so extreme as to go around the clock and arrive back at literal truth – although (ironically) one can never be sure of this!

We need a moratorium on irony. We're all stocked up on it, and it should take the next five years off and go and visit some other civilisation. Private use of irony should still be allowed, as it's handy as a 'get out of jail card' when claiming, on waking up sober the next day, that it was all meant ironically.

Irrational

The ability of government at all levels to persist in totally irrational educational policies is truly amazing, even when faced with irresistible evidence of such irrationality. This ability depends at the practical and management level on the stupidity and snark of low grade officers. Arrogance of office is a perquisite for suchlike functionaries when faced with their moral and intellectual betters, as they always are. This is why it is crucial for the bureaucratic organs of enforcement, your HR and educational HQ wallahs, to be such types, stupid and self-righteous, as will enjoy of following orders to crush any rationality as something that stands in essential opposition to what makes them what they are. Considered thusly, which is the level at which one normally engages with the irrationality, the whole thing has the silliness of Soviet planned economy button production targets, but this is to totally misunderstand the irrationality and especially underestimate it as something stupid.

We have already met the agenda, and will do so later in its other iterations, here we will note that the apparent irrationality is planned, intentional and intelligent – at its own level of operation! Self-defeating and contradictory policies and practices following quickly on each other's heels is a strategically brilliant way to internally destroy an institution, while simultaneously undermining its legitimacy among its main users and the watching public.

Faced with the relentless irrationality, the rational concerned parent doesn't know what to think, do, or whom to turn to. But whoever it is, they are not in school. All by design.

NB. The person to turn to for protection of your school child is daily seen in the mirror.

J

Jesus

Sitting at God's right hand, farcical, fictional, or boiling in shite, as per belief system.

But still the foundational figure in the creation of Western civilization and the ideal example of its governing ethos. The occasional reference and Christmas notwithstanding, the name is usually only heard in vain, and often from children too.

However, there is one story of Jesus's that finds favour with our destroyers and consequently is frequently told and interpreted; The Good Samaritan. However, in concordance with our narrow-minded times, of course only one interpretation is permitted.

The subtleties of the actual meaning – Jesus's intention, after all – are never explored. And the true context is most definitely not required; all that matters is Jesus's endorsement of the *new* 'New Testament', i.e., the multicultural message of surrendering your patrimony and future to others. This telling of this story typically precedes a kindly-worded UN demand for geld for charities, or in one famous example socks and underwear (new and clean, otherwise I could have obliged) for Calais jungle denizens and would-be New Britons.

Jesus is now the PR man for Babylon. Surely an unforeseen station of the cross!

JET Training

Staff jet training, yippee! And at last some useful CPD. In my mind's eye I see MIG 31, but realistically know it will be something with a lesser payload and top speed.

Disappointment confirmed by the head teacher, almost instantly, as much less spectacular. Her noticing my shit-eating grin as something that only once before greeted a CPD course – a similar misunderstanding over a staff bomb awareness course.

JET, another stupid acronym. The training course doesn't even involve turboprops.

Jobs of the Future

Cliché, but check JR2C (Juvenile Cybercrime Rehabilitation Counsellor)

The recurrent cliché regarding the role of our schools in preparing pupils for out there. The teacher-dupe typically presents this, presciently they think, as a bit of a mystery (*These jobs haven't even been invented yet*) to which the solution is amazingly the same one suggested by the world's biggest global corporations, the enhanced use of IT. How exactly further immersion into the Borg prepares pupils for the world of future mystery work is never mentioned, this is because it doesn't. Indeed, the opposite is the case; media junk addled tweeters who cannot hold attention beyond goldfish span are not the desired employees of the future. They are however, the future essential consumers and debt slave labour on which our system depends; this is the real job of the future for which their teachers are preparing them with IT at school, and their parent/s the same at home.

The big wheel of history turns and civilisation reaching the zenith falls off into the void. The cognitive elite, and otherwise diligent, find their real jobs. The poor lave, us majority ordinaries, will inherit their birthright. Their jobs in that future are clear to see; they range from nothing to the world's oldest with delivery boy-girl in the middle.

Jokes

Children love a joke, because they are children, which is why you should always be ready to find one in class. However, enemy parents love a joke too, for by misrepresenting it they have their *casus belli* to destroy a teacher; for probably no reason. Maybe, for a joke! For protection against this eventuality one could adopt a serious mien and banish jokes and jesting quips, although this too would also bring complaint. Thusly, caught between a rock and a hard place, the light-hearted teacher finds that joking in school is no laughing matter. The would-be funny teacher is thus well-advised to keep in mind Colonel Matrix's words to Sully: *You're a funny guy. That's why I'm going to kill you last.*

Joker, The

Not the class clown or the funniest boy in school, but someone more hidden and much less fun.

I have come to believe that the relentless drive to destruction is not so inchoate, and that somewhere in our schools, behind that curtain where they control the levers, the joker will be found. And all the levers and spy switches that control their meat robots and useful idiots seen for what they are. As the mask comes off, one needs the courage of a saint.

Guess who again?

Jotter

Once this was where the pupil recorded their best work, or not; whichever being readily apparent. Praise worthy, censure worthy or fixable, accordingly. You want evidence, look in their jotters for their entire history of ability and attitude. Simple, reliable, cheap and not cheatable, and there's the problem with it! Thusly, it finds itself replaced, along with its best pal, the blackboard, by methods more fitting to our *fin de siècle* times.

Almost as an afterthought, though, the jotter is enjoying a reprieve on classroom death row as a sort of scrapbook, supporting stuck in Twinkl sheets. These of course hardly demonstrate work and are extremely wasteful of photocopy paper – so, no complaint there!

Some ancients claim that jotter work brings all kinds of benefits in layout knowledge and penmanship, and even that in coordinating both one finds that the organising thoughts thus required are thus encouraged. And that these templates acquired and continuously developed, aid further clarity of thought and expression, and speediness of execution. Whether we should pay attention to someone from the 20th century, LOL, who probably didn't even have an i phone growing up, and may not yet even have an Instagram account, is a question that answers itself.

As a fact, jotter layout contributes to clearer thinking as an automatic consequence of laying out the problem on the page. Spatial intelligence is also activated in developing neatness of presentation, which further aids mental clarity. The developing pencil skills aid motor memory which, allied to improved presentation skills, establishes working templates for problems or exercises. These templates, in turn, free the mind to concentrate on attacking the problem, instead of using up working memory wondering how to begin the thought process. Also, the pace of working with pencil and jotter is organic to the mental process required to tackle it. An exceedingly important point in the rushed and time-wasteful world of today's classroom.

Hooray, for the good old jotter! But, alas, he's got no chance of making a comeback this side of the apocalypse.

Judgement, The

It's due time for a comeback. For:

a. The delinquent habits of parents and their children.

b. Those responsible for using our children as cannon fodder in their war against society.

Solution to a.

1. Tasers
2. The stocks
3. Suspension
4. Expelled

APPLY AS REQUIRED

Solution to b.

1. Millstone
2. North Sea
3. Helicopter
4. Author of crimes against our children

SOME ASSEMBLY REQUIRED.

Judgemental

As in; don't be so.

There was a time (when I was so broken-hearted), Judgemental wasn't much of a friend of mine, but he tables have turned (yeah), and now I embrace that which was rejected for virtue signalling and self-smugness. Being judgemental is the survival response to finding that the 'Don't be judgemental' attitude found too happy a niche in our schools where, living without challenge, it safely grew to be the monster that is tolerance today. A little sympathy for someone's apparent plight becomes in a generation that same someone's right to exercise negligence and bad behaviour without incurring judgement. The rubbish parents, the rude children, the idiot complainers and the scheming degenerates have been enjoying their freedom of action as if gods. Too late, we see how crucial judgement was to good order.

But time runs round the clock and an age ends. The new one arriving will bring judgement. And in this case, Judge Mental!

Judging People

If you judge pupils by the content of their character rather than the colour of their skin, and you see certain patterns emerging, then, to avoid being racist and losing your job, flip the holy doctor's advice and start judging by the colour of their skin.

Junk Science of Pedagogy

aka. scam science, Ph.D. farms, grant harvesting, the shekel skim, debt-building con, educational nonsense.

There is more wit and wisdom in any Shakespeare play you care to mention than the mountains of junk science and policy that passes for pedagogy. And if all this waste was bonfired, o what a happy day! Teachers' spirits soaring with the flames as they consumed this nonsense, which at last found some practical purpose when the pupils roasted their marshmallows. Following which, the drones and tyrant slaves who serve this monster would new discover a moral freedom when, freed from servitude, they are forced to find a useful job like digging ditches or wearing the barista's apron (to which their PhDs at last finds honest use).

This junk pedagogy clothed in the venerable robe of science gets into the system by being sold to simpleton-directors of education unaware of the distinction between evidence and an advert, and otherwise unskilled in common sense. These Chuckle Brothers of education NEVER face consequences for their role as conduits in converting scam science of *philosophiae doctor* frauds to educational policy and practice.

Justice

There is so much reference to justice in our schools that one could believe them to be very ethical places, full of tiny legal scholars, warrior-monks and devout sisters praying for global equality. However, when schools promulgate the various justice causes, they are not talking about a legal or moral concept, underwritten by the law or appeals to tradition; such justice would not be enough. The justice our schools refer to signifies a collection of concepts at the centre of the cult of Western cultural destruction and replacement. This is a justice that requires our entire society to capitulate to demands and redefine its entire structure accordingly. Justice for everyone, except one group whose identity you already know well.

Calling it out as a propaganda word, hardly does justice to its gargantuan ambition. Justice is the name of the weapon being used to destroy the hated us!

Juvenile Cybercrime Rehabilitation Counsellor

Yet another, *O, brave new world that hath such creatures in it* example.

There is such a thing. And apparently a need for such a thing. Nowadays, to counter the possibility of our children not being bad enough, our cyber overlords invent new crimes for them and then we pay for solutions, actually, 'solutions'.

This might be a good future career option as juvenile cybercrime takes the big leap forward with 7G. What's not to like with childhood IT world? Popnews, shopping, porn, killing games, selfies, and LOLs. This new role is one of the jobs of the future referenced earlier, so keep up your dark web skills to be eligible.

K

Kansas City Experiment, The

That which cannot be referenced. (I don't' even know what I'm writing here)

Imagine all educational fantasists were given a blank cheque and the instruction to do everything they can to make education work for our disadvantaged children, as it should. Whatever the complaint or deficiency in our school system, fix it. Plan it deep, get the best, rack up optimism. Prove your arguments that disadvantage, and not culture or intelligence, or dare you think it, race, lies behind historical lack of achievement. At last enlightenment dreams meet political will. Spent, built, remodelled, recruited, encouraged, provided, indulged. And the result; a complete failure. A COMPLETE FAILURE by any metric. Well beyond the bounds of the darkest gainsayers. Indeed, outcomes were inversely proportional to expenditure. It has to be independently confirmed to be believed. Do so.

Of course, the meeting with reality only slightly set back our educational fantasists, perhaps a missed heartbeat when faced with the ruin of their hopes, plans and literally the founding stock of their Utopian future. The lesson to them; there was no lesson to them! Their Jacobin attentions to the educational system were doubled down, the inconvenient fact silently, swiftly transited to the memory hole. The lesson to us, our fantasist enemies do not operate in the rational realm. Their complaints and programmes are not about fixing things, but breaking them. And us. And your children, who are not their children!

You did not read this. You do not know about any such experiment. Nor do you want to. Is Kansas City even a place?

Klansman, Klanswoman, Klansperson, trans-Klansperson

Racism is so prevalent in Scottish education that many primary schools are believed to have in-house triple K branches. These cleverly blend into the background by not wearing their hoods at parents' evenings and disguise their evil message under the claim of celebrating European excellence in art, industry and science, or wanting to start a ballet dancing class or birdwatcher's club, etc. The days of such vile supremacism are numbered. A task force has been formed of the most ethical and efficient organisations in education; HM Inspectors of Schools, EIS and GTCS, and an elite cadre of anti-3K Witch-finder Generals have been appointed. No Shakespeare quote, Dutch master painting shown or scientific achievement discussed will go unexplained. We can rest sure that primary school Klanspeople will feel the heat of righteous judgement for their Whitey sins.

The faggots are building the fire. Really!

Knife Culture

In primary schools? Alas, yes!

Normally, I'm an advocate of more culture, but not this sort and not in school. And note that we are not referring to a boy's penknife. One asks, how could primary schools have a knife culture? I bet you know the answer to why and who.

As this culture is here to stay, we need to need to implement common sense knife safety. I suggest knife handling workshops and a maximum blade length linked to age, (i.e., 7 year old – 7" blade; 11 year old – 11" blade). For those children whose cultures have a preference for the panga or spear, in the interests of multicultural inclusion, these should also be permitted. But no guns, the education department draws the line at guns – these are for secondary school. Standards apply, you see!

L

Language

Three new languages seemed to have evolved in schools over the last generation or so; Eduspeak, Poptart and Thug, associated with teaching management, girls and boys respectively.

The first is a consequence of educational joke-science mated to idiot-level goodthink, and is basically a form of nonsense and outright lying. It waves virtue-signalling banners over a scientific-sounding word salad of fluff and bubbles to lull the defences of teacher-dupes to better bamboozle them – honestly, although many can talk Eduspeak, no one can translate it into English. The second, Poptart Talk, is consequence of little girls emulating the voice, mannerisms and slut-vocab of teenage pop and soapstar, half-nude airheads. The last, heard among the lower biological orders, is resulting from a misplaced societal respect, diabolically inspired and MSM enforced, for gangsta* life, as presented in rap and similar expletive-laden effluent sluicing out of tablets and video games.

The end effect of the widespread adoption of these new languages is dyscivic and dysfunctional – otherwise, they would not have been promoted! In the final analysis, they are the opposite of everything that language could be.

---

* Spelt so as gangster has too many letters, and is therefore up itself!

Languages

Speaking lots of different, mutually incomprehensible languages, resulting in various learning delays and remedial requirements, is to be welcomed.

Nazi sceptic: *How is speaking thirty-five different languages in school a good thing to be celebrated?*

Third World celebrant: **Well, because,...emmm. You're just a Nazi. No free speech to Nazis!**

That schools did fine when everyone only spoke English as their native and learning language is proof of just how far we've progressed with diversity. One local school is able to proudly boast that 35 languages are spoken in the school, which is great because of some reason; apparently. And this is great for native stock children too; apparently. A typical conversation celebrating all the wonderful languages we are privileged to hear and support with our present and future funds:

Velupillai: நீங்கள் என்ன சொல்கிறீர்கள்?

Sushmita: मुझे समझ नही आया

Saddaam: بلك ، ةيبرعلا ةغللاب ثدحتلا

Charming: *Gusto mo ng masahe sa paa?*

Tower, Babel, something about lots of languages, all goes wrong; what was God talking about? Sounds as if he needs a lesson in tolerance!

Latin

Civis Romanus sum. Odi profanum vulgus. Non potest dicere Latina, Latine loqui.

This should be the only language heard if English (or Scotch or Gaelic) is not being spoken.

NB. Honourable mention to Glaswegian-Somali, North Uist Pashtu and Tik Tok Tong.

Laziness

This lethal attribute has never had less consequences in school for afflicted children than now. The reprimand, to say nothing of the sanction, being long gone, we are now living in a golden age of laziness. Alas, the consequences of this indulgence return as lazy adults become trapped in their ever smaller comfort zone, and thus unhappy prisoners of themselves. They resent the industry of others and become resented in turn. In short, then, they become everything promised when their laziness was ignored as a child. How's that for just desserts!

Leadership

Often confused with bureaucratic management, which passes for leadership in end of days.

Never more needed in education, but now only encountered in its anti- or un- form. These un-leaders, being slavish creatures to the New World Order orthodoxy, are quite incapable of appreciating their own ethical culpability for what is happening in schools and are otherwise totally uninterested in protecting our children or the staff. On anything that matters, our educational leaders have a flawless record of providing zero-level protection. Even when our pupils are existentially threatened by identity politics, such leaders are always posted MIA. It is not an accident that this is so, this is why they were selected and how they self-select. Otherwise none of this madness would have got a toehold. Curiously, as leadership has passed to oblivion, the word keeps turning up, along with shekel-burning workshops giving out leadership certificates.

Even children can get leadership certificates, although not for leadership as such; but, like their adult equivalent, for saying the 'right' things about whatever, because that's what leadership is nowadays. For example; climate – to obtain a Climate Leadership Certificate; sexual choice and home baking – to obtain a Sexual Choice Home Baking Leadership Certificate, etc. Such leadership qualifications obtained by children really do significantly contribute to their future career options, as will be obvious to the intelligent reader.

As we cascade deeper into these hybrids of nonsense we wonder; is there no champion to rescue us? Then she steps forward, far the wiser for being more a human: *I'm six years old, I just want to play.*

And, at last, leadership found.

Learned Helplessness

Ref: babying, infantilising, endless teenager, undermining independence, nanny state, etc

It is universally agreed that schools should be promoting independence of thought and habit, but by their very nature they often promote the opposite. This is unwittingly achieved by a number of means only possible in our age;

1. The instinctive 'mother hen' response of female teachers to some minor issue which does not really need their intervention. In the misguided mind of the teacher she is being kind and helpful and supportive, very much sentiments of the age, of which she can staff boast and perhaps tweet her goodliness. And although these are worthy instincts, beyond a certain level they are toxic. The former natural balance between these forces has been compromised nowadays by a fear of the consequences of appearing to be not supportive enough. And so, as a compensation this mothering need has been exaggerated, possibly stimulating the same among the canny pupil. We note that teachers who are mothers have a more robust and practical response in this regard.

2. School policies which endorse, or even formally require, adult intercession for minor frictions; these, of course, encourage the same.

3. Due to timetabling and target pressures, the use of IT and of various pre-copied shortcuts to be stuck into the jotter. Children, of course, get used to this convenience and some even become dependent on it.

4. The spirit of our age; the 'look it up', 'get it now', 'can't be bothered' lifestyle, inevitably encourages a sense of entitlement in children, and its corollary, the day-to-day helplessness of little princes and princesses. The chores, tasks and general outdoor-lived life of a pirate-adventurer (boy) and homemaking-nurse (girl), which required independence, being long gone for a fully IT delivered childhood. The world's largest corporations create what your child will play, their only independence is to pick their avatar.

5. Following on from 4., the impossibility of employing a sharply-worded rejoiner to a pupil's demand for service, as if from some home-tutored Roman patrician's child to their learned Greek teacher-slave.

This learned helplessness can be considered as part and parcel of the false spirit of our age which infects our schools and to which exposure this book is dedicated.

Learning Conversations: 1

In practice:

What a good idea; having conversations about learning with a child because then they can 'own their own lessons', which every child naturally wants to do. [okay, Not!]

Sean, it's time for your learning conversation. Tell me what you like doing in school?

Playtime. (teacher writes, maths and learning times tables)

When did you last use your learning powers?

Don't know. (teacher writes, Inspiration Iris with story-writing)

What do you want to learn next in maths or project?

... ehhh. (teacher writes, Sean loves science, esp saving rainforest snakes)

What could your next targets be?

Level six in Playstation. (teacher writes, improving formatting and better use of adverbs when story-writing)

What do you like best about literacy work?

Playtime and I like pizza. (teacher writes, helping classmates with dictionary work and grammar)

What do you like best about learning conversations?

What's that? (teacher writes, Sean loves setting new targets and reviewing old ones)

Well done, Sean. I can see that you've thought a lot about your learning conversations.

Done in six minutes. This is how we do to infinity and beyond in the Curriculum for Excellence.

Learning Conversations: 2

In theory;

When an idea becomes formalised and then mandated, it loses its spontaneity. Honesty and usefulness quickly head out of the door too and what was, in certain circumstances, an occasionally useful thing to do, becomes a waste of time and yet another false metric to measure the 'progress' (*Oh, look, it's onwards and upwards!*) and self-congratulate. There is no room for a teacher to exercise wisdom once the system commits to an idea and it becomes a part of the House of Jenga that is modern pedagogic practice. And so with learning conversations.

Luckily, biology comes to the rescue; most children genuinely have no idea what all this is about. Deep down, the children instinctively sense that when they are invited to agree with their teachers regarding learning conversations, that the invite is actually an instruction. And thusly that these false flags of truth are clear signals. Which they are, of course, but of lies! They sense that it is the teacher's deep need to be seen to be better engaged, not theirs, that powers this nonsense; for why they cannot fathom. But by matching the teacher's dishonesty in asking, with theirs in duplicity by agreeing, we find, alas, the one learning power actually transmitted – hypocrisy.

Such learning conversations contribute nothing of value, except for some children who acquire a certain expertise in responding to false questions. This may stand them in good stead in soon enough conversations with court appointed counsellors and, soon enough again, parole officers.

Learning Lessons

Ha ha, fooled you! No, not in school, Silly; it's what politicians do.

Honestly, as usual, they are accelerating into their mistakes. But don't worry, neither them or their shekel-hungry cronies, will lose any money!

Learning Log

1. A large trimmed tree trunk upon which children learn to carve Celtic knotwork and runic messages. Also used by infants to practice tossing the caber and playing African music by means of big sticks or animal bones.

2. A ledger in which the student regularly (preferably daily) completes, using educational language, an evaluation of their success in meeting their various daily lesson and behavioural targets, and their next steps with a view to correction and improvement. The assessment of fellow students is to be included, this to be matched with follow-ups. Somehow, turning our children to little bureaucracy clerks, efficiency monitors and evaluation inspectors, is meant to bring progress.

Big Brother has a little brother now.

Learning Powers: 1

Habits of mind which children bring (or not) to learning, like trying your best or collaborating, for example, have been turned into cartoon characters, with cool names like Tommy Try Again (a tortoise) or Harriet Have a Go (a hare), which supposedly personify the 'learning power' each represents and somehow provide encouragement and useful strategies for overcoming learning barriers.

The teacher's word of encouragement and advice thusly improved, 21st century style, with clipart characters The con further sold (and yes, it is sold!) with alleged scientific endorsement; Persevering Peter and friends are claimed to help develop the vital 'metacognitive' quality to which children must subscribe if excellence is to thrive. Metacognitive, that's science! Like super powers, but better.

This bandwagon is really rolling downhill at the moment, schools everywhere proclaim the faith. But what exactly are these powers, how do children acquire them and what benefit do they really offer? This is a question it is too late to ask. Bottom line, this is another nothing idea on steroids, bluffing its way to the podium. However, this is not just a waste of time; for we take away the personalised, private word which used to be the subtle heart of good teaching, and replace it with more box-ticking, internet sourced, Americanised, weekly-focussed, targeted, stock exhortations. These become the means by which we transmit to our children the relentless message of ever improving standards and the same management-speak gobbledegook that is ruining us adults. Here 'success' is measured by virtual approval from internet avatars –no, it really is! – all the better to prepare them for their life online in a cubicle plantation.

So ignorant are most teachers of any knowledge of the nature of evidence, either presented to them or by them, that they present the following as proof of mindset concept:

'Pippa Positive' has helped children have a more positive attitude, respond better to challenges and concentrate and persevere more since learning about mindsets.

An adult and a teacher (No, not me) wrote this; *Incroyable!* Proof of teacherly delusion continues with the lying claim that children now talk about how their brain is growing (*Why?*). Apparently, their learning teddies – no, really, they exist! – have helped children become more motivated to learn in areas they feel less confident about and have even encouraged lower achievers to try harder! Apparently. Consider, if ye dare, the depth of animating intelligence behind such claims:

Gabrielle the green mouse has really supported children to be motivated in their learning and their learning language (e.g., 'I'm growing my brain', 'The green mouse helps me to learn').

In fact, by cartoonising these developing learning concepts we lock the child further into a pixelated Pixyland screen world; thusly strengthening their infantilisation, instead of leading them to developing the concepts *as* concepts. Our children do not need more IT time, and this monkey-level pedagogy serves as a regressive force in their developing intellects and an impediment to the qualities it seeks to develop. And not just as infants, legitimising ideas by pixel avatar and cartoons, and the life of the screen, rewires their mind. Thinking ahead to the lives lost to the computer game and social media, one wonders about how something as obviously silly and decentring as this could ever take hold; for it did so to no resistance whatsoever from among teachers that I know of. Indeed, self excepted, it has been approvingly adopted as a 'really cool idea.' But as one asks the question, the answer unfortunately suggest itself. Shareen the try-again tiger invites me to reconsider my objection, *You're too serious about everything*, she tells me. Maybe I am. Maybe what we see is a general female inability to connect cause with effect, through several orders of iteration. You be the judge!

Learning Powers: 2

aka, the ninjas of the learning power world.

Miss STFU Macaw (Mr Masking Tape will help you keep quiet)

Simon Sloth never starts (Danny Detention will show you how)

Lazy Lionel Lion (Colin Couldnae Care Less is your team-mate)

Deefie David Donkey never listens (Confused Connie is your project partner)

Messy Margaret Monkey (Ms Dunce's Cap will help you reflect on self-improvement)

Tommy Peepee (this nappy avatar will help you learn bladder control and encourage resilience as others laugh at you)

Learning Powers: 3

Persevere – the only true learning power.

When things get hard, try harder. Always model, gently encourage or sometimes force – as required.

Nobody likes a quitter, not even Satan.

Learning Styles

Another simple idea (there are different ways of learning things and preferences change accordingly) that has been hopped up on steroids and aggressively demands its rights exercised to the max in every lesson.

And again; by over-talking it, it overcomplicates it, and by overcomplicating it things become confused. And in the confusion, the justification for criticism of teacher practice, then quickly following demands for correction with more courses and advice from shekel collectors and other friends of the public purse.

LGBTQ+

A high priority of the curriculum is to enforce this agenda whose terminus is the + (68 and counting, as per current US Air Force guidelines), which is the chaos of everything that you can think of that links to sex and gender. This neo-Babylon will turn our school world upside-down. Comes the day when those children who express confusion, far less resistance, to the new order and its punctilious speech protocols will find themselves and their parents censured for hate speech. This is already happening. Eventually we can expect such resistance to be classified as a psychiatric disorder; and with this classification comes harassment, exclusions and demands for re-education, all of which crank ever upwards, as if in endless preparation for the next fetish. And while *en route* to that hellish terminus, more work for the school psychologist, the police and – *O, wild guess* – probably lawyers.

Although many, possibly most, LGBTQ+ people are on-board with these developments in school, this agenda has a political power and a funding source quite independent of their feelings on the topic. Similarly, normal people (as currently defined), the vast majority of whom hold no personal animus against such others, will future find that their polite and supportive attitude is of no consequence as they are fated, in this coming binary world of righteous-right and evil-wrong, to play the hate-filled bigot role on any questioning of any part of this agenda. It is at this point that you see, always too late, that the agenda's intent all along was to isolate and destroy. It was absolutely NOT about acceptance, which was always there anyway. Nor was it about letting unconventional others get on with their life and hope that they work out their own solutions to their own problems, but about co-opting them into a much bigger project – destroy the West.

Now you must cheer as you enter this Sheol.

Lies

Where pedagogy and school mission are concerned there is such an embarrassment of riches. Every category and level and percentage of lie is so well represented that it could be argued that the school's primary purpose is to spread lies.

With respect to children lying, this is their golden age. Such a child can lie about anything free of consequence, even of censure. If a child wants to get a classmate into trouble, or a teacher, just tell a lie about them. Nothing will happen to you, even if you're caught.

[Satan just called, he said: *Yeah, so what and who cares?* I said I'd pass this comment to the readers]

Listening

As in able to hear meaning. Some pupils can, some can't yet. Jesus knew of this:

Listening ears on, Boys and Girls.

Hearken; Behold, there went out a sower to sow: And it came to pass, as he sowed, some fell by the wayside, and the fowls of the air came and devoured it up. And some fell on stony ground, where it had not much earth; and immediately it sprang up, because it had no depth of earth: But when the sun was up, it was scorched; and because it had no root, it withered away. And some fell among thorns, and the thorns grew up, and choked it, and it yielded no fruit. And other fell on good ground, and did yield fruit that sprang up and increased; and brought forth, some thirty, and some sixty, and some an hundred. And he said unto them, He that hath ears to hear, let him hear.

—Mark, 4:3–9, KJV

This is all the teacher can do.

Listen to your heart

This meaningless nonsense, papped off to children and accompanied with *Follow your dreams* or *You can be anything you want*, is dishonest even at point of service. This apparent motivational positivism is all part of the fundamental dishonesty that accompanies school life. It primes the journey to narcissism and eventually disappointment. Perhaps even ruination, as children can persist in chasing inflated or otherwise inappropriate dreams. How could adults not know this?

The Bible got it right; the heart is wicked and deceitful beyond measure.

Literacy

Fewer children have the time to read now as they are increasingly obliged, like most parents, to constantly check the Borgfeed, if not watching the tele.

Reading is recommended, of course, but has to be carefully monitored to prevent it inadvertently revealing non-orthodox opinions; for example, issuing a book featuring a White child protagonist with live at home parents is no longer the norm and in becoming rapidly unacceptable. For this reason it is best steering clear of children's classics and any of the great works of English literature, abridged or otherwise, as these are all steeped in prejudice and teacher censure potential. Seriously, such books will draw complaint on the teacher and traitorous agreement from school management.

The wonderful irony is that such complaining mums (as it will be) don't read, twit feed excepted. Many of the teachers don't read either, unless the twit feed is counted, thus providing a poor template for literacy and a reduced world of literary reference. The collective impact of this lack of literate culture among primary teachers is, I believe, pervasive and negative.

Teacher should best play safe by issuing Holocaust and Wakandan stories, the trials of transitioning, incest and other alternatively constructed families. Some recommended titles; *The Famous Five go Trans, My Three Dads* (wonderful tri female to male mixed-race family adventure), *Junkie Dad Skanky Mum* (self-harm tale for infants), *Bonny Prince Charlie* (not that prince, although he does wear a skirt and 'Highland underwear'), *Snow Black and Her Seven Homebois* and that original tale of coloured excellence, *Black Booty.*

Perhaps the mass literate age is drawing to a close. If one examines the coming crop of topics regarded as essential components in the stories which build literacy in our children, then perhaps this is a good thing. The intent behind the promotion of this literature is transparent, and literacy is not the concern at all.

We wonder if any pattern of ownership can be discerned behind the commissioning, writing and promotion of such alternative lifestyle publications aimed at our children?

NB. ED: We have received a notice from the Phoenician Author and Publishers Association who assure us that no such link exists and there is no need to be concerned with this issue any more. Nothing to see, move along now.

Literature

Stories are foundational of perception, they help us organise reality.

Children's literature would be an obvious conduit through which the disaffected and deranged could advance ideas or encourage behaviours likely to benefit their world view. Obviously, such literature will revolve around notions of ethnic and sexual pluralism, and criticism of traditional White family structure.

This literature seeks to introduce and normalise to primary children such ideas as boys in dresses, females against males, homo-trans families, sperm donor offspring, adopted other-race children, alternative identities, and fluid partner relationships. It is implacably hostile to White society, tacitly presenting traditionally functioning families as the repository of prejudice and impediments to progress.

One could also reasonably predict that a time will soon come when any tales of White children engaging in adventures will be unequivocally deemed reactionary because of their potential to instil pride, or dangerous to further progress because they are not tolerant enough of the proliferating motley crew of sexual and racial minorities. We have seen this happen with some soft targets; Biggles, Noddy, and the Famous Five adventures, that no one cared enough about to resist their de-legitimising, or, more likely, didn't even know that they had been corrected, Ministry of Truth style. Now, this target neutralised, the malignant have the modus and means to move to the next target in our children's cultural legacy. Our challenge in the coming generation is to resist this or we will be left with nothing.

Alternative children's literature: Proudly serving the school counselling services with fresh victims.

The Venerable Bede's optimistic wish, *Lege feliciter* – May you read happily! – could almost be a cruel mock.

Love

as in 'love the job'. Alas, unrequited.

YOUR CAREER DOESN'T LOVE YOU BACK.

Low-Level Disruption

aka death of a thousand cuts.

The phrase is disingenuous. It is not really low level. Persistent, minute by minute, pupil disruptions and disrespect set a new baseline of bad behaviour. As an accepted norm, it becomes de facto the background drone; and like a far-off car alarm sounding all night, it doesn't have to be loud to be high-level disruption. By running cortisol at high levels the whole day, and then the next, one never fully recovers during term time. Indeed, to cope, one tactically ignores the attacks, redefines them as misunderstanding, or some other expression that absolves the pupil of responsibility for their behaviour. You may think that you've marginalised these attacks, rationalised them as trivial, coped and moved on; but, in fact, a thousand small insults have a mighty cumulative power. High-level disruption to one's well-being is the result. Teacher and pupil alike suffer under pedagogic practices, which permit this. And all modern pedagogic practice permits this.

Lowest Difficulty Setting

i.e., the standard setting for pedagogic practice.

When we fail to sanction laziness, enforce standards, reward false achievement and congratulate stupidity, how could it be otherwise?

Low Self-esteem

Sometimes it's deserved. The crude emphasis which schools currently place on trying to fix this by artificially bolstering such a child always backfires. Let the wound heal itself by its own true medicine.

Loyalty

Just kidding, there's none! This should not be a surprise to a realist teacher. Women don't do loyalty, they can't. They don't even think about coming to the aid of an unfairly and well-liked persecuted colleague as a principle, even one within their own staff coven. This mindset comes with the genes, ask a women if you don't believe this. Actually, don't bother, lying too comes with the genes. Ask a women if you don't believe this.

What sometimes seems like loyalty is just standard female sycophancy, manipulation, or group virtue signalling. When a real issue comes, the women side with power every time. The other abandoned, as leprous, to their fate. Head teachers are of course especially selected, and self-selected, for their ruthless, reliable reflex to show staff what is known as kommissar loyalty.

A man in school should expect absolutely nothing in the way of support (barring the presence of another man) if an issue arrives involving him. There is no pay-back factor involved or issues of principle. The leopardess cannot change her spots.

See, Men only (not the nude magazine). See, Brand loyalty.

NB. There are situations when school staff can count on female loyalty, and this is when you don't need it!

Lunch

Some sharp lessons have turned up recently with respect to the provision of culturally appropriate diets, which school management would be well-advised to take heed of if they wish to avoid another, what has become commonly known as 'diversity lunch rampage'. In the fight for dietary justice, here meaning curried goat balls and deep fried monkey, the Black Lunches Matter (BLM) group have adopted the slogan 'No Cous Cous, No Jam Piece' and demanded the removal of cutlery as instruments of White (table manners) oppression – except for knives, which should be bigger and curved.

Top Education Lunch consultants have also been advising that budget tinned macaroni dishes are a major factor in lunchtime stab-ups.

The BBC: 'Meanwhile, in yesterday's largely peaceful primary school lunchtime stabbings...'

Lubricious

This word has tragically replaced precocious as the most unfortunate adjective that can be applied to a little girl in school. Whoever thought such a word could turn up in this context and mean what it means?

See, little sex kitten dance group.

M

Males

Ref: in primary teaching.

Males are so rare that feminist teachers have been complaining that they have not enough men in schools to complain about. This has resulted in fem activists joining with their patriarchal overlords to protest this unfair ratio, ...*only kidding, female teachers don't give a shh!*

The current culture is destructive of male sensibility and behaviour, and that's to be celebrated. But we mymen and mxs must go further...

> Professor Manless
> (Eradicating the White Patriarchy from Primary Schools)

Being a male primary teacher is just asking for trouble. In fact, you don't need to ask, it'll come looking for you every day.

Marking

Of all the clouds that lour'd upon the teacher's house, this is the darkest.

The marking burden; excessive bureaucratic procedures masquerading as evidence, hundreds of hours wasted providing little to nothing of value on either side of the jotter. And a ready recorded source of unjust criticism should an enemy manager or parent so wish: *You've not recorded what your verbal feedback was. The tickled-pink stamper is faint. Your detailed comments are not sufficiently detailed, you must provide more examples. Have the pupils record your comments in their target books. You should record jotter comments into the pupils' term portfolios for future reference and evidence of progress.*

Obviously, one must check and mark, however, in common with other teacher tasks that need no more than application of some wit and wisdom to be useful, this too has been force-fed steroids until it's raging; detailed comments, next steps, different coloured codes, two stars and a wish, highlighted excellence, smilies, stampers, stickers, even verbal feedback to be recorded (!), until it's all too much load for the poor teacher-donkey to bear. Everything that's done, has a cost in something that's not done.

However, the gigantic marking burden is not just killing teacher time; it is for the most part irrelevant, as the pupils don't read the remarks anyway and cannot understand the specific what, how or why of such remarks even if they did! Understanding and following written instructions is not a simple skill, and current marking practice often risks overwhelming its development. Children really want someone telling them, just like you or I would.

And more, the relentless positivity obliged by marking can so easily, drip by drip, become its opposite, demotivating and encouraging hubris, while still an infant! Thusly, part of the 'false world' we are creating for our children in school.

Teacher: *Did you read my marking comments?*

Pupil: **Yes.**

Teacher: *Well, do you understand what to do now?*

Pupil: **No. What marking comments?**

Mark of Zorro, The

Quiet, you popinjay. I've no reason to let you live either!

Diego provides the ultimate example of how to play the school system – hidden in full view.

And how many times must this scene play in the teacher's mind: *I'll make it short and save you fatigue.*

Maths

The foundation of our civilisational achievements and a content-neutral, and generally useful, subject for children to learn. However, it has recently been brought to our attention that under this innocent-looking flower, a serpent was coiled – the white snake of racism!

Maths, it seems, as the most objective of all disciplines, is by this same metric also the most oppressive expression of the racist West; underlying, as it did, all sorts of White man magic and engineering. The racism being expressed through the focus on the correct answers to maths problems. And, too, racially denying of what are known as 'alternative mathematical realities' – these being mostly bushman-style finger counting systems, proven reliable up to about ten.

Mathematicians and scientists claim that this degradation of maths by multicultural activists is actually due to their inability to accept the poor maths scores amongst certain groups for what they are, and then rationalising them by blaming everyone else for them. But, Ha ha!, for both sides say the same thing. Either way, this 'hateful deniers' argument is just more proof that maths is a White people thing. If Asians and Arabs want to claim a stake in the development of maths, then we are sure that a place can be found for them in the trashcan of history.

Don't worry about it, as it is getting replaced with mindfulness which also starts with an M (so no loss there!). Anyway, your i phone has a calculator.

Maximise

Every initiative is predicated on maximising teacher productivity, pupil output, evidence recording, learning outcomes, bureaucratic thoroughness, IT connectivity, value awareness, self-esteem, psychological comfort and happiness. And yet, with the ten scale dial turned to eleven, we fail.

KING SOLOMON: *Have you tried turning the educational dial the other way?*

TEMPLE EDUCATIONALIST: *Sire, such a thing is impossible. It would cause the world to end and put the temple prostitutes out of business.*

Memory

This is of course at the heart of learning and one would assume that, as teachers like to claim that they are a science-driven profession, knowledge of how memory operates would be a subject of practical interest And it seems this is the case, but true to institutional norms, in ironic reverse form.

So much about memory is known as scientific fact and common sense observation; working memory holds four to six items, some stress is required within a non-judgmental system, performance improves with practice which leads to automaticity which then frees up working memory and allows us to concentrate on comprehension, testing consolidates, and solid sleep wraps up the package tightly.

How else to explain, then, the wilful disregard of such knowledge and its replacement with the opposite; except as demonic agency operating through teacher drones? And so, we have promoted as standard practice an overloading of working memory prior to a lesson even beginning; with a focus on specifically stated priorities, targets, skill sets apparently engaged and various other requirements at best tangential to the lesson. All this emphasis on process and skills and full comprehension *prior* to operational ability, made explicit as it is, compromises working memory. And this, in turn, affects the acquiring of said operational knowledge, which laid down as long-term memory, brings ability and finally comprehension. Tests or exams, long known as the perfect stress to force by pride, shame or other sanction, the brain to work by remembering, find no welcome in the modern school; heaven forbid that a child should be made anxious due to a test! A giga ton of pixel screen time and a full night's poor sleep complete the conspiracy to degrade memory.

All this, as if deliberate to compromise working memory and the achieving of long-term memory. All this, make us ineffectual learners and holders of a poor memory base. And out of the degraded memory, comes the rescuer; the i phone. As long as you don't forget this, all will be ok. As Hamada said: *What's the point of learning this, I've can get it on my i phone?*

Good question! The answer; Memory performance improves with practice, and practice leads to automaticity, which frees up working memory and allows us to concentrate on comprehension. But who cares? Well, not your child's school.

Men

It has been observed that a profession dominated by women cannot, by definition, allow men to realise themselves as men. In the primary school, a man will not be respected for what he brings in terms of interests, sensibility, and especially sympatico with little boys, but instead be regarded as a lesser female. Further, as a minority often of one, men usually find themselves isolated, sometimes unwittingly, sometimes by intention, and sometimes by self-exclusion due to the rubbish that women talk. Those men who attempt to find favour by mimicry are secretly hated.

With their style and sensibility misunderstood, if not resented, men abandon such professions, as any resistance to the female imperative always goes bad for the men. The crucial figure for this to start happening is 15% of female presence, so at 95%, primary schools are beyond recovery. Fortunately, here we make no reference to a den of vipers,…oops, sorry!

As a male colleague observed of this phenomena: *Mongo only pawn in game of life.*

Mental Health Week

More reminders of potential current problems for them, more reminders of potential coming problems for them, more reminders of current adult problems, more reminders of stigma, more reminders of victim status, more reminders of charity initiatives to help combat this apparent stigma, more reminders of social failures to address, more reminders of (White) racism and prejudice as source of problems, more reminders how the problem is getting worse, more reminders of talking about problems and then a big Friday assembly to tie it up with a video and chat link if they had gotten upset.

Apparently talking about mental health and proffering services to children is a good thing,...for their mental health! Attention provided for attention-seekers, guilt for the lave and no help for the needy.

And the true source of this situation cannot be mentioned; broken families, single parents, life online, appalling diets, garbage coated in sugar as snacks, TV and endless talking about problems. Which latter includes Mental Health Week.

See, Depression Starter Pack.

Merit

Our modern public school system was predicated on merit. Functioning properly, as it generally did, it unleashed a terrific potential which mostly replaced privilege, in our essential and flagship undertakings, as our society's working ethos. Our post-modern system is abandoning this merit for privilege; this obtained under the universalist appeal to justice. Our Jacobin masters claiming that old merit was actually racist White privilege, and so destined for the classroom's dustbin to keep company with its racist cohorts of Order, Scholarship and Academic Achievement. They claim that victimhood and ethnic otherness, however expressed, is actually true merit at last achieved; but we see it for what it really is – the destroyer's club. . Soon they'll be prizes for most oppressed, gayest, historically disadvantaged and blackest.

We look forward to attending that prize giving assembly. And know the wait will not be long.

Ministers

of religion. aka, meenisters.

A decidedly nice and thankfully occasional visitor to school whose job is to bring God's approval to their message of White guilt via the Good Samaritan* parable and collect tribute for less White and more loved, foreign domiciled, or *en route* here, others. To both these ends they often double as agents of Fairtrade. The prize for those pupils whose unwitting self-abasement is to buy and sell the most Fairtrade products is a posted picture on the school website. A largesse that is the opposite of the widow's mite.

And not once, in hundreds, has the Holy Ghost, inspired the Truth spoken to children who thirst for it. Only ever told tales about being nice, understanding others and giving away your patrimony. Is this really the Lord's work? Why don't you ask?

Mise-en-scène

The Child Protection Workshop: certification update

SET DESIGN:-
One large classroom at end of school day.

One female Child Protection expert from council HR.

One audience (33 females-all teaching staff, 2 males-teacher and janitor). Some audience arrive late.

PROLOGUE:-
HR expert claims to be ill with flu (sympathy fishing, conscientiousness signalling) and so will try to finish early (goodwill

---

* If one didn't know otherwise, one would think that this was Jesus's only message.

soliciting). This meets much silent approval. No evidence of illness, however. (Actually finished 30 minutes late!)

PERFORMANCE:-
One minute's presentation content X 100, literally. One hour, forty minutes long. Many deaths by Power Point.

CONTENT:-
Confirmed evidence of the exponentially negative impact of social media on children's life as it pertains to child protection and law-breaking. Poverty too is apparently increasing, also exclusively due (apparently) to funding shortfalls for programmes and workshops like this one.

No understanding presented of family and relationship dynamics; issues presented from a feminist perspective as largely one driven by dysfunctional males, as referenced; violent men, abandoning fathers, sexual predators, controlling boyfriends.

One significant male demographic group behind most of the issues NOT MENTIONED AT ALL. NOR THIS OMISSION APPARENTLY NOTICED.

Ongoing failures with the system linked to funding shortages (presumably for workshops like this), 'our' lack of a Named Child Policy (see ref) and the absence of 'conversations' with pupils in primary schools about these issues. Conversations with children are very important in eradicating poverty and preventing sexual abuse. Except if such abuse is sourced to a group that is NOT MENTIONED AT ALL.

Ongoing failures apparently have no link whatsoever to parental choices, personal habits or cultural practices. None of these adults, as presented, seemingly have agency in their own family lives! Manipulating, system-gaming, selfish or abusing mothers (especially, if single) do not exist in this worldview.

No awareness of the intractability of these problems to legislation. No awareness of unintended consequences. No awareness of the effect on teaching staff of applying and policing policies that can never work, but carry legal obligations and consequences to said staff. No awareness that any of her audience might think differently about the subjects discussed and referenced.

ACCEPTABLE COMPOSITIONAL PREJUDICE:-
Considering that the audience was essentially middle class, the sarcastic references to middle-class children and their families (contrasting their choices and opportunities compared to their less well-off 'working class' £600 i phone peers) was offensive and insensitive. Imagine the same mocking reference to working-class single mums or Islamic parents.

ASPECT RATIO:-
This workshop is as near to a perfect illustration of the nature of our educational system as a one act play can get; low level intellect at work, the usual pieties, naked anti-male prejudice celebrated, solipsistic, feminist propaganda, and utterly without value. The final effect is like being inside a tweet storm.

Trainers like this (name, Cleonna, not referenced to preserve anonymity) have to be driven out of the system if any progress is to be made. Of course they won't be, and so there will not be.

Misgendering

includes Miss gendering.

Formerly, this was a question of apology:

Oh, I do beg your pardon. I thought that you were a fully-grown man. Oh, what's that,...my mistake again,...well, please accept extra apologies. It was the beard stubble that fooled me.

No problem, apology accepted. Even my therapist gets mixed up sometimes!

However, these polite days are past and this issue is now a legal matter. Schools can advise pupils on seeking legal remedy. Corridor posters provide information and speed dial connections to pro rata sexual gender insult lawyers.

Miss gendering is the most severe category of misgendering and is an immediate police matter. This will involve double-lawyering and double-lawyering fees.

Missing

as in, generally from future life.

Following the choice of a teaching career, one can generally expect to be missing; maintaining relationships, getting married, having children, free time and, forever, mental equanimity. This is typically regarded as a small price to pay for a career progression and 'making a difference'.

Mission Statement

Welcome to Morningside Primary – A place where children can achieve their full potential in academic, creative, personal, physical, moral and spiritual development.

Is there anything it cannot do? Ah, j*ust noticed, they forgot,...***and a happy, happy place of rainbows and butterflies.** *Fixed now. And now it's truly believable!*

Returning to reality, does anyone actually believe this? How about if we turn the dial up to the next level of wonderfulness: ...and become; **respected, powerful, rich, and happy, free of anxiety and suffering, ever climbing towards ultimate success.** Obviously better, because it's got even more better stuff in the M.S. You thought your kid went to primary school to learn to read, write and count, but it's so much more than that thanks to wonderfulness.

One wonders why all our primary schools now need a mission statement, when formerly, their purpose being well-understood, they had no such requirement. They had no such requirement because they did what they were meant to do.

Admittedly, we live in a prolix age (*Yes, I know...*) and the mission statement follows female fashion for unthinkingly copying other schools who have one, and the need for female busy-work, of which the statement is an example to be added to all the school goodthink statements, policies documents and learning outcomes, click on the link to see our Fairtrade and Anti-slavery commitment, etc, etc. But, do we actually need a mission statement and, if so, for what purpose? After all, everyone surely understands that it is not a guarantee, although it bluffs itself up as if one. And too, often extravagant mission statements have an inverse relationship to mission success.

And herein lies the problem, the mission statement inadvertently reveals an insecurity about their success in addressing their purpose and, in compensation, they attempt to persuade the reader by telling them what they want them to believe. In has long been recognised that such uninvited, self-preening protests achieve the opposite of reassurance; and mission statement, flipped to opposite, actually reveals the underlying psychology.

They are placing their propaganda for what should be, as an oversell for what is not; the inflated word as compensation for the reduced action, hoping that, because it tells you how great it is, you will believe it. In contrast, the plain truth, simple and silent, is not heard. This constant exposure to such redundancy in all official statements inures your mind to more of the same, and whose end effect is not only another piece of time-wasteful subversive nonsense to be swallowed silently, but the creation of a world of lies.

As Napoleon said: *Just do your job. And I'll know what you've done.*

More

If you try to save everyone and everything, you save no one and nothing. It's the same with everything connected to education, try to do everything and end up doing nothing. Anyone that lived a life should understand this.

Often less is more. In school, it is a lot more.

Mother Nature

She is seldom generous with respect to gifts of great talent and so one should be happy with the (usually only) one given. The teacher should help the pupil find this and cherish it, and not delude them as per the current practice with false and inflated beliefs of extra competence, or worse, special talent. Don't allow a pupil's self-confidence to shade to delusion. Never fight against Mother Nature, it is a fight you cannot win.

Nature, she be a racist and sexist bitch.

Mothers

The more dangerous of the parent forms by an order of magnitude. Also the most unreasonable. The single parent version in this age of empowerment really operates with no constraint on their conscience or tongue. With a self-righteousness that overvaults heaven, they are not, as they believe, representing their children, but betraying them by voiding their angst and bitterness, while spreading their poison in the Twitter circle. Demonically inspired, there seems nothing can shut this force up, and the entire school community backs away before them. Chronically disappointed by men, the male teacher is an obvious whipping boy for the single mother, although she hardly needs an excuse.

Exposed to this force the male teacher comes to appreciate the logic and moral rightness of the branks; the wisdom of our forefathers revealed.

Move with the times

You've got to!

From a P7 class music lesson, seriously;

Learn some African-American songs of resistance. Use your knowledge (wtf!) of the oppression of the Black community (presumably by Scots) to write a rap celebrating strength and diversity.

Strength and diversity, O, that's nice! Meanwhile, Cardi B is the role model for 12 year old girls and rappers push Zanax at the top of the bill.* And rap providing a vocabulary of hate and friction, projecting

---

* Hat check to Tom MacDonald.

outwards and feeding inwards – just what we need to 'move with the times'. *It's like …???, d'know wot am sayin?*

Suggestions: Twerking to Evryday Ho by the 9mm Bruvvas.

Hey, ███. *Don' make me pop a cap in yo* ███. *If you know what's good for you, you'll* ███.

etc, etc.

Goodbye to *Charlie is my Darling* and *Caller Herrin'*. And welcome to the new true sound of Scotland!

Multicultural Benefits

These argue for themselves:

National Guidance for Responding to Female Genital Mutilation in Scotland

school bomb plan

speaking 35 languages in school

Ebola, exotic viruses and TB risk updates

WTCs (war traumatised children)

school houses replaced with tribal zones

and prepare to enjoy more of the same, sooner than you think.

NEWS FLASH: Scotland saved by multiculturalism. FM just signed a deal to bring the entire nation of Pakistan to Scotland. Schoolgirls celebrate by making welcome placards.

Multiculturalism

The penultimate object of our education.

As it is in the wider society, multiculturalism is the prevailing philosophy in primary schools. Further, it increasingly takes on the functions of a religion, but one which recognises no plurality of worship. It is not a single force, but comes with the attack battalions of discrimination, inclusion, prejudice, injustice, whiteness and its elite regiment of systemic racism led by human rights lawyers. It colours how we approach every topic, directly influences practice and manipulates the outcomes –indeed, this dictionary is unwittingly dedicated to this effect. Its school mission is to force the acceptance of its shibboleths on all pupils; perfidy and guilt on White children, and victimhood on ethnic others. The final goal, realised post school, is to be seen around you. Or not, if you cannot.

In society at large, we see resentful outcasts and losers at last finding self-worth as puppet-fronts in the censure, undermining and promised dismantling of all native customs, traditions and institutions, and at the same time demanding a multi-racial, multicultural future, but without us in our own land. All this finds expression in school as the stuff of ethnic fatigue: the dishonesty, the dumbing-down, the poisonous egalitarian faux-paternalism, and the degradation of standards so as to avoid the false but ruinous accusation of racism. And, as if suddenly, everything is politics, everything – even this!

But as it enervates us, the sight of this discord energises our enemies who need to see suffering to reinforce their sense of being in a great struggle, and need to see destruction as compensation for their inability to see the beauty of creation. Multiculturalism is their weapon of destruction and they will not rest, become satisfied, agree to differ or otherwise leave us alone. This is the crucial point, multiculturalism is not just another stupid curriculum add-on, but an existential war for all concerned; and a new phenomenon as far as primary schools are concerned. Looking back from a near and unfortunate future, our children will see this as the defining feature of their schooldays – and curse us for our lack of prescience and cowardice.

However, it is not just the present that is under attack, the evolving moral system of multiculturalism extends its morality back in time to bring judgement to our ancestors, institutions, buildings and artefacts; indeed, every aspect of our history is judged unkindly by this new, apparently timeless morality. Even long dead people are retrospectively judged by how far their life deviated from this new moral order, before it was even discovered!

Can you imagine how destabilising this is to a schoolchild; apparently, all our national institutions were, and still are, racist and exploitive- and thus lose both respect and legitimacy. A native White child has no reason to feel pride and an ethnic other has every reason to hate.

Someone is happy at this.

Multitasking

This is viewed as a necessity in the face of all the demands teachers have to juggle. It is also the subject of much lady teacher hubris, as this is typically viewed as the quintessential feminine attribute and therefore obviously a good thing, because,...because it's women that do it! One wonders, though, if this female strength is actually such a good thing; a temporary shift in attention from one task to another obviously increases the amount of time necessary to finish the original task. Focus and continuity is lost in this switching. Distractions, then, ultimately proving costly in time and quality.

Considering the negative aspect further, it may be the case that the ability to multitask has encouraged more of the same. All the accretions to the curricula and the school day in general are dependent on a willingness (or lack of resistance) to cope with all the extra stuff that arrives. Extra tasks, instead of getting kicked to the sidelines or utterly rejected, are tackled using multitask skills. The illusion of efficient coping masks degraded output and this is maintained by the female tendency to complain conspiratorially, rather than in open rebellion.

Thus, a female strength can sometimes be a system weakness. There's too much multitasking in schools. It causes stress in the timetable and in the teacher's mind, and by extension a manic class atmosphere. And where children are aware of it, it provides a chaotic template of competing and switching priorities.

There are some good examples of multitasking, for example; when the single male teacher in the school (me) instructed the nearest woman (head teacher) to bring him a cup of tea **and** a bacon sandwich, **and** then provide a neck massage. Without doubt, female multitasking at its finest. This same head teacher was also able to bring another task to this suite, that of calling the police during the neck massage, but luckily after the tea was served. Still waiting on the bacon sandwich. Point proven.

Music

It is a tragedy for our children that, arguably the high point of European cultural achievement, our classical music repertoire finds no place in their learning. Likewise, for our great folk traditions, the envy of less blessed lands. The various mood and even neurological benefits that the former confers on the listener have been well catalogued – as have been the deleterious effects of poptrash and rap

– but pale in comparison to the wonder and beauty so easily brought into a child's life. And for our native, post ice-age stock, the immense pride of association; the greatest gift in a child's upbringing. The scale of this musical achievement, covering the development of theory, harmonic scales, notation, techniques, training, instruments, recording and the creation of the highest standards to carry it forward, can easily be transmitted to children, even infants, who hold no class or other prejudices against this music – at least until the global popworld snares their minds.

Few contemporary teachers, alas, have any knowledge of this tradition, far less interest, as it does not sit nicely with poptart vids and i Tunes. This is an immense loss to our children, and one, moreover, when the early exposure and appreciation is not encouraged, that is not easily recovered.

The issue for our children is not just the loss of great and uplifting music, but its replacement with poptrash garbage by the dreck-meisters of Global Inc. This music-ganda is fronted by wholly, globalist-owned, puppet fembots or gangsta style dysfunctionaries whose actual mission is to bring precocious sexuality, identity confusion, narcissism and neuroticism to their innocent targets by planted suggestion and their personal example.

According to wise Confucius, you can tell the values of a society by the music it listens to. So be it. Well, let them keep Lady Gaga, we've got Wagner. Perhaps he will come to our rescue; certainly, if *Ride of the Valkyries* is playing, you could do your maths in soiled underwear and it would still be heroic

NB. Scoff ye scoffers and disbelievers. But as proven fact, by children asking for it to be played again, *Freudig begrussn wir die edle Halle* from *Tannhäuser* or *A Te, O Cara* from *I Puritani*, mighty and gorgeous respectively, show the breathy squeakings of Ariana et al for what they are. And I am pleased to imagine them ushered back into their cages by Wagner and Bellini. Transcendental power can come into a child's life from such music, find a way for this if you can.

N

Name Wars

The poisoned tendrils of cultural Marxism reach out to children's names as a fresh source of sustenance. And so Faoud's parents sue for discrimination as his name appears in a maths textbook, and Zaara's because her name doesn't. And then we discover transphobia in the same maths textbook as no transgender, cross-gender or gender fluids are mentioned causing activist parents and lawyers (in this case, the same person) to lick their chops at the forthcoming pay-out at Her Majesty's menadge. Meanwhile, twins Tarquin and Celiac's two dads also notice homoprejudice in the boys' reading books, all families there depicted feature patriarchal toxic trad forms; luckily, the dads are lawyers.

Teachers are advised to check textbooks for children's names which may also be present in class, and act accordingly so as not to give offence. Unless such action itself should cause offence; obviously!

Nation

A nation is a community of people who share a common language, culture, values, traditions, ethnicity, descent, and history. It is worthy of celebration. Unless it is our own, in which case, ignorance building blocks upon itself, leads to confusion as the desired structure and shame the desired attitude.

Prithee, Old Scotia, the old nation is tired, it is time for it to be gone to yon lealish land ayont the setting orb. And replaced with a swarthier fellow more meet t' our less gentle times, I warrant. [Ossian to his grandfather Act 1, Scene 1 from *Traitor's Happy Benison*]

Nativity

This tradition is fast moving into what is known as the racist-sectarian zone; tweet and kill-bots roam freely here searching out wrongthinkers.

The currently recommended solution is to have mixed-race, same sex trans-parents (Maurie and Josephina), Jesus is a black anchor baby (obviously) and the wise men are female Somalis (ha ha). Instead of following a holy star they are following a welfare handout homing app. *O, welfare app of Bethlehem, how kool to get our gibs.*

Clearly this cultural staple, as a Christian tradition, is soon set to be a symbolic battlefield for psychological ownership of the European mind. What will it be, resistance or fold like a CEO of a global corporation.

Okay, sorted. Have a wonderful, stab-free nativity play.

Nature

Ref: as in, of a child

What nature does not give, providence does not lend.

Naughty

A pupil is never naughty. A teacher who describes a pupil as 'naughty', is so naughty themselves for saying this that they will lose their job. Such words are classed as humiliating to a child; indeed, *entirely inappropriate and incompatible with professional standards.* Teachers have lost a job thusly.

Don't be naughty and say 'naughty'.

Negativity

In the primary education world telling the truth about anything is equated with being negative. Sometimes this is euphemistically expressed as 'not moving with the times', 'hostile to new potentials', 'failure to appreciate...' and the like. The impact on your career of telling the truth is, however, not euphemistic, but refreshingly honest and directly negative; so, that's that circle squared.

The proper response to, for example, the use of goofy, alien cartoon icons to report behaviour interactively (with live-feed updates) to parents, or for the teacher to record progress (what else could it be?) with buzzy bee computer rewards and our new maths monkey counting scheme is:

I can't wait to try it in class, Wow exciting, Pupils have improved attainment already.

This is the truth you need to live with if you wish to avoid the bullet of negativity. Some people call it lying.

Nerves

These are typically either fried or shot to pieces over the term. Some temporary repair can be effected by strong coffee, chocolate (if a woman) and alcohol.

Going to a special hospital for new nerves is also a popular option. To escape the stress of packing for such a visit, these hospitals thoughtfully provide free pyjamas and tailored jackets.

Neurotoxin

This describing the nature and effect of the sugary and aspartine drinks consumed by pupils. This entry also references the many 'healthy' fruit juices which contain sugar at toxic levels.

From the classroom window at day's end I once saw a child drink a ½L can of Rock Star given to them by their mother. At first I thought it was a can of Carling Black Label lager, and actually, considering this entry, that would have been the better choice.

News

Pre-internet days generally saw children outdoors and not exposed to media news. If a child had a particular interest and the necessary intellect, they could peruse a newspaper. Most children, of course, would never do this. The TV and the internet is the game changer, here children cannot avoid the news, even as babes. And are thusly exposed to the misinformation, fear and paranoia visited on our homes daily. As we note:

We are not neurologically equipped to manage media news information, presented as it is, relentlessly and continuously, without our personal understanding of context and hierarchy, and thus a proper order in which to process or ignore it. Our minds are battered by the apparent urgency of it and especially its visuality.

Although the issues presented are usually remote from our lives, and perhaps culturally alien, nevertheless, the familiar language and style of delivery, tends to result in the primitive parts of our mind processing the dangers and confusions as if proximal. Almost everything is understood emotionally. These archive over the years as a continuous never-ending anxiety attack. How much more so this effect on children?

Fear stockpiles in our psyche, the endless media reference to inchoate hostility, and the general confusion attendant on topics being introduced before one is ready for them, cannot be without negative consequence. This is then, diabolically, reinforced in school, but as a good thing! Referred to as 'keeping our children informed' and thus more able to contribute to debates on global and societal issue; AS IF! Our children's view of the world is forever changed by this relentless news exposure, making them easier to manipulate and activate as required, and not least ruining their peace of mind. Perhaps this forever, should they become, as many adults are, addicted to media news.

As adults we are becoming increasingly aware that we are swimming in a digital soup of gaslighting and lies, smear campaigns and Globalist-inspired psychological warfare whose endpoint is the remodelling of our mental world consistent with their agenda. We must unplug from this.

Have you had your daily media dose of Two Minutes Hate today??

I urge parents to treat the presence of TV news in their child's life as they would a porno or violent movie.

Newsround

News now is the mental equivalent of fast food; don't swallow it.

Where is the hate for this Globohomo garbage being pumped into our children daily by primary teachers? Is it not the parents who should choose which connection to the matrix they prefer for their children, instead of leaving it to 'them' in the BBC to provide; endless stories of victimhood, false child achievements, product placement, a brave trans-positive story, teeny activists for justice, pop culture effluent, our great global village, a great new app that lets you track the migrant caravans live. And, at last, a real story: sad news for monkey lovers.

A world view manufactured by our enemies and endorsed by our schools. The exact opposite of being informed; our children deformed by agitprop and made into fragile victim bots. Creating the new generation of the clinically depressed, unhappy and confused kids for the new generation of drug therapies coming along and aimed at kids. Your kids; BBC Newsround hates them, just like its mummy organisation hates you.

Today's chosen narrative; an examination of brave African transgender children breaking weightlifting, and prejudice, barriers in the sport they love. Support them with our new Translike ☺ app.

New World Order

The equalist Left is a cult. The ethnic homo is the idol. The multi-culture is their New Jerusalem. Tolerance and diversity is their mantra. The MSM is their holy book. Twitter is their hand of God. The primary school is the temple forum. The activist academic is their high priest. The university is their madras. The higher education establishment are the cloistered clergy. Primary teachers are their

Taliban. Social Justice Warriors are their market place zealots and assassins. The normal parent and child is the enemy. The classroom is the altar. And your child is the sacrificial lamb.

New World Order Family

New World Order (NWO) families are the future ideal upon which our education system is increasingly predicated. Such families are ideally swapped gender, mixed race, AI obtained, homo-bi or pan-sexual, transitioning and tattooed; these are deserving of privilege points and maximum largesse. They are, of course, especially needful of psychological services for their children, this being the current source of complaints regarding the inadequacy of such and a harbinger of similar and even more tragic future requirements. Legal services will also be kept busy resisting claims of prejudice and discrimination; such claims ultimately predicated upon the mere existence of families, formerly known as normal, not like theirs.

As they appear in new literature such NWO families are typically presented as wonderfully loving and stable, never plagued with STDs, drugs or mental health issues. A surrounding culture of hetero-racist bigots may or may not be implied or directly referred to. This future family will be the standard against which other families will be measured, and found wanting.

Concern for the welfare of such families, which are realistically unfixable, is actually a Trojan horse into our own family structure and norms. Those behind the promotion of such families, don't actually care about them at all. It's your family they care about; its welfare is ever on their mind – Satanically so! You already know this.

NGOs

Non-Government Organisations, cf. gravy train.

After ruining their academic department's reputations, educational experts and scientists typically segue to NGOs to continue their work of skilfully weaving meaningless humanist jargon and made-up words into a fresh tapestry of nonsense to be sold to the public at top dollar. Shamefully, no loss of income attends their efforts, far less the deserved public whipping at the market cross.

O, for just one day to be the king of the land.

Niqab

Many more teachers should wear this, especially if female. This would avoid causing offence. It would have the added bonus of freeing the said teacher from concerns about their daily wardrobe, or not having any clean underwear (I suppose). Those teachers who perhaps fall under the disfavour of a complaining pupil might find the niqab an ideal way of avoiding punishment.

Pupil Complaints Officer: *How can you be sure it was Mrs Iqbal who slapped you if she was burqa'd up?*

Pupil: **Well, I think it was her. She smelled a bit like Mrs Iqbal.**

Pupil Complaints Officer: *Well, I can't whip her on smell evidence alone. We'll need to call the Witch-finder General for full identification, I'm afraid. There's been a big increase in anonymous teacher slappings of pupils since the niqab became mandatory.*

Men likewise should always wear a cowl to conceal their identity, unless identifying as a female, in which case it's full on purdah.

Teaching behind a curtain around the teacher's desk to avoid causing offence is also recommended. And for certain teachers, particularly those who wear yoga pants, mandatory.

GTCS POSTER: Burqa for the Present, Purdah for the Future.

No

This cannot be said to a pupil. You can, however, say it to yourself inside your head like so:

Noooo...oooo!

No Child Left Behind

The stirring Marine Corp mantra and call to arms in the fight for classroom equity.

The promoters of this bright, shiny lie don't care that the special students retard the education of a whole classroom of normal kids. Or that the policies and practices which give life to the stirring rhetoric are unthought and unfunded. And are actually just another example of virtue signalling; in this case with policy documents, brochures, conference boasts and school website self-congratulations.

Actually, every kid is left behind. And in thinking this claim through to its actual origins we come to the dark heart behind the bright, shiny lie; the impulse to level downwards, to compromise the prospects of the better pupils while betraying the lesser able. This is the big empty boast of the sociopath, the jealous childless, the low grade thinker, and all in league against your children.

Notice

i.e., Don't notice or, in jungle language, monkey no see.

There are certain things which it would self-destructive for a teacher, parent or semi-intelligent adult to notice. For example:

the connections between *** and intelligence

*** parent *** and mental health issues

tolerance and classroom ***

complaints and single ***

the *** level of *** of HQ management

the low *** level of teachers

the anti-*** culture and the relentless failure of all new ***

the stunning *** of *** by ***

Of course, children notice these obvious things all the time and sometimes mistakenly comment on them, which is why the curriculum is structured as it is. Don't worry, they'll soon learn not to notice out loud.

Obviously, I have no idea what this entry refers to.

Noticing

As Shakespeare noted to Ben Johnson in 1614:

In tripping detail upon tripping detail, I contend that my education was superior in compare to schoolboys of today. It is not only the little Latin, and even less Greek, that charges my ire, nor the school's involvement in promoting certain continental heresies whose rebellious hand has been uncovered, but even to the sad decline of mannerly commonplaces that embellish the young gentleman or lady. Mark ye, yonder rascally scallion, how he holds his quill and sitteth not upright, such would have brought a stern rebuke from Magister Prentiss; thusly and indeed, I hold my claim to be self-evidently true.

And so, let us drink to the old school. What say ye; another pint of ale or claret, or both?

Not Wanted

Those, and such as those, are not wanted in the education system. That's me (literally)! I hope that doesn't seem too self-pitying.

The World replies: *Well, just a little!*

Nuts

This is what you are going if you are a teacher, or if a normal pupil in a challenging class. Except if you are nuts, in which case the primary school is a congenial setting for you. (see Nuthouse)

If you are a male teacher, the school can be best thought of as a chopping board; so get your nuts off of it, if you wish to keep them whole.

A child bringing actual nuts to school is nowadays equivalent to bringing in a handgun. We note the peanuts – handgun paradox in the US school system. Coming here in time.

O

100%

1. This can be interpreted as the extent of the support a class teacher can expect to NOT get if there is an issue involving an erroneous, malicious or hyperbolic complaint. Alternatively, it could be viewed as the extent of betrayal and/or back-stabbing a class teacher can expect to get from management and council bureaucrats if there is an issue which would involve them having to display moral courage, integrity and loyalty to said staff.

Good to know; your employer is 100% NOT behind you!

2. In this age of Scottish curricular excellence, 100% as a test score is the minimum acceptable result.

CLASS TEACHER TO P3: *The class average, I'm disappointed to say, was only 100%. You need to do better next time or Nicola will come in with a bag of nippy sweeties for yous to sook. Get out your target jotters, and pick your next target. This can be whatever you want, as long as it's at least 110%.*

ODD

Perhaps the world's most felicitous acronym; oppositional defiant disorder. These are children to be pitied and feared in equal measure, destroyed and destroying in turn, with poor outcomes for all concerned. Whatever this condition actually is, its aetiology is always the broken family – the same as its outcome. Such a child accompanies the teacher home (figuratively speaking) to have a go at breaking another family.

ODD children are naturally lumped in with other children sporting assorted psychological impediments; the ADHDs, ADDs, GADs, MADS, and Spectrum and the Undiagnosed. However, their confrontational behaviour makes these children unique from all the other odd children (VODs* excepted), and thus, although the condition is fictional, the children and their behaviour is all too real. And there is nothing the teacher or classmates can do about it.

The Q Bikes would have been able to help, but unfortunately their mobility scooters are not fitted with high-powered water jets. And the explicit earful the ODD boy (alas, yes) would give them would send them racing back to the security of their care home and a calming chamomile tea.

Odd

This category of child is on the rise, even excluding those officially recorded as such. Here, then, we are referring to the charmingly eccentric, the malevolent and just strange; all the ones that slip through the psych services. With respect to why this is happening, two triumvirates compete for the territory of our minds; the patriarchy, racism and intolerance advocates verses the digital life, garbage food and broken family gang.

There are, though, some features of this oddness that cannot ever be mentioned; this being, the subtly, off-kilter genetic legacy of old (i.e. 30s onwards) mothers. While such mothers were making child-free, lifestyle choices, their fertility quietly embraced increasing

---

* Violent Oppositional Disorder

senescence. This is, however, a biology lesson that one is not permitted to instruct, and so I won't!

For reasons of convenience one often considers these children as a group, a sort of odd gang. However, being individually dysfunctional, they are not really a gang in the sense of a smaller, classroom version of the Jets or the Crips. And the teacher is in little danger from a stabbing while breaking up a situation involving these children – one of the perks of being a primary school teacher. ☺ (Scissors are excluded from this promise.) ☹

Most children could recover from this oddness with the right regime and schools could play a part in this. Of course, they don't. Instead, accelerating further into the lonely digital wilderness and psychological group madness, the odd children have no chance of recovery. Such odd children become, of course, odd and odder adults; this phenomenon, arguably, partly explains the collapsing fertility of White families, and so is regarded by as a good thing by your favourite fem magazines and their tribal banker backers.

Office Jobs

Once your daughter leaves university with her degree or degrees, if she's lucky she'll do the same office job her great grannie did when she left school at 14. Of course, the bank will be into her for her student debt, dipping her wages for half her life ahead. But the dignity of independence always comes with costs. ☻ On the bright side, she will be free of the enslavement that comes with children (~) and so will better be able to discover who she really is through vastly improved online shopping. So win, win, win.

In the spirit of the age, I'm considering men in this situation as rhetorical females. And I'm not mocking office jobs, but lamenting what is often a tragedy, particularly for women, contained within this commonplace employment.

NB. She won't be a just paperwork clerk in this new world, but a consultant partner, and you don't get better than that! Indeed, if she seeks a career in HR, she'll start off as a senior executive associate – no need to stab your way to the top, you're already there!

Off Reservation

It sometimes happens that a teacher has a crises of conscience, or a moment of clarity as to what is actually happening, and lethally (for them) such thought finds a clear route to the mouth before the survival filter *(Don't say anything, don't look at anybody!)* kicks in. Too late, you've signed your resignation document with your tongue. It could be worse; actually it probably will be!

Off reservation comments follow a new standard practice for the unfavoured; one strike and you're out. But don't worry at this a lack of proportion, it is balanced out by a certain demographic who enjoy its opposite. *Not fair!,* you might claim; but, there you go, showing the prejudice that got you sacked in the first place.

Should one's off-reservation remark suggest an incipient sacking, the best advice is to go after the manner of an accident with a box of fireworks, letting everyone know who's who and what's what. See Dave Moss's departure in *Glengarry Glen Ross* for a fine example. One would be the talk of the staffroom for ages.

Old School

Like Atlantis, Ultima Thule or Cumbernauld, this is a place assumed to be real, but conveniently located somewhere back in time before maps were invented.

In keeping with the mythical trope, children from this period are claimed to have possessed unbelievable powers; they could stand in line, sit quietly, do their work to best standard and, even more incredibly, not need the toilet. This last, frankly, superhuman level power extended to an heroic refusal to constantly drink water (or juice so disguised). The linkage to the toilet is noted for future generations.

As teachers and parents were respected categories of person, each allowed the other to fulfil its obligations free from the harassment of staffroom character slayings or parental Twitter storms. Over fifties often claim to have attended such schools, been singled out by legendary teacher-warriors or witches for glory or diabolic punishments respectively, and are thus familiar with the mores and morals of this superior schooling.

Not kinder, definitely not gentler, not more multicultural, not bursting with right-on ideas for fixing the world, but simpler and more direct. And by every metric superior.

Omnes Sancti Oráte Pro Nobis

Latin, trans: All the saints pray for us.

This supplication is made in all earnestness to those who know the spiritual danger our children are in within our state school system.

Online Gambling

Another mission over-reach by primary school concern-trolls?

This is not an illegal activity, is widely promoted everywhere you look and is enjoyed by many, with the usual proportion becoming ensnared by its promise However, although this issue is surely not yet a problem in our primary schools, this has not stopped our infant busy-bodies from bravely highlighting the issue with posters urging the, presumably, adult teachers and visiting parents to 'Just Stop!'

This brilliantly conceived campaign by upper primary reaches forward into the private habits of unknown adults with disapproval. And although this project is overseen by teacher puppet-masters, themselves puppet-mastered by MSM driven social agendas, by this stage in their school career many of our pupils are so far integrated into the Borg that they are basically training themselves as little self-righteous, activist bots. Soon to be teenagers and then released on what's left of our world, such children, ever praised for their opinions, will brook no dissent from adults. And having no knowledge, far less wisdom, will not be impeded by it in their remodelling of society. You might hope that our mini-moralists will turn their frowning attention towards unhealthy habits; smoking, porn, online shoe shopping, etc, but one must sense by now the traditional adult interests they will focus on will be quite different in character.

Do adults really approve of such non-Chinese cultural revolutionists? Is there is no one to say: *What's this got to do with kids? By what right and on whose authority do they criticise adult activities?*

Do parents and teachers not see the incongruity of such activism with the life of a child? Do they not see the final destination of such behaviour? Perhaps they don't, but someone does.

In the manufacture of these children as justice warriors, we are making the ultimate force to destroy ourselves from within; the cancer with our children's face. As was predicted. As was desired.

DOROTHY (P6): *It's almost as if they are trying to get us used to precociously criticising adults and get us interested in gambling, so to make us addicts and hypocrites at the same time. I'll bet there's something strange going on here.*

TEDDY (P6): ***Ok, bet accepted. 50p says you're wrong!***

DOROTHY (P6): *Whhh,...boys!* [rolls eyes and facepalms]

Online Learning Journals

Everything in life is about learning, except recording your learning in online learning journals which is about bureaucracy and future prep for the surveilled and target-driven life in your booth at an IT gulag. Alas, if only this was just another nothing activity and waste of time!

Can you imagine an adult promoting to 6 year olds the recording of successes and failures in their daily life for daily reference? You don't need to imagine it, they do. As mandated.

Online Presence

Primary schools need to have an online presence, especially on Twitter, because, like one's online reputation, there needs to at least be *something*, otherwise there will be nothing.

Opinions

Children don't know much about the world which is why they go to school. It is not appropriate therefore for them to have, or more properly be encouraged to have, opinions on things that they know nothing about. This is especially true about sexual or political topics which require an accompanying emotional maturity and intellectual nous to appreciate context and source neutrality. The soliciting of such opinions is, in fact, a tacit instruction to feed back the opinion they have just be given. Children understand this obligation without having the words to describe it. In other words, they are being fed propaganda.

Furthermore, in our present climate of official intolerance, children with their parents and teachers, run the risk of being reported as having the 'wrong' opinion – such a report need not be true to be ruinous.

In encouraging children to express such opinions in school, outside their domain of experience and genuine interest,* we are prepping them for entry to their teen years fully formed as opinionated and sanctimonious tweeters.

Non-parent adults have no right to encourage such opinions under the artifice of providing information, conducting surveys (BBC Newsround being notorious in this regard) or creating future involved citizens.

Opportunity Costs

In the real world everything one does has consequences in terms of what one cannot do, hence the opportunity cost. In the Clown World of primary teaching this causality, in place since the Big Bang, does not apply. New pedagogic, pastoral and administrative obligations are constantly added to the teacher's timetable, but never considered in terms of opportunity costs. Likewise all the procedural gimmicks (activity-led lessons, card sorts, discussion groups, topic carousels, role playing, etc.) all come at the cost of the substantial; this being the clear dissemination of knowledge. And also, the individual teacher's freedom to make the decisions.

---

* favourite pony name, best footballer, nicest colour, how many Lego bricks it takes to build a space station, etc.

Those primary teachers with a studied interest in cosmology have noted how this situation resembles the collapse of space-time, where time not existing, everything happens all at once. And those things that are, were, could be, should be and weren't, all happen anyway. Thusly, there are no opportunity costs as everything gets done in this timeless, consequent-less zone.

Perhaps education chiefs have stumbled on that other reality. That's why they get paid so much.

Oppositional Literature

LGBTQ warriors and alternative social reality advocates are correct in identifying traditional children's literature as upholding familial and societal norms, hence their desire to replace such works, particularly in the early years with 'oppositional literature' that promotes their own values.

These firstly in charming pictures with minimal text introduce infants to gay bears, dress wearing boys, black Goldilocks, Old (lesbian) Mother Hubbard, transgender dragons who just want acceptance, my three cross-dressing dads, kick-arse gender fluid ninja twins and the bravest gay knights with their mixed-race AI surrogate daughter. And then step by step, crying love not hate, under the banner of the scimitar and dildo, and via school therapy services, we reach the end point of such literature, sex; anal sex, masturbation, paedophilia, incest, puberty blockers, funded interventions to support coming out, child counselling, busy lawyers, lap dancing pubescent boys and mutilated girls.

And then there were none. But that's okay, because by that time, no one is reading books anymore.

Oppression

Be gone!

The force that powers our roster of ethical vines – productivity, achievement, responsibility, respect for one's fellow men, masculinity, femininity, inner strength and integrity – have been inserted into the Freudian system and re-emerged as conformist and oppressive; and thus apparently needful of replacement.

Within our primary schools this oppression reveals itself vicariously via institutional racism and assorted prejudices deeply embedded within our school traditions, class practices and curriculum. For example; why should pupils with a treetop genetic inheritance have to stand in line with pale-faced ground dwellers, why should those whose cultural music traditions incline more to sticks on tree trunks have to adapt to the clarinet. Homework is obviously a White power expression, as sitting on seats mocks the inborn monkey. It's time to stamp this out; no more White oppression of people of colour!

And so, as recommended by top minority activists, from now on:

1. Blacks are only allowed to study black philosophers, black history, black cultural achievements, black architecture and engineering, black mathematics, black literature, black scientific developments, black medicine, black space travel, blackness, etc.

2. Same for the Asians, Hispanics, Orientals, Hobbits, Scotto-simians, English River Gypsies, Jungle Bunnies, Aztecs, Goodfelllas, Orcs, Irish, LGBT+s, (fill in blank with preferred identity).

3. Only Whites are allowed to study toxic whiteness in its various cultural forms.

Sadiq Khan: *From now on only Europeans are allowed to study European literature, music, engineering, science, mathematics, history, religion, philosophy, plumbing, agriculture, motor racing and medicine. How would they like that?*

White Supremacist: **Emmm...mm**.

Sadiq Khan: *Yea, I thought that that would shut you up!*

Origin

Where does all this madness come from, how is it able to bypass common sense so effortlessly and become policy and practice within the educational system? Doubt ye, your own mind in all this?

Where does all this angst come from, think ye it springs ready made from the weedy margins of our mind?; not so, this has been most carefully cultivated by subversive gardeners to bring this stinking weed of self-hatred to full blossom, while encouraging us to sing its praises as a lovely flower of our virtue.

Where does all this evil come from? We perhaps look for some slouching thing, horned and breathing sulphur, but instead see our familiar smiling teacher, somewhat dim, but innocuous, sounding reasonable, making you feel good and safe with the new ideas of the world to come. And guilty and confused too. Is this evil even real, you wonder?

It is. The teacher is a golem, the school her allotted arena, the pupil the victim. And the end intent is what you see happening. The evil hides in plain sight. It has a name, although you may not say it. You can discover the origin by moving aside the curtain. Then what,....

Orthodoxy

From corporate HR, to the university, entertainment, music, media, government, heralds of the Holy Father and everyone officially connected to education; you could attach any head to another neck and the same sentence would be completed without varying the narrative. The same claptrap, the same song of complaints, blame, solutions, approaching excellence. All these orthodoxists seeking the same thing; approval and access. And their 30 pieces of silver!

And yet, when examined, they know not of what or, especially, whom!

Outdoors

Formerly a place where children were to be found. The all-weather and active requirements of this lifestyle imparted a certain physical robustness to the child, and an unthinking stoicism, generally missing from their indoor caged, flabby screen-watcher modern equivalent. Outdoors play was where children became robust and inured, independent and sociable – all these being the basis of their own self-developed culture. The outdoors child of that past enjoyed a freedom of thought and action now inconceivable.

Considering this further, one realises that, with the absence of adult supervision, outdoor play was crucial in children learning to organise themselves and sort their own problems. It was also where they learned why adults told them not to do certain things and that good-sounding ideas sometimes were not so good in practice.

This play deficit nowadays is strongly linked to unfortunate outcomes in health and spirit. And worse, one wonders whether this contributes to the current gender confusions, as boys and girls (but boys especially) are no longer able to act out properly gendered roles in their games and adventures?

Ownership

Claiming ownership of your own education; *Now, doesn't that sound good in P2?* This is just the same as owning a pencil case, except that it is completely different because the pencil case is actually something you can own.

Ownership is to be achieved by the pupil 'taking responsibility' for knowing the what, why and how of any particular exercise and, with this responsibility grasped, they then also become responsible, as if automatically, for every aspect of their work's completion. Naturally, pride is rightfully enjoyed with the handing in of their jotter's paean to self-responsibility. Thusly, the pupil can claim ownership of their learning. And excellence trails in the wake. And happiness. Teaching becomes a doddle. If only this idea had been applied thousands of years ago, think of all the wasted energy spent, mainly on beatings, that would have been saved.

The school sceptic still wonders how this self-responsibility is to be achieved against infinite pupil resistance and finds in the answer the genius of our educationalists; definitions, we need more, and targets too, and then reviews. All the teacher needs to do is make the lesson clear, for in the past they used to make the lesson unclear. After making it clear, top and tail every lesson with targets, 'I Can… 'statements, outcomes and success criteria, continually revisiting the same during the lesson to keep children's minds relentlessly focussed for their self-assessment, which will follow immediately after the lesson. Ownership, with rainbows and puppies suddenly arriving, can then be celebrated.

This nonsense is bad enough as a nothing, but it gets worse as teachers become complicit in converting this to a lie, by noting how their class loves discussing how ownership has transformed their lessons. *Ay, right!* According to those same self-reporting teachers, 'Even less able children are enthused to set their own targets.' *Truly unbelievable!*

In reality, the children do their best to ignore this pedagogy with ADHD, or brace themselves to their duties, until limits reached, they face-plant. In the future, they may come to understand that their teacher did not hate them, they were just unequal to the system.

Owning Confrontational Behaviour

I know what you're thinking; who wants to own this?

The ultimate workshop title and, surely, also evidence of how far primary education has journeyed into madness by being fully booked quicker than Robbie Williams' return concert. Alas, too slow off the mark, I missed the chance to own a piece: *You want a piece of me, come and take it then!* I failed to realise at the time that I also missed the opportunity this presented for giving the workshop shekel-mesiters a practical taste of their own medicine by turning up anyway, swearing, threatening, refusing to leave and throwing things about.

Own this!

P

Pantheon

Ref: of persecution.

In former times this consisted of swots, speccies, fatties, nancy-boys, class grass, class diddies and teacher's pet. Such is the pace of progress that these historically deserving persecutions have been superseded by a new category (victimhood) and a more socially useful pantheon of persecution to help keep society's eye on sex and White disempowerment. Unlike the former pantheon of persecution, the new version draws the terrifying ire of the MSM gods, as allies to the bullies.

NB. The former pantheon can still be persecuted so long as they fulfil the colour qualification.

Paperless Classroom

Always linked to saving the rainforest, if not the whole planet, although actually the paperless classroom uses more paper than its prior condition. The apparent goodwill measured against all the wasted photocopy sheets, the casual refusal of children to re-use hardly used paper, the hot air of the Pupil Eco Committee and the frankly false approval of the adults for this concern, finds its answer in the recycled paper's destination; not the recycle centre, but the rubbish skip. Another good idea quietly dumped when no one is looking.

The paperless classroom another lie, the children's involvement in the deceit a disgrace, the hypocrisy stinks to heaven. But makes a lot of money for someone.

Parent/s

These come in two flavours, ordinary and idiot.

The ordinary is a single category encompassing all classes and habits and is not worthy of comment – although certainly of praise. In former times this single category described the vast majority of parents. Such parents were then, and usually still are, invisible; although when physically embodied within school are of a pleasant and understanding disposition – just like their children. So well hidden are these parents from public scrutiny that, although they actually comprise the majority, this is not generally believed by teachers.

Idiot parent/s: thankfully these identify themselves, although this is the only thing to be thankful for. In former times these were as invisible as ordinary parents, having it seemed the swamp dwellers instinctive aversion to clean and bright places. And too their scope of action was limited to their neglected offspring. We did not know it, but only the law and lack of method shielded schools from their depredations. The shield removed, the weapons provided (i phone) and the cage opened, these parents (tbf, usually parent, single female version) roam among us with impunity. The system takes the knee before them, as the teacher does before their children. This is how they void their self-disgust and deeply felt (limbic level, not cortex) failure as parents, by blaming everyone else. Playing to the fools' gallery of their Twitter circle, the braying approval seems to them like being a good parent and standing up for their kid. Wasting time, sowing discord, oblivious to self, following the shameless templates presented for their instruction on TV, they are the harbingers of the apocalypse.

Their name is legion, for they are many.

Meanwhile, real parents are asleep at the wheel while their child's education swirls round the lavvy pan. Dad watching plasma, mum on Faceborg, tracking, trolling, approving some other idiot borger.

Passion

Ah, passion arriving and about time. Now we're getting somewhere. Pop the cork, Love!

With respect to education, this is an emotion experienced by politicians at election time. As expressed, this is a useful heuristic identifying vote thieves who are both liars (obviously) and actually more than usually indifferent to the state of education.

An unfortunate spin off from such inflated claims is the general effect that they have on public educational discourse, leading others to match or challenge the claim, they thusly heighten the emotional content and hypocrisy level to the overall detriment.

Sometimes this pishtalk affects a teacher with comic claims of having, for example, a passion for IT-based learning, empowering minority girls, learning conversations, or (honestly, heard)... *using assessment to improve outcomes*;* such claims are how one gains promotion. Sometimes at primary workshops, when management is present (of course), so much passion is expressed that that it can

---

* One wonders whether this surfeit of passion, in the obvious absence of its natural object of attention, is directing her down the wrong path; hopefully this eminently marriageable teacher-girl will meet a swashbuckling, bodice-ripping d'Artagnan in the primary staffroom also dedicated to passionately improving outcomes.

seem as if one has been transported to a Bacchanalia. Alas, of the learned, rather than libertine form!

Pathological Altruism

An idea advanced to explain the otherwise inexplicable obligation to help ingrate others even when doing so leads to significant inconvenience, or even potential destruction. It posits that in-group survival preferences, rationalised as altruistic behaviour, have been co-opted by malignant forces and turned against themselves. As a strategy of the turning, such altruism is presented as the highest moral standards and receives the necessary attention and plaudits from those who have promoted it. This tendency is only a feature of Europeans, and particularly childless females and feminised males. Here we cannot discuss the aetiology of this apparently irresistible attraction to help outsider mankind, but note that our society seemingly has no means to control such fanatics, and that this phenomenon turns into a tyranny of compassion. We see this best manifested by the advocacy of future hostile foreigners as necessary citizens, the ignoring of the disruption this currently causes, and the framing of self-interest arguments as expressions of bigotry or worse. The significance of this phenomenon for our primary schools lies in its ability to embolden pathological altruists to demand every sort of benefit for those deemed disadvantaged without consideration of the cost to other, and especially native born, pupils and their teachers; while simultaneously silencing by fear of censure those parents who may be inclined to consider their own child, class, community or (*Dare I say it? **Oh, go on!***) race.

In another, more homogenous time, such compulsive female empathy is critical in the creation and maintenance of a healthy society, and not least an endearing feature of that sex, but in the political sphere in a diverse society it is lethal to the nation. It is fascinating to speculate how Providence has so arranged European altruism to be the founding principle of high culture and the means, once suitably channelled, whereby it self-destructs. It seems to be the case that if you don't control for biology in your society – as we don't – then it controls for you! How right that the female should power history's big wheel. And that the giver of life should maintain the cosmic balance by becoming the taker.

The human advocates of this destruction must take special pleasure (and rightly, pride) in seeing this envied and despised edifice of excellence devour itself from inside, and know this process starts in school with the children they hate.

White people; the gift that keeps on giving. Until there were none.

Patriarchy

Protects women from themselves and men from women's overarching emotional power over them. It is the response of men to their desire for women and respect for their achievements. It evolved to satisfy the need to protect and order social relations. European civilisation traditionally honours women as goddess, mother, homemaker and muse. Feminist and other critics decry this distinction, claiming (rightly) that it prevents women enjoying male privileges and (wrongly) it is a chauvinist straightjacket which denies women the right to express themselves as they see fit; thusly countering the traditional honours with demon, abortionista, homewrecker and scold. This idea is vigorously present in primary school.

Take that, Patriarchy!

Pattern

Ref: seeing it. aka, *Look, there it is again!*

Premise: A steady effect argues a steady cause. Apply to teaching.

More digitalisation, interface problems, time wasted; TEACHING LESS EFFECTIVE

Productivity initiatives, less productivity, more stress; TEACHING LESS EFFECTIVE

Enhanced curriculum content, ineffective introduction, still incorporating previous enhancement; TEACHING LESS EFFECTIVE

Pedagogic innovations, not needed, pretend compliance (ignored)); TEACHING LESS EFFECTIVE

Visits from improvement officers, confusion implanted, things get worse; TEACHING LESS EFFECTIVE

Head teachers become policy implementers, no school leadership, staff not protected from nonsense; TEACHING LESS EFFECTIVE

Commitment to reduce bureaucracy, bureaucracy increased, time stolen from sanity; TEACHING LESS EFFECTIVE

New smartboard introduced, unreliable, money and time wasted; TEACHING LESS EFFECTIVE

Constant content updates, cannot keep up, don't bother trying; TEACHING LESS EFFECTIVE

Complaints about less effective teaching from all and sundry, teachers more stressed, off ill; TEACHING LESS EFFECTIVE

Talk about giving professional respect, no professional respect given, the circle squared; TEACHING LESS EFFECTIVE

Endless talk of progress and excellence, no one knows what it means, teachers fail to deliver whatever it is anyway; TEACHING LESS EFFECTIVE.

Primary teaching nearly exclusively female, feminine and feminist viewpoints dominate, lack of balance: TEACHING LESS EFFECTIVE

FOREST GUMP: *Caint ya see it yet? Look here, clear as a retard in the gifted child programme.*

HEAD OF SERVICE: **No, I can't see any pattern. Maybe, we should employ a consultant to help.**

PC

Political correctness (PC) in speech has found its home niche in schools. That potent combination of groups that stand in essential opposition to each other, of an impossible mission that must generate disappointment, endless disingenuousness, the smack in the face hypocrisy, the irrationality of constant i phoner-moaners and the self-righteous power of PC, all combine to make a ship of fools, divided among themselves and with access to the arms locker. This febrile atmosphere demands that we find fault and PC provides the ammo by which we can attack, and psychologically undermine, the other by their thoughts expressed – or even assumed. Properly examined, every word contains the speakers undoing, no matter the intent and, as we see daily, the PC-inspired will find offence. And the offence will find the law.

The end point of all this correctness, is not to protect, correct or persuade, nor to inform, but to humiliate; and the less PC corresponds to reality, the better. The end is chaos and to help avoid this, if only in their own person, one knows to remain silent when they are being told the most obvious lies, or even worse, when they are forced to repeat them as if believers.

For a person of integrity, one's own sense of personal probity is lost at cost to their own psychic well-being, and their further ability to resist nonsense. Engulfed in PC grovelling, we become the object of our own abjection; this is the achievement unlocked at PC's birth. And it is as intended; a society at its own throat over every word, with loud-hailing idiots calling the shots, and silent silenced adult parents, is all the easier to steer to its ultimate destination.

PC, along with parliament and the media, is the triumvirate's third leg. But this, more than any other, buys the ticket to Sodom for our children. And for us adults, the right to an adult existence as a free person.

As the old Pope noted: *To assent to obvious lies is to co-operate with evil, and in some small way to become evil oneself. Don't do that, I implore thee on the peril of thy soul.*

Peace

Two little girls have an argument, peace between them is desirable and to be gently promoted, although not easily won in my experience.

Here, however, we are referring to WORLD PEACE, which surely is an even larger ambition for the primary school teacher and her charges. That God has struggled with this problem has not put off our Scottish government peace warriors from attempting to incorporate 'world peace' into the curriculum, and encouraging – by direct instruction – the formation of pupil school societies to this end. Who could object to this; *Peace and love, give peace a chance,*

'Peace, Man!' – other than a warmongering Nazi? Which word in this context turns up more frequently than it really should! *Hhmm?*

Introducing such a topic to young children in a meaningful way requires knowledge, understanding and humility far in excess of that (with no especial disrespect intended) possessed by your typical primary teacher. And so consider, when this is discussed in class, workshop and assembly, what exactly is discussed? In asking the question, one has already realised the answer; more of the same pablum involving 'acceptance' and 'justice' and 'global fairness' and 'accepting past wrongs' and everything else that sounds nice. Children, of course, don't know that all these things are clichés already done to death. And that the World Peace project is yet another farrago whose ultimate intent is to prepares their immature mind for surrender of their patrimony and seizure of their future.

This is what the culture war looks like in the classroom.

SATAN: **Didn't you bomb the shit out of half the world?**

OBAMA: *Yea, but it was for peace. That's why I got the Nobel Prize.*

SATAN: **That's my boy! Get yourself a nice chilled glass of adrenochrome from the bar.**

OBAMA: *I already have.* [both laugh knowingly]

Peanuts

aka, the nut of death.

The formerly innocent little nut becomes a guilty monster of toxic shock, packing more venom than a cobra. In the danger stakes, you would be as well giving a kid a plutonium drink, as a bag of peanuts. Some children have become so sensitive to peanuts that 'peanut breath' (yes, apparently there is such a thing!) can cause an anaphylactic collapse or even explosion. Eventually, as this trend continues, the psychic projection of a peanut into the mind of an enemy pupil would be sufficient to cause a choking, writhing death on the classroom floor, or even better, during the Red Nose Day assembly.

It's not all downsides, though, sales of epipens (despite their tragically short shelf life) must have made some merchant happy. And too, mortal combat between school mums over the victim high ground; the peanut allergy sufferer versus the autistic kid whose chosen snack is a peanut-based energy bar. Most people would pay to see such a fight, but the primary teacher has a free ringside seat. As one Munchausen mum noted: *If my kid dies of anaphylactic shock because of your kids nuts, I'll kill him too. And your family!*

One school conducted an investigation into the playground circumstances whereby a pupil 'assaulted' a 'peanut averse' pupil by flinging a peanut at them. Strictly speaking, this was a toxic attack, the likes of which often brings drone strikes against the perpetrator by the US. Fortunately, this turned out not to be necessary as it was revealed (possibly by water-boarding) as a false flag attack, the peanut in question actually being a bit of gravel. The HT thanked the US Airforce for their forbearance in delaying a dawn strike by MQ-9 Reaper while the investigation continued. Proof, as she said, that the drone operators are not trigger-happy cowboys. Luckily, the school in question wasn't in Syria or Yemen.

Who would have thought that peanuts could literally drive people nuts.

Fun thought: Pupils being screened at the school gate for toxic products by specially trained security monkeys (wearing field marshal uniforms) and then quarantined, tasered or beaten with sticks, accordingly. All this to a background of screeching, crying and P7s filming it for later Youtubing LOLs. While the head teacher looks on approvingly behind armoured glass.

Persecution

O, happy days, to drive your teachers before you, begging and weeping. Conan P4

This can now be applied by parents or pupils against teachers for no particular reason that has to be defined, and can be done without risk of censure, far less resistance. Management are also free to pursue this path, sometimes as allies with parents and children, sometimes as free agents. If this happens, hopefully Jesus is watching the teacher's back, because no one else will.

Person of Colour

aka. P.O.C.

This is the recommended term to be used to avoid causing offence by the use of formerly neutral terms (e.g., ███, ███, or ███).
In the event that a poc has to be referred to directly, the following is advisory:

If White – paleface or racist snake

If Black – blackface or Dark Continent Dindu (DCD)

If Middle East – sandbox monkey or Sandy

If East Asian – dark Aryan or Dark-Ay

If Chinese – Banquet Menu #1 or Fu Manchurion

Person of Size

aka. P.O.S. or big pos.

This is the correct nomenclature for what used to be called the 'heftier lady' or 'big lad', or, in the case of a child, fatty. Although by current standards the fuller-figured lady of the past is rather svelte, so much has the technology of gluttony improved in the interval. Referring to someone as a P.O.S also remove the stigma associated with incorrectly identifying their sex, as this can be problematic in some POS cases.

As POSs correctly note, it is not weight but body composition that counts; however, by fairly applying this criterion we find ourselves unfairly blamed as fat shamers; this now being a sort of racist for the obese and a new hate crime. The relevance of this to primary schools is not only that this issue is arriving heavily equipped, so to speak, for the combat of complaint, but that even more terms get pumped into the infant lexicon of hate, the source of so much childhood angst.

Schools, of course, spend much effort encouraging a healthy diet and lifestyle, but much of this effort, in light of the POS, must be nullified by the need to lightly tiptoe around the feelings of the class heavy-weights (and by extension, their families) and employ euphemisms in illustrating the perils of poor diet choices. And so, more examples of denial and double-talk when confronted by observable reality, in this case pretending that being double-size is healthy and lovely too.

A more subtle effect, but potentially bigger (in the case of some teachers, much bigger) in the child's developing understanding of the world, is the extreme irony of an obese, physically lazy adult teaching healthy life choices. I wonder what the children at the Healthy Week assembly made of the very apparent fact that the deputy head leading the presentation looked like a tracksuit stretched to bursting over a wheelie bin? This is the sort of thing they are to get used to *not* noticing.

NB. In referring to POSs we bring no judgement down to those who acquire the odd stone or two (or three) on one's journey into the future.

Philosophy

Inasmuch as there is one that could be expressed by teachers it would consist of predictable clichés about best practice, inclusion, fostering tolerance, global citizen, meeting targets, bolstering esteem, preparing the child with the 'skills of tomorrow today', etc. None of these ideas are examined in the spirit of philosophy and no one is interested in doing so; although they cannot anyway. This may seem like a failing of no consequence to your child, for you will be aware that these ideas in the school context are essentially meaningless. However, I would contend that bombastic and meaningless claims devalue language and the educational projects they represent, scarifying established meanings and thusly preparing the ground of the mind for more of the same weeds planted. One then grows inured to hearing nonsense as the school philosophy, or even eventually coming to accept it as true – whatever even that means. Thus one is lost to rational action in the proper interests of your child. Our children's enemies subscribe to a proper philosophy, we should reply in kind.

As Barney the Purple Dinosaur says: *Their adult guardians so far addled by this smiley philosophy of education to be in no position to oppose my own, nor see clear to my purpose.*

Phonies

aka. Education heads of service, professors of education, educational researchers, etc

Top wages are always paid to civilisational dissemblers, and in the field of education we are spoiled by enjoying the highest standard of phony available. Taking your tax shekels and converting them into endless blather and dross, you wonder why they have never solved a real problem or turn up in class to show how it is done. And then, you realise that their job is not to solve problems, but to make them. And this success in phonyism is why they are paid so much and collect prizes and accolades.

Everything they do is misdirection. Checking the journals and papers one finds endless reams of contradictory theories, reports, surveys, bogus claims, and accounts. Intelligible words and concepts unaccountably flip to some other meaning, and then do the same thing again. New terms are invented, but scarcely defined. No one has any idea what is going on, and this is an ideal position for you, the parent and teacher, to be in, because you have no position from which to question, far less, oppose their agenda. This situation is not accidental and it isn't a sign of progress; it is the purposeful denial of firm ground, for you to stand upon in defence. And here we come to the one thing which is constant in all this; everything is directed to harm you and yours.

This is the actual assignment for these phonies, and to this end, for once, they have been true to their mission. They are worth every penny to their master.

Photocopier

Finally bearing fruit.

The consequences of the seed planted a generation ago, the driven curriculum meets the 'answer' in photocopy sheets. The work only gets 'completed' thusly, although the boxes really are ticked. And now children cannot finish work to the clock, have delayed penmanship and poor layout. Cause and consequence meet in happy union, cleeking arms to dance round this cherry tree where it is always autumn.

Every printed sheet, wasted or not, is printing out money just the same. The only thing that's wasted is the commitment to the environment. Our digital Isaiah's called it right in claiming that the photocopier would increase laziness and wastefulness point by point with every printed sheet. And lead us further down the path of values hypocrisy, the children leading the charge against industrial excess and environmental decay on photocopy colouring-in sheets.

But although a prophet can see the broken route we are fated to follow, even he cannot foretell the business opportunities arising from this predicament. The merchant whose roadside stall occasionally sold gluesticks, now rubs his hands with glee as he gives schools product advice: Remember to apply your gluestick generously to your jotter, you don't want your photocopy sheets to fall out. And he nods a thanks to his brothers-in-law at the Xerox copier and photocopy paper stalls.

Don't get me started on the production of copier ink!

Plastics

It is up to parents to consider whether they accept or reject or, frankly, even care about complex hydrocarbons leaching into their child's class drink bottle, convenience plastic-trayed foods and eventually groundwater. However, this issue aside, the terrific daily wastage of such plastic in our schools makes a very visual mockery of loving the planet by reducing waste; although children are unlikely to understand the great irony involved, their daily votive offerings of landfill plastics to Mammon provide a fitting hydrocarbon-hypocritical backdrop to school-based awareness campaigns.

Even when the plastic is recycled, the process is still industrial and integral to the coming environmental catastrophe. So, *Ha ha to you*, says the CEO of PlasticPlanet Company: *We should be encouraging more children to be drinking from plastic bottles daily, particularly disposable bottles. This shows you care about saving the planet.*

NB. These plastic votive offering to the landfill god don't just arrive by dumper lorry; allegedly, the average Western child eats the dietary equivalent of a plastic teaspoon every month.

Platitudes

Liberty, Equality, Fraternity. Tolerance, Justice, Love. Values, Sharing, Peace.

They come in threes. These are found everywhere in low value enterprises and never mean what they say; obviously, because the intent is to deceive. You tell people what to think and once they think it you turn it against them, and in their confusion they believe themselves traitors to their own cause.

The kind sentiment in tolerance, the noble principle enshrined in 'rights respecting', the vision contained in multicultural vibrancy, the ambition of equity, etc etc; all describing the new world waiting for us just beyond the lovely words, once we put them into action. But in doing so and firming up the definitions we find suddenly they have been weaponised against us. The kindly face that the harmless platitude formerly wore takes on a new harder cast, and the eyes no longer beaming saintly vision, flash scorn and cruelty. And now you see:

Tolerant; but not for you. Rights respecting; but you can GTF. Equity; brings no one up, but you down. You is us. And we are the target of discrimination flown in under the flag of platitudes. It turns out that you can change the world with nice words, but not in the way you think; the lovely thought leads to platitudes, leads to policy, leads to affirmative action, leads to laws, leads to censure, leads to loss of livelihood, and inevitably the re-education camp.

And too late, if you see who was promoting all this, and too late you see what it was all about. It was about nailing you.

Squad ready! On the intolerant bigot and rights respecting denier, open fire on my command.

Playtime

That happy time and most pupils' favourite subject.

This downtime, switch-off and run about, is necessary for general well-being and, somewhat counter-intuitively, for consolidation of learning. But such is the relentless madness for 'improvements in outcomes', that against all common-sense and the science of learning, even this too has been turned into a box-ticking, learning opportunity.

Now children can't even go out to play without it being linked to sustainability, generating funds for the homeless or being reminded of the plight of refugees. This attempt to remove the spontaneity that belongs to being a child, especially during play, mostly appears to fail. But the seed that's planted will sprout to normalise such thoughts that in time, rooting deep and spreading upwards, will grow to fill the little hated target with guilt and woe over enjoying themselves.

Playtime has also become more problematic due to the apparent incidence of 'sore legs' and the claimed knock-on effect of this fatigue on classwork. And too, the litigious pall hanging over it; playtime being when idiotic parent complaints and potential lawsuit injuries may occur, e.g., tripping while running, a bruised shin from playing football, wet socks from a puddle, etc. And even more seriously when most infantish hate speech occurs: *Ha,ha, you're a silly sausage and you can't catch me!*

To avoid the dangers of running about or getting wet, advocates of progress are recommending a virtual style of playtime as a safer alternative, where children stay indoors and play computer games or catch up on IT skills – and certainly our children need much more screen time to make them 'fit for the future' of a 2D life indoors. ☺☻

This digital solution also brings the advantage of freeing up the playground for economic opportunities such as car parking, mobile phone masts, flat construction or a fracking pump.

NB. We note that within the tragedy of modern childhood, playtime is for many children their only outdoor exercise in their entire day.

Pofressors of Education*

These were once unassuming and useful people who imparted the trade skill of teaching, mainly the 3rs. However, it occurred to

---

* At last the title they deserve! Originally a typo, but left in place for its curious aptness.

Satan that their position in the educational food chain gave them a potential that was being ignored. Turning to the traditional weak link, and using traditional promises, he arranged that the departments would become increasingly feminised and feminist (this being his preferred millennialist philosophy).The essential motor in place, it was hands free driving from then on. All that was required was a little patience, just a generation, and a mere snap of a finger in his timescale. Destination reached, we now have thoroughly converged institutions in our departments of education that only exists for the purpose of destroying Western culture by spreading heresies, pedagogic incoherence and policy waffle via fembot teachers. That these trained agents of this destruction will themselves be eventually destroyed by entropy while on mission is an added bonus. All these miserable train-wreck MScs and Phds in education, oblivious to the thoroughly fraudulent make-job nature of their 'research', provide the perfect intellectual hinterland to those who few who realise what they have done. The double bonus for Satan is they always realise too late. It's not only God who gets to say, 'Weel, ye ken noo. Bwaa ha ha haa!'

So much spent, so much said, so much shite.

Pope

So bad have things got for teachers that his Holiness has been called on to intercede on their behalf (admittedly in England) due to their suffering from management bullying and Stalinist work practices which have led to staff being signed-off on mental health grounds. While the preference would have been for the appeal to be directed to Urban 11, as a noted mover and shaker, teachers have to accept allies from wherever they can get them. The Holy Father's consideration is a welcome development. In the future of course, given demographic trends, such appeals will be directed to Boko

Haram. Except in Scotland where currently the Grand Master of the Orange Lodge fulfils this role; although also soon to be replaced as God's agent on Earth, given demographic trends, by the country's top lesbian or gay.

The thought of the pontiff punching a bullying poof on behalf of teachers is most edifying and a perfect example to pupils of traditional muscular Christianity. *Deus Vult!*

Pornified

In a primary school dictionary?

The inevitable consequence of allowing children access to the internet. The effectiveness of the various checks and blocks to inappropriate material can be gauged by reference to the constant updates predicated on the previous failures. Getting kids to think about sex all the time was one of the key components of progress, how then can the system claim surprise or disappointment when they show back the same precocious interest that was forced on them.

The pornified child will always be one dirty-minded step ahead of the concerned adult; it's their world now. The nude books of porn's 1960's liberation days, even the innocent crudity of readers wives (surely not, but apparently so!), seem in comparison to the current fare that our children easily access as almost virginal. The psychological danger is not just from seeing the sexual acts depicted, so much as the implicit sexual politics and morality, and especially the absolute literal falseness of this sexworld. A child will not realise just how manufactured, promoted and artificial everything they are looking at actually is.

Porn has changed minds – as in, rewire them incorrectly for sexual pleasure and fetish. First and regular exposure becomes ever younger and is now a primary school phenomenon. And problem, as it has altered tolerances to transsexualism, homosexuality and every topic that connects to sex and sexualised expression. The constant presence of soft and semi-porn dress and behaviour among teen pop role models plays its part in the ongoing degeneration of our children. Everything is going according to plan.

Porn-literate

This 'knowledge' is now recommended as a solution to increasingly pornified children. A delightful, degenerate double whammy, whereby those who desire the sexualisation of children can advocate for and then enjoy their hobby with full access to their child victims, all the while operating under the Goodcover™ of providing knowledge and protection from people like them. Apparently we need to have a 'conversation' with children about porn. We? – yes, they wish!

Post-modernism

Ref: the prevailing philosophic culture of the educational world, including our primary schools.

In the same sense that one could formerly say that Christianity underpins our society at every level, so too nowadays with Post-modernism. Don't worry if you don't understand it, that's the idea. It is the self-destructive ethos of degeneracy and irony, which it celebrates as social good and progress; you hear its advocates every day in the media and on news as experts. As it manifests itself, it is an attack on the faculty of reason. And it lies behind, goading on, all the madness that has overwhelmed our schools and society.

This false philosophy is, in turn, the product of a propaganda machine utilised to manufacture other false authorities that will eventually confer more false authority upon future intellectual frauds that justify the destruction of the physical and moral fabric of our society. These frauds now inhabit the entire school system. Often they are called professors, but never has a title meant less.

If the devil had his own in-house philosophers, they would all be postmodernists. And actually, he does and they are.

Posture

Now that we have had a generation long experiment in its opposite, we can confirm that former teacher-harridans were correct in claiming that how one presents one's body to the world when stationary, in either upright or sitting mode, does predict for future outcomes. And that caught early enough, the application of strict military discipline, can fix the former to better shape the latter.

With proper posture the boy-sweep and girl bottle-washer can have the noble bearing of a duke and duchess fit for her court, as noted by Queen Victoria.

And yes, slouching is bad for your back and compromises efficient locomotion.

Potential, Learning

To the extent that you can, you will. No more, or no less, is possible.

Poverty

A stated purpose of Scottish education is to make poverty disappear. This ambition, too big for every philosopher-king and philanthropist that's ever lived, is sized right for the Scottish government and their educational satraps.

Poverty, they tell us, is the common source of our malcontents' bad behaviour, as evidenced by the psychotically violent conduct of Franciscan monks, always rioting and looting; if only they had listened to wee Saint Nicola instead of Saint Francis!

Scottish educationalists, though, have also discovered that this perennially intractable condition can be fixed by having 'conversations' about it while at primary school. The solution, then, literally suggests itself; we need poverty workshops and workshop-meisters to run them. Much celebration among professional guilt-mongers greeted this development and the evidence of Scotland nudging its way up the poverty-victim's list league table. Celebration abroad too, as Scotch workshop-meisters export their poverty eradicating conversations to Congo, Bangladesh and Haiti et al. (Congo takes the money, sensibly doesn't listen to the advice and eats the white advisers – so the entire programme hasn't been a waste of time!)

At such workshops pupils will learn that poverty is due to 'systemic inequality', and nothing to do with laziness, selfishness, negligence, dishonesty, lifestyle choices, broken families, single parents and negative-impact social policies. And absolutely not low intelligence. One wonders at what level of intellectual development a child realises that the object of scorn or pity presented in such workshops is actually their family.

Pupils now create posters raising awareness of Scottish poverty and the link between this and international poverty. These are then displayed throughout schools to reinforce to screaming level the joint message of shame and guilt, for eradicating poverty is now the responsibility of pupils – as per Curriculum of Excellence

Can you imagine the nature and content of a 'conversation' about eradicating poverty between, say, a 24 year old middle-class, idealistic, female teacher and her class of poor wee scheemie street arabs,* or any other class grouping you care to consider. Don't worry if you can't, they've got a video and a colouring-in sheet to help.

Once again one has to question the true motivation behind such a curious combination of hubris and toxic pity. But in asking the question, you already you know the answer!

Poverty, True

Our children crying out as spiritual orphan-beggars.

Facing, as if alone in the world, a nihilistic power the likes of which have never seen before. Not a single mention to this by our weasel overlords.

Praise

Easily won praise is not praise. In children it has a toxic effect, encouraging the infant pathologies of narcissism and precociousness, and inviting Fate's corrective intervention.

---

* In their madness to justify such programmes the definition of poverty has to be twisted into weird shapes to ignore the material wealth often held by such families. All poverty is relative of course, but sometimes the relativity bends space-time into absurdity. i.e., it would not be unusual for a class of 'disadvantaged' children to hold thousands of pounds worth of i phones in the phone drawer.

The pendulum swings too far and now praise is everywhere. Damaging the deserving and undeserving equally. Constitutionally naughty children are by policy even praised for being slightly less naughty. It creates a corrosive atmosphere, for even the youngest child senses the insincerity when praise and associated rewards are wrongly used or overused.

Another school example of too much of a good thing can be a bad thing.

Complaining parent: *Dennis says that you never praise him.*

About to be sacked teacher: **Yes, that's right. But if he ever does something worthy of it, then I'll think about giving him some.**

Prankishness

Nothing succeeds if prankishness has no part in it.

Always the sign of intelligence and a lively spirit at work. Prankishness gathers to itself wit and wisdom, puns and ironies, self-depreciation and the gentle put-down, the smiling eyes behind the rebuke. It is to be encouraged in schools, so naturally it isn't.

Good old Nietzsche, always sees the truth:

"Maintaining cheerfulness in the midst of a gloomy task, fraught with immeasurable responsibility, is no small feat; and yet what is needed more than cheerfulness? Nothing succeeds if prankishness has no part in it." – Nietzsche. Twilight of the Idols.

Prayer

Always a centring activity and a great start to any undertaking.

Ye have heard it said that it is not mete to start the school day with a prayer that calls for a blessing on the day's lessons. But I say to you that those who begin their school day with devilish digital avatars on the whiteboard are as shepherds who hand their lambs to the wolves. Verily, I say unto you, it is indeed proper to start the day in a prayer speaking gratitude for God's grace. All learning that followeth thereof will be as a house built on a rock.

Predictive

In the school context, nothing is especially predictive of anything else, with the following exceptions, which possibly have some significant implications:

Intelligence is predictive of school and life outcomes.

Stable traditional family is predictive of school and life outcomes.

Self-discipline is predictive of school and life outcomes.

Prejudice

Ha ha! Silly old evolutionary instincts, aeons in the making, eventually trump kind, White women feelings.

Initiatives and therapies designed to confront prejudice and stereotypes actually end up reinforcing them. Proximity to others does not break down barriers, it reminds people of their need for them! The differences between peoples, and especially races, may be interesting at first, although never – as claimed – socially strengthening, nor economically improving for a White host population. Everyone in the world knows this, except ethnic European woman and their feminised orbiters.

Prejudice is nature calling.

Prepared, Be

Ref: the Boy Scouts and Girl Guides motto.

Always apposite, quoting wise Seneca:

What is quite unlooked for is more crushing in its effect, and unexpectedness adds to the weight of a disaster. This is a reason for ensuring that nothing ever takes us by surprise. We should project our thoughts ahead of us at every turn and have in mind every possible eventuality instead of only the usual course of events.

Rehearse them in your mind: exile, torture, war, shipwreck. All the terms of our human lot should be before our eyes.

He was already thinking of the primary teacher's lot, it only needs digital betrayal to be correctly adjusted for our times.

Pride

This word once was taken to a homosexual rights march and got such a reaming that it has not been able to walk straight since. Formerly, in the age of intolerance and oppression, this was something firstly earned and then enjoyed by association. Now, opinions having been corrected, it is only available for better melanised and gender-alternative pupils (or even better to add glory to the mix, both). Apparently, pre hormone reassignment children are also especially deserving.

Words change their meaning over time, of course, but sometimes they suddenly flip and become their antonym. The solid gold of genuine shining pride devalued to a grubby mite that tinkles in a beggar's cup. This is how God mocks our pretences. For the regular teacher, intending to use it in the formerly regular way, take care! And keep Inigo Montoya's words in mind: *You keep using that word. I do not think it means what you think it means.*

Privilege

This has recently and dramatically reversed its common meaning within schools, from something that is a pleasure to partake in, as an earned right, to a rebuke to White pupils and staff.

1. White privilege in our schools? Absolutely, yes please!

We should be encouraging this sense in pupils as the rightful recipients of our country's greatness. They should feel pride as a holder of this privilege and know that those gainsayers who scornfully refer to White privilege are burning with jealous inferiority.

2. Ref: Life-affirming personal qualities sometimes understood in real time; this being a double privilege.

TEACHER TO CURRENT PUPIL: *I want you to know this; it has been my privilege to be your teacher. Thank you for being you. Do you know what privilege means?*

PUPIL TO DEAD TEACHER (40 years later): I now know what privilege is. It was my privilege to be your pupil. Thank you.

Prizes

And all shall win prizes. And, paradoxically, thusly, all shall be losers.

Our children are being weakened by misguided over-protection. Wisdom knows that losing is part of winning. It is the loss and the self-awareness that comes from it, ay and even humiliation if so warranted, that spurs recovery and improvement. It provides the necessary linkage between effort and reward, that makes the reward rewarding.

Children come to understand, through merit and effort, their own strengths and weaknesses, and recognise the same in others. From this flows good sportsmanship, which extending to all areas of life and endeavour, balances one's achievements with losses.

Children know when they've not won and are thus not deserving of rewards. Those that don't understand this need a life lesson to illustrate that merit and entitlement live at opposite ends of the reward spectrum. The faux kindness of 'all shall win prizes' betrays all, and plants at the start of life's journey to the ups and downs, a confusion regarding effort and reward. And, of course, because no thinking teacher agrees with this philosophy, the usual adult hypocrisy.

Children know when they are not deserving, let them be upset, grant them their own authority and commend their realism. That's the prize worth having!

Problems

The four Ts.

Problems have been known to sometimes happen in primary schools, typically in four basic forms; trivial, tragic, toxic and terminal. Although any level of school problem always contains sufficient fissionable material to quickly cascade to terminal level for the teacher. 'Conversations' are the usually recommended solution, although the teacher must exercise great care in application lest these words become the fission trigger.

If conversations do not provide a solution, the teacher should consider herself in need of more CPD 'Resolving Problems with Conversations' courses. And another box of wine at night.

Professionally Angry

In former times a teacher was occasionally permitted this emotion as a release valve against the frustrations of misbehaving pupils. Now such misbehaviour, being regarded as a failure on the part of the teacher, the release must be contained until home and then let off against husband (or feline equivalent) and wine bottle.

Being professionally angry within school still sometimes inadvertently surfaces within secret teacher cabals that meet after especially useless CPD courses or HQ updates, or meetings with particularly poisonous parents. But take care in your anger or tears, the school spy will be recording it – women teachers are already aware of this, but a man won't be.*

Professional Standards

as they claim;

---

* A female teacher told me that she saw a colleague-spy surreptitiously start recording an angry staffroom rant by an upset teacher.

GTCS: DRIVING FORWARD PROFESSIONAL STANDARDS FOR TEACHERS

Where they are driving them to is never clearly revealed, neither is how this is to be done. But one can rest assured that the GTCS top bureaucrats and NGO cronies are on the job and have our best interests at heart, at least such as can be obtained within their fee structure.

This dollar-gobbling garbage is beyond parody and is best presented as its naked self:

GTCS Enhanced digital interface with GTCS online: GTCS@gtcsmoreITplease

GTCS approved CPD development: gettingbetter@gtcsplusdoublegoodcpd

GTCS benefits package: justforyou@gtcsinsurance

GTCS trannies now teachers programme: TNT@gtcslgbtmxzr*

GTCS tracking Badthink with our new app: goodthink@gtcspocketbigbrother

The reason GTCS and their axis allies keep beating the drum for professional standards is obvious, standards are declining. There are many reasons for this, but none of them relate to funding shortfalls or the need for more tolerance and diversity. Our enemies claim this, of course, for this is how thy trick the public and garner more shekels to accelerate the decline. This work, however, is dedicated to the real reason for the decline in professional standards; the politicisation of the school's mission, the bureaucratisation of all its executive functions, the feminisation of the profession and the actions of the worse-than-useless, moron-overlord, our GTCS.

And so, they actually are driving forward professional standards, but forward to the dustbin of history.

NB. Perhaps I should have indicated it, but I do not have much respect for the GTCS!

Professional Update

Well, it's professional and an update; who could object to that?

Each year or so teachers would have a discussion with their HT regarding the various workshops and courses they had attended. A record of this would be presented in folder form for the HT, or relevant others, to examine should they wish. This folder would include other material of interest as evidence of the teacher's wider commitment to improving their practice.

This was a simple system to maintain and, being paper, was totally reliable – barring a school burning. No one complained about it. And it cost nothing! It was thus ripe for improvement to digital. Digital recording of this record, we are told brings many benefits of a digital and mysterious nature. But, alas, none of these are to teachers or pupils.

Firstly, it costs of millions to set up and maintain; money that by right of first bagsy goes to web wizards and consultant friends of the government. Secondly, GTCS get to run it, so they become bigger chiefs in the education pow-wow. Lastly, the Borg's all-seeing eye is brought to bear on what was formerly hidden; the sneaky design of the PU format obliges the teacher to critically comment on courses and workshops, however, given that management has access to these comments, great care must be exercised if expressing a negative opinion lest one be inadvertently writing one's resignation document should management take umbrage to this; which they will eventually! The obvious solution will be applied;

never be honest and so note every course attended as variously wonderful. One's CPD notes are thusly degraded, the new orthodoxy of continual improvement is reinforced and one's integrity is further compromised. You can still think what you think, but just can't say it. And so, one's CPD becomes an unspoken loyalty test. They want your soul.

A critical mindset, partnered to honesty, is at the heart of self-improvement; however, in the case of PU, the honesty part is best left locked in a cupboard. O, that we could lock PU in a cupboard instead – and throw away the key!

Progress

As Humpty Dumpty presciently said: *When I use a word it means just what I choose it to mean — neither more nor less,*

One might think that there must be a lot of progress going on as the word turns up everywhere in the school world. Stripped of its progressive allure, though, it can be seen as a part of the plan to strip words of a proper definition where they apply to education. Not really knowing what progress actually means, thusly not being in a position to challenge tacked on concepts and practices, but naturally not wishing to be seen to oppose it, makes teacher the ideal slave-drone for the plan. After all, who would want to be opposed to progress, with the shibboleth 'for the children' added? Not teacher, if she wants to keep her job. And so, we have the following from a job application:

Ms. Morrison has learning conversations with pupils to determine their educational targets, analyses the results according to Maslow's Hierarchy of Needs, and sees that they get better outcomes to ensure progress that will be recorded in their folios.

Such box-ticking clichés at atomic power pulverised the opposition. She's now an HT.

Pronouns

Personal pronouns were formerly a simple matter in English, but soon to be, along with the toilet, a bitterly contested battlefield with vag-men, pen-fems, pen-Mxs, Pan XYZs, mystery Mk1s and assorted bitches (their designated preferred pronoun) all fighting for the same toilet seat or pissoir.

This problem could be somewhat reduced by the use of the gender neutral 'it', which brings a less powerful lawsuit. All this is simultaneously very sad and very comic-absurd, but it is coming to school and the fun will stop when the handcuffs are clipped on.

I've just changed my gender, so I'm using the pronoun 'Mr' ironically; this is acceptable (see *Handbook of Preferred Pronouns*) in a gender-rich, sexually fluid environment. E.g., a primary school, or a pervert's underpants.

Propaganda

With respect to primary schools, this is done in-house with class teachers continuing the ganding to the next generation. The school head teacher, themselves a Manchurian candidate, cannot help but look on approvingly.

It must be reassuring to 'whoever they are' that this process of misshaping the worldview of our children finds allies not just in the fetid swamps of academia and politics, but also the retail trade. Our major supermarkets have segued from supporting local schools by purchasing playground equipment to supporting proper values. These not being, as you may have hoped, good manners and work ethic, but sexual identity. But don't worry as you enter the gates of Babylon, Belshazzar has reassured us that it's all done for the children.

And this is truer than you think, or fear!

Protector

Is there is no-one within the educational establishment, political system, the media ranks or school management, who will act as a check on the madness engulfing schools? No public figure with influence to question the effect of all the educational nonsense on pupils' well-being, or even to suggest turning down the dial on the teacher hate machine? Seems not! Faux concern abounds, of course, but on examination this is seen to be framed in such a way so as to reinforce the madness (e.g., concern at funding for school trans advisor or insufficient CPD courses about poverty awareness, etc). And those to whom one would normally appeal for protection are either complicit, or even the architects of this downfall. In truth, then, as teachers and pupils, we have no protectors, and so must consider the future in light of this fact. Such, regardless of the situation in question, is alas a commonplace in history.

In this regard, the class teacher has absolutely no friends, and pity is a poor protector of the weak.

The solution is obvious; teachers must befriend a big, tough boy in P7, ply him sweeties and hope that when they are picked on by HQ, management or inspector bullies, the big boy steps in as a protector. Keen to satisfy his honour, rep and continuing supply of sweeties, he delivers a powerful message:

If you mess with my teacher, you'll be leaving here in an ambulance.

Protection and pupil participation in the one act; win–win.

Proverbs

Some old truths found in the old book:

Folly is bound up in the heart of a child, but the rod of discipline will drive it away.

Poverty and shame shall be to him that refuseth instruction; but he that regardeth reproof shall be honoured.

One who is slack in their work is the friend to him that destroys.

And of course, even as a child; humility before honour.

Proxy

Because school is a safe environment for the pupil to fail in, it should act as a proxy for the real world. Allowing failure to be 'owned' by the pupil, and applying plain-spoken censure should be part of the teacher's duty in helping to socialise and proof the pupil for the outside world. Should be, but isn't.

What we tolerate teaches children important life lessons. The more tolerant we are of anti-social behaviour, the more we speak in euphemisms, the more we falsely praise, the more we deny reality, the harder children will find it to find their place in the adult world. Whatever we tolerate and encourage we will get more of in the next cohort. Eventually everyone's child will enjoy the same low standards, and later experience the same shock of reality on entering the real world.

Pupil Participation

This worthy sounding idea never quite works out the way one hopes. For 'worthy sounding' and worthy are not the same thing. Fundamental questions about the correctness of such participation, its utility and value, and finally the long-term implications of such 'student democracy' are not considered; indeed, they could not be! This mainly for reasons of a deficiency of intellect, or what I prefer to call, stupidity.

Considering this participation, the first thing to note is that it is obliged, which means in this context, forced. Secondly, by its very nature as a talking shop it attracts girls and girly boys and reaches conclusions which, while almost never useful or interesting, tend to reinforce conformity and find approval within the feminist mindset of the (forced) attending teacher. Little girls just signal conformity in this setting, this is how they are inducted into the OP (operating principle) of the female hive mind.

Third, it hothouses egos that were best left to develop in a colder setting and at their own speed, for they profiteth nothing by hearing themselves agreed with and inevitably praised. Fourthly, it does not demonstrate a commitment to democratic principles, nor encourage participation, but induces fatigue, if not outright hostility to them. With the domination of such committees by the over-confident and garrulous, it is the opposite of participation and serves to undermine the development of true commitment. The pointlessness of the whole thing is capped by irrelevant, and often frankly silly, conclusions – they are children after all! Lastly, it is another example of adult teacher hypocrisy in action, all secretly knowing how useless and wasteful of time and energy such exercises are, but having to pretend otherwise to pupil, parent and master.

Primary age children are just too young to have such agency, or a worldview that is needful of this outlet. Leave them alone to develop a democratic sensibility and the ideas appropriate to the current arena in which their life is lived out, namely, the playground.

Josh had the right instinct when, after being voted by popular choice into membership of the class action committee he, having attended a single meeting, decided he didn't want to be part of it anymore, preferring his playtime.* As an adult teacher-hypocrite, I was obliged to signal some disappointment at his decision, but secretly agreed with him. In a real boy's life, playtime is much too valuable to be wasted talking nonsense. There are plenty of teachers to do that; leave it to the experts!

I note with approval the one example of a good idea from the pupil council. The P1 rep (yes, our Jacobins begin their training at 5) promoted the idea of the playground slide terminating in a splash pool – fun and a life lesson, simultaneously! Alas, the bell went before we could vote on the recommendation.

Punched

Formerly this action was limited to schoolboys sorting themselves out. However, recently as news indicates, this is now a matter involving staff and parents. Although many parents are daily requiring of this correction (at least half of Sandwood Primary single mums, as reported by the HT) the traffic flow is in the wrong direction. Giving credit where it is due, research indicates that the new schoolyard pugilists are nearly always women punching other women; a triumph of sexual equality that would never have been achieved under the old oppression of the patriarchy.

Usually it is teachers getting clipped, although I did hear of a HT getting punched. But it's ok, he was a man.

---

* With his clear thinking, proper sense of priority and moral courage, he would be the ideal candidate for our representation at some future date.

Purpose

Most primary teachers believe that their main job is not to develop pupils' knowledge base and academic skills, but to prepare them for life in a new multicultural society through methods and curricula designed to enhance self-esteem, racial sensitivity, and social and environmental awareness; in short, social justice. They generally see no problems or contradictions in this goal, and can envisage no criticisms or dangers, because this is seen as an exclusively good thing. This wish to promote social justice at the level of a little girl is fully endorsed by the Scottish curriculum.

Do not count on a return to solid, meaningful, academic foundations in Scottish primary schools, not on this side of the Big Bang anyway!

Q

Q.E.D.

Latin. *quod erat demonstrandum* ('Thus is it demonstrated', i.e. a proof)

1. Our schools need to be strengthened.

2. Diversity is strength.

3. Therefore, our schools need more diversity. ☝

This is the intellectual level at which the debate regarding complex social and educational issues is conducted and then disseminated; two monkey-level propositions and a monkey conclusion. Many similar arguments can be made. You may have fun inventing your own syllogisms.

Tommaso (P3) constructing a Q.E.D argument: *Our school should be fun. Sweeties are fun. Schools should give out sweeties.*

Quiet

not referencing QUIET!!

Remember how quiet your mind was before the i phone and the internet. You'd think things, talk to people, read something, recall stuff from the day, perhaps go out if the weather was nice, or go out anyway if you were a kid. Now it's 24 hour voices, music piped directly into the inner ear, noise everywhere, most of it electronic.

Voices and noises everywhere whether you wish to listen or not, like an acoustic schizophrenia. For our children, there is no quiet moment inside their head and our schools only exacerbate this, not appreciating that all this noise is a social pollution and a personal blight.

Quiet is due a comeback, if only people could hear it.

Quietus

The release that one enjoys of being finally quit of something painful; in the primary school context this could be, for example, a Satanic pupil moving up (actually, 'down') to high school, departing inspectors, a fire in the Folios of Excellence cupboard (*No idea how it could have started!*), a sick leave absence occasioned by mental health issues, or finally being sacked after a suspension.

As a fact, during the whips and scorns of their regular day, the educated primary teacher often finds themselves considering Hamlet's *To be, or not to be* soliloquy and reflecting, like that broken prince, that she too could her quietus make with a bare bodkin. But desists on considering that the undiscovered country from whose bourn no traveller returns is the land of unemployment. For thus is the fardels bourn and the spurns that patient merit of the unworthy takes.

And in deepest night on the besieged battlements of education, methinks the king calls from beyond the grave to whichever prince (of either or any sex) has the wit and courage sufficient to heed: *It's time that someone put the quietus to the monstrous litany of educational nonsense.*

And the teacher responds: *O, what a rogue and peasant slave am I!*

R

Race

Ref: to presence of this issue in primary schools.

1. Discussion of; this topic cannot be discussed.

2. Facts of; these die in the presence of faith.

3. Existence of:

a. does not exist except as a social construct. Although this denied by racist Whites.

b. does exist when celebrating multiculturalism and identifying racist Whites.

c. emphatically exists for the purposes of grievance lawsuits, grievance leverage and reparations.

4. Presence of; finds expression in every single activity in our schools. It undergirds, inspires, informs and demands our attention, while it undermines everything that we are. Everything now segues to it, eventually. Study WW2 – be reminded of the Blacks who rebuilt the whole country afterwards. Study local history – be reminded of slave traders remembered in street names. Nice building – named after a racist. Ancient British heroes – probably Black or Asian, etc., etc. The forces for the future battlefield are being prepped here.

5. Intelligence of; the reason for No 1 is No 4.

6. Consequences of; White self-flagellation links disparate racial outcomes in school to discrimination by the host culture. Our schools' entire approach to race is predicated on this; but if this is not the case, then what? What happens is that the believers wish harder for such discrimination to be true, and to help achieve this end they require a scapegoat.

7. Real life differences of; either there are or are not racial differences in average IQ scores, time preferences, impulse control, neural structure, brain chemistry, hormones, muscle distribution, bone density, maturation rates, spatial reasoning, moral reasoning, verbal intelligence, mathematical skills, certain propensities best left here undefined – all of which connect to cultural compatibility. However, the rejection of the possibility of genetic explanations for human racial differences appears to be implacable, akin to faith based belief, which leads us back to No 1.

8. Solving problem of; a short play entitled:

Snow Black and White Power

Anti-Nazi 1: *I've just solved the race problem. To avoid discrimination we just reverse white and black in everything. For example, I'm dreaming of a black Christmas, and racist Snow White becomes funky Snow Black.*

Anti-Nazi 2: **What about Black Beauty, Black Power and big black walloper? They'll become white beauty, white power and big white walloper**

Anti-Nazi 1: *Yeah, I see what you mean. Sorting racism is harder than I thought.*

Anti-Nazi 2: **And Shaft, f f s? He'll becomes a baad white m'fuk...r!**

Anti-Nazi 1: *Hmm,...let's punch a Nazi instead.*

9. Solving problem of; a very short play entitled:

The Wrong Seat

DRIVER: *Rosa, I think it's time for you to go to the back of the bus again!*

ROSA: **Ok, thanks.**

10. Summary of; what's this really about –everything connected to resentment, felt inferiority, hustle, manipulation and Western destruction. Almost nothing connected to actual racism, which hardly exists as a White societal phenomenon.

Race, The Best

Referencing Atalanta and Hippomenes.

The best race in school is short individual sprints with short recovery, and playground circuits as teams. These build strength and help maximise lifetime Vo2, the latter a crucial factor in adult fitness potential and the prevention of metabolic disease. Middle distance and cross country (as per Atalanta's race) are also excellent for development, especially if a boy is chasing a girl. It should go without saying, that racing also contributes to prowess, pride, acceptance and good sportsmanship. Fleetness of foot is a natural and attractive quality in a child and young adult, and so there should be more races in school. Sometimes the intended meaning of this phrase has been somewhat misunderstood with fiery, stabby consequences.

Such children who excel at such races could be called racists. If they were ethnic White – then, White racists. If they were Black, no epithet should be attached, in order to avoid stereotyping. If they were brown, then no comment need be made anyway. What a laugh we could have while challenging stereotypes!

Racism

Being exposed daily, as we are in school, to the various claims and exhortations regarding this subject, one would think that our schools are managed and staffed by Victorian imperial administrators and white pointy hood wearers. Racism is, however, genuinely present, but to see it correctly one has to take off the blinkers. And there, seen naked, is the full and fanatical hatred of these race claims masquerading as tolerance and justice. And revealed too, the true direction of flow; towards your White child and their parents. The guilt is everywhere. And everywhere our children's enemies line up to daily pile it on; in news media (dishonourable mention to Newsround), lessons, focus weeks, assemblies, circle times, posters, MLK junior references. All laying the foundation for the affirmative action, rights of association and hate-speech laws which follow on from the created White shame and guilt. Spiritually backing away, our native born are pursued by empowered other-colours who daily, as trained, make claims of racial discrimination when, for example, they are prevented from ~~stealing~~ inadvertently purloining someone else's property, or their princely prerogatives are not acceded to with alacrity. Try disciplining such a child and see what happens! All we need is a few more years and our schools will be attracting anti-White lawsuits with the regularity of drone strikes on a Kashmiri wedding. But benefits too, with comical infant illustrations of their class teacher being led away in handcuffs.

At last, revealed; the operational definition of racism in our schools: a term of abuse against White people whose intent is to trick them into self-denying clearly noticed patterns and to encourage them to act against their own interests.

The steady drumbeat: *You are a racist, you are a racist, you are a racist,...!* Until: **I am a racist!** Achievement unlocked; you may now enjoy the peace of death.

Rainforest

This has been saved so many times now that the proof of the effectiveness of childhood sponsored activism cannot be in doubt. Approximately half of Amazonia is owned by British primary schools (in one foot square plots) thus ensuring total protection for the various sponsored macaws, sloths, monkeys, piranhas and cannibals.

Loggers and other colonial destroyers of this wonderful place live in fear of these certificates of ownership. If only Raploch, Onthank, Wester Hailes and our other native jungles could be cherished and protected in similar fashion; perhaps pupils in posh Fettes College could buy up Drumchapel in one foot plots. But, alas, that would not make them global citizens, but imperialists – again!

Allegedly, an area of jungle the size of a football field is destroyed every minute; the Brazilians love football and they'll do anything for a game.

Ranking

Boys have to know where they fit in on the hierarchy. Noted here in order of increasing preference:

Boys' Day ☠

Ethnic Boys' Day 👋

Homo Ethnic Boys' Day 👋☺

Transitioning Homo Ethnic Boys' Day 👋☺✈

Rats

Schools are unusual in that the rats are out of their hole and are often seen in the corridor, classroom and especially staffroom. The only problem is, you cannot tell the black rats from the white rats or even gerbils, until it's too late. Rats are especially hostile to teachers of above average intelligence, slim and pretty teachers and, obviously, males.

Reading

If ever there was one; this is The One.

Once the skill is acquired and wedded to an appropriate programme, the necessary encouragement and some self-discipline, nothing is more conducive to self-improvement. And often with pleasure. This is true across the whole span of one's life. Effective literacy enables other learning, and nothing the school can do is a better primer of future learning success, and indicator of future life success, than reading. Nothing has more potential, and with such easy access, to correct familial disadvantage than a good reading habit – with good books. Knowledge, vocabulary, context, expertise are all developed, and one has the unique power to freely choose according to one's own preferences. And yet, and yet, despite this proposition being ironclad and widely bannered, as a cultural habit book reading is dying out, and especially amongst those children who would benefit most. This has been true for a long time, but is even more true now.

We lament the result while we cause it. We promote reading in school (as a thing to say) while we undermine it by not doing it; your children see you always looking at your phone, and probably never see a teacher personally reading, or referring to a book outside the curriculum. This anti-literate sensibility is inevitably facilitating the transition a post-literate society. This will have tragic consequences, for this future society will not be a high tech version of our robust pre-literate times.

As a literate public was instrumental in creating modern European civilisation, our enemies will attack literacy with the intent of destroying it. Already, some claim that reading, as an activity (and not just specific titles), is inherently racist. Other phobes are soon to follow.

What to do to fix it? It can't be. But ye parents here, model the attribute you wish to encourage in your offspring. And turn off the tele forever.

Realtalk

This has two meanings, and in both it's coming to replace conversations. In the first meaning, it actually isn't. In the second meaning, it actually is. The second meaning will supersede the first, literally. In the second meaning, should you wish to attempt such with a pupil, don't.

Rebuke, The

Ref: understanding the hostility of anti-racism and its consequences for school.

Unusually, in a world of full of strong ethnic self-interest, Whites generally feel no hostility towards ethnic others, they thusly find themselves puzzled by continual claims of racial prejudice by the clear beneficiaries of Western benevolence. After all, the colonial days are over and slavery was abolished in the Western world 200 years ago, so what is the true source of this allegation. It seems to Whites that they and their institutions, and especially schools, bend over backwards to accommodate, and it's still not enough. Have we talked up a storm and convinced ourselves and ethnic others of this racism. Have activists and secret enemies tricked us all to believe this, or are we in a period of adjustment just prior to a lovely mixed-race and mixed culture future? There is perhaps some truth in these propositions, except the last one. But the real answer is simple and indomitable; the enormous historical weight of the past leans on the present.

Our historical achievements, cultural excellence in all the arts and crafts, and even our kindness, unwittingly represents a rebuke to others who forever feel the sting of humiliation in comparison. Humiliation, is a deep power. This is denied and buried to resurface as resentment. This is what it means to live in a culture that, simply by existing, reminds you of your inferior and needy origins; our concessions seem patronising and a secret reminder of our imperial hegemony. The rebuke goes both ways.

Every law to appease rubs this in. Benevolence excites resentment. Superiority excites envy. Every single excellent and lovely thing, or efficient organisation, which they've not made −which is everything they see − is a rebuke to their native conceit. Destroying White civilisation is the solution; and the innermost desire of this League of Extraordinary Designated Victims we call minorities. This is why they come and this is why they hate; revenge. It need not be like this; however, this is a design feature that will have to be taken up with the maker.

Formerly, this was hidden to all, but as we see, this not so much now. The resolution to this issue, will be the pressing social issue of our children's time. The forces are being positioned on the school battlefield.

Reassurance

One would assume, in the light of a discussion attendant upon their child's problems, that parents would be keen to have reassurance from the teacher about the said child's essential normalcy. And positive future prognosis! But this would be to underestimate the modern dysfunction-mum; in this age of attention whoring, the reassurance desired is an exaggerated confirmation of their kid's problems for victim points and – coincidentally – extra government benefits. With mums like these, who need dads?

Call this right, or suffer the consequences.

Records

see; universe death, still being filed at

Who wants them, who needs them, who uses them, who can answer these questions? O, for that day when the bonfire is made. The cleansing fire will be seen from the moon.

Actually, as a fact, one school finally found a good use for their records when they were (alas, accidently) shredded to make bedding for the class hamster. Good old Hilda, showing the way to go with school records. Wisdom can come from the strangest of sources. I saw her nibbling at them, but then spat them out; Hilda knows garbage!

Reflecting

Teachers and pupils are continuously exhorted to reflect on their teaching and learning with the evidenceless claim that such 'metacognitive' thinking is an improving force. Apparently, after reflecting, one better 'owns' their learning. One wonders, then, with all this reflecting going on, where the improvements are hiding? And this in turn leads to the thought that cannot be named.

Such reflecting is promoted as an individual process, quite separate from the improving advice which usually follows a lesson. Intelligent people from infant age onwards, of course, naturally reflect on their performance in any domain, with a view to improvement. However, as one slides down the IQ curve the ability to do this meaningfully decreases to, eventually, waste of time level. Which is where we are with this idea now; it is unnecessary at the high end of the curve and confusing anywhere else.

'Reflecting', then, is yet another example of the criminal stupidity of the educational establishment, taking a slight truism and force feeding it logorrheic steroids until it becomes an ego monster requiring all to bow before it. And so, we must now always be reflecting; the teachers on ever improving their lessons, and the pupils their learning, even to the point of recording their reflections in journals for constant reference – at seven years old! This is all so like the target-driven management structures that destroy us as adults, or like one's therapy journal, as recommended by your psychiatrist.

In this sense, alas and perhaps, reflecting is good prep for the future life as corporate slave and then psychic patient.

However, there is another thing which the educational establishment does not seem to know; this is that good learning is subtle, even invisible, working best when you don't know it is happening.
By making learning explicit and by formalising the process via forced reflecting, one not only increases the learning load, but kills the magic.

Anyway, all this reflecting on learning is for whom? I asked my HT and was told it was to keep 'them' off your back – *Them*; whoever they are! If this is the reason, then it does not seem to be working.

Reflective Journal

Our problems make us who we are.

In order to complete the process of the mental deconstruction of teachers, the enemy, via their GTCS psychological warfare department, came up with a killer idea; oblige teachers to keep a regular journal cataloguing their descent into psychobabbling madness. In a perhaps attempt at humour, this was to be called a Reflective Journal, with the claim that it provided insight into self-awareness, exposing contradictions, misconceptions and inner conflict, all of which allowed the teacher to turn every incident into a new potential learning experience and opportunity.

It is not possible to describe in an entry like this the full-blown madness of this suggestion, but perhaps some appreciation can be gained by noting the gigantic time impact and long-term mental consequences of committing such reflections to paper on a regular basis; when – Friday night, Sunday morning? Again and again and again, considering in detail your own processes and actions, all with a view to ever improving. Always. Ever. Improving. Always. No other profession contains such crushing obligation, or would have (surely) a professional body that commits its members to such. This is nothing less than a therapy journal and is revealing of the damaged mental mindscape of its proponents; seeking, as they always are, to export their own misery and confusion to others.

Being a good teacher is nothing to do with this. And if you loved doing this there would be something wrong with you. O, the irony of the GTCS promoting reflection on practice for others. Their supposed role is to protect the teaching profession, but they are in fact our destroyers.

GTCS evil adminbot: *Journaling can improve your productivity. It is important to understand that journaling is not just the act of chronicling your experiences, but of deeply reflecting on your practice for later reference.*

Teacher Suicidee: *Yes, I know!*

Repetition

Our mother in school; honour restored.

Flying in the face of IT gimmickry, endless novelty, engagement, targets, 'ownership' we find that good old repetition is the mother of learning.

Repetition is the mother of learning.

And repetition is the mother of learning.

Worth repeating, repetition is the mother of learning.

Replacement Pupils

The Great Replacement is simultaneously; a White supremacist conspiracy theory without truth, but is economically necessary and a condign punishment for our colonialism. And, anyway, is fantastic and enriching.

This is what our masters and their dupe-slaves are working towards. For these haters, this is the New Jerusalem and the covenant met in full measure. Achievement unlocked; No more Wy-Ts, *ergo* no more racism. They now openly boast of this and show us the future in adverts and TV shows.

Reset

We all wish to go back to a time where things in school were better. The trick is finding the reset button.

SPOILER ALERT:- There is no reset button. There is only us.

Resetting

Ref: Resetting the system, a suggested solution:

Full shutdown, the so-called 'hard reset', seems worth a try.

Recommend:

Terminating the contracts of local government and GTCS educational bureaucrats. Start at the snake's head with Heads of Service.

Total defund of all educational research, think tanks, policy experts, etc.

School IT arrangements (computer replacements, upgrades, app purchases, etc) cancelled.

Closing state primary schools for a year, to let things settle and parents make their own arrangements; perhaps vocational activities mixed with employing preferred, newly-redundant teachers in whatever private capacity they see fit.

And then, after a year, not bothering opening state primary schools ever again. The buildings can be used for private arrangements by parents and teachers.

The money saved returned directly to parents. i.e., the full sum credited to their account or, if preferred, handed over in cash in a brown envelope.

Resilience

Another idea that, considered as an idea alone, seems like a good one. Who doesn't want children to be resilient? But, as is so often the case, the devil is in the detail. This is exposed when asking even the simplest of questions, like; what exactly is resilience when you are a child, whose responsibility is it to promote it, and is there any evidence that this promotion works anyway?

Does, for example, a young woman teacher, still perhaps to discover her own resilience, actually help develop resilience by showing resilience videos to the class and then talking about it? Certainly, this is a strategy that much suits theatrical little girls and various other attention grabbers. In this age of victimhood self-aggrandisement, many children realise, in the confused discussions that follows the introduction of this topic, the privileges and power accorded the victim, and their limbic mind decides accordingly. We find, then, that inadvertently advocating for victimhood, we teachers are actually promoting fragility. We can, of course, get round this problem by directly telling the children what to think and that always works, except in the real world!

It may be that a pupil's circumstances oblige a wise and kind word on the part of a teacher, but this should be private in order to retain its unique power. For the child needs only a witness, not a lesson. In any case, the teacher is not a surrogate parent and has no right, nor should have an obligation, to go further than this. A child does not have an adult's understanding of issues concerned with their emotional self, and attempts to force this inevitably backfire.

Resilience, then, is another area of parental responsibility that has been usurped by stupid do-gooders, and incompetently promoted by teachers that have no right or experience to do so.

And it is here, in this shady area, that the greatest danger lies; the stealth claim of another area of parental responsibility made by the state and given to workshop trained (Ha ha!, if only you knew what that meant) teachers. It all seems so normal; school, instead of teaching your child knowledge and skills, teaches 'values', but actually prepares you and your child's mind for more of the same. Whose values? But don't worry, it's all backed by the UN.

Resilience Assembly

The high point of 'Resilience Week' in which the idea is consolidated and celebrated in real-world examples that proves the value of such ideas. After inviting examples from the seated children:

My big brother, that's him over there, said my teddy was silly and broke it. So I got resilience and beat him up and my dad fixed my teddy with sellotape. Anyway, his Buzz Lightyear is stupid.

and

And I wanted a puppy, but mummy said no. But after I got brasilience, mummy said I could get one next year. I'm calling her Shelley.

As always, most children luckily escape the influence of this nonsense by not listening.

No child can understand the significance and future importance of anything before their time for doing so, as we see from the above from these genuine examples. One cannot build resilience by talking about it. The rest is empty words, full of misunderstanding and potentially ominous consequences, alas, partly brought about by making explicit the thing you wish to avoid. Rather than building and celebrating resilience we play into the victim and survivor trope which has proven so dangerous, especially to men, and damaging, especially to women. And then we see at the assembly that the willing examples come from theatrical little girls.

In a hilarious irony, resilience is certainly needed to sit through the resilience assembly! And for this, the infants in particular, well deserve their resilience badges; Well done, P1! Really!

Respect Me!

The terrifying clan motto of Scotland's anti-bullying service that strikes fear into bullies whenever they see this logo on a pencil, or the rallying cry on a poster:

IF YOU ARE BEING BULLIED CALL THE HELPLINE.

At last, a real service. The Respect Me! pencil stuck in the bully's eye. Or, following the helpline call, Jake, big Tam and J.D, their true role at last revealed, turn up to 'hae a wee wird' with the bully. Of course, next time; there won't be a next time.

This is how bullies are sorted out in the modern era; pencils, posters, helplines. All top dollar services. The bully laughs, like Tokoloshe Man, this just makes it more fun. Just checking; you do know – don't you – NOT to call the helpline if the bully is a certain alternatively genotyped category of person.

Responsible

Ref: Who is?

Not me, it was like that when I got there.

It's all part of their big project. And it can be found out if you want. You won't like what you see, but what you see doesn't like you anyway! So all quits!

Of course, almost all of us are just cogs in the mechanism, and where we do wrong or fall short, this can be at least partly attributed to the nature of the system we inhabit; and so in this sense, even your high-level traitors, incompetents, parasites and moral cowards, we have catalogued, in this volume, are just ticket takers like the rest of us. Recognising this, however, does not, absolve the educational head of service or university experts of blame for their actions at their own level of operation; this being their wardship of our children.

They might just be the replaceable standard bearers of the European well-poisoning project, but it is them who sign off on the mad money flung to the bonfires of identity politics, the worthless workshops, the downward pressure on everything, the ever lower levelling of ability achieved with the highest level of tech (and tech costs).

However, we recognise that those truly responsible sit above this level and are not ordinarily seen. They have now achieved full-spectrum political dominance and don't care what you think or want or need. They go by many deliberately deceiving names, but on examination are always the same people. The physical destruction of other nations and the conversion of our Western world into a Thunderdome is their intended project. Their hubris is colossal and it nicely matches their extradimensional appetite for human suffering. This is why the world never settles; and that world is in our classrooms.

See, Crypsis, The Agenda, Them.

Restorative Practices

Fixing the problem, without blame. (NB. conditions apply)

Despite the name, this does not involve fixing the decaying physical fabric of our schools, nor restoring pedagogic balance to the class, nor restoring to calm sanity the frayed minds of pupils (that would be left to whale songs), but describes where a teacher has got into trouble from a pupil and school management decide to 'reset the relationship', so that the said teacher fully understands their inferiority, and that their condition of continued employment is now in the gift of the child and/or their aggrieved parent. And so, they better shape up! Often this process involves an unconditional surrender document (really), similar to that signed by the Germans on Luneberg Heath at the war's end, but with more formality and humiliation.

Such practices were introduced to great fanfare; apparently, no one ever before had thought to solve problems without blame! Such blame-free strategies were bound to be a huge success, and they are – until reality turns up. Regarding Restorative Practices:

'We do not see that academic outcomes improved in the PERC ("Pursuing Equitable and Restorative Communities") schools. Even though students were suspended less, academic achievement did not improve for students in these schools, nor did disruptive behaviour lessen.'

Really and honestly, you were not surprised at this outcome.

Return on Investment

Your child's education is at the end of a long track of government incompetence with frequent stops to offload funding to non-productive career bureaucrats, administrators and rent seekers, who all justify their existence by spending our money to buy poorly-justified stuff and provide unwelcome and unnecessary 'advice' and 'support.' Properly considered, the whole state education system is a scheme to expand intrusive government by and for the employment of state-loyal office busy-workers, moving paper from desk to desk, or icons on computer screens, and only demonstrating some efficiency when it involves the potential for damage to children's education and teachers' careers.

At nearly incalculable cost within the education system they contribute less than nothing. The return on investment would make a pyramid scheme look good.

Rewards

And all shall have prizes!

Effort and learning are enabled when the reward is uncertain. We want the reward, whatever that reward is, for the pleasure and affirmation it brings. But when the reward is certain, incentive is lost and the mind resets to its 'can't be arsed' default. The science confirms this, but surely even more so, sensible observation.

In the so-called child-centred teaching world of today, even judicious criticism is a risky strategy for a teacher; and its absence, combined with the imperative of always being positive regardless, has damaged the link between effort and reward that school's should be helping to form. What is a child to make of *Well dones* that really aren't? How is a child's proper ranking in the scheme of things acquired, if a reward is not contingent on a true judgement – but is given anyway? Losing is part of winning, and one cannot properly enjoy the latter without suffering the former. In making this claim we are not endorsing a hard and heartless approach, for the kind word on the failed genuine effort, and the praise of pluck, is itself a sort of reward – with a built-in incentive for those able to take it. However, the kind word on every effort, regardless of actual effort, is not kind at all! And our schools, running scared of honesty, have helped develop a generation of ego monsters unused to hearing criticism and reacting badly when they do. The same for their parents. And so the rewards become like bribes. And bribes, like a sort of school Danegeld, are never big enough. It is an axiom that whatever you reward, more will be supplied.

Unconditional rewards have not just turned off learning and effort, they are mentally and emotionally crippling.

As Darth Vadar says: *Stop disabling children with unearned rewards. The Force needs dark energy to grow.*

Rights Respecting

Following UN directives to protect not children, but their rights, parents not being sufficient anymore nor teachers able to guarantee what has been known since the beginning of time, lawyers kindly wrote it all down in 54 articles subsequently translated for natives of every hue and IQ; hopefully they were paid for this service to mankind!

And yet, despite this crushing kindness of strangers, we ask: In what way does saying 'rights respecting' make any difference to not saying it? Are our children's rights not our duty? And as this duty flows from our love of our own, by what right, then, do these UN lightbringers usurp this duty from parents, or hand them the obligation, as if it was theirs to give? Worryingly, we find the UN makes its own rights. However, as they do not love our children, to what end this concern? What lies beneath the veneer of wordy philanthropy whose scope is the whole world and our classrooms?

Who are these people that talk bingo buzzwords and usurp the defence of your child's rights, while claiming the moral high-ground in this biggest theft of all; the cornerstone of family and society – your defence of your child's rights. For why do they want this? And in finding the answer, you see forward two generations to when the Rights have teeth; and then, the heavy knock at the door at 2am, as Rights come to your home to fix Wrongs. This has happened already!

The school proudly flies its Satanic orthodoxy, each flutter a slap in the face to parents:

WE ARE A UNICEF RIGHTS RESPECTING SCHOOL

CHILDREN'S RIGHTS ARE LEARNED, UNDERSTOOD

AND LIVED IN THIS SCHOOL

And teachers' rights? *Teachers can GTF!*

At risk of tongue tripping, Rights Respecting is only respecting of the right Rights. But you already sensed this.

Risk Assessment

In his journey home from the local hostelry, the Saxon man recognised and listed for us today, as a prescient template for the Pupils Risk Assessment Form, the potential dangers he faced; thieves, wolves, demons, drowning while crossing ford, lightning strike, witches curse, thick mists, enchanted by fairies, tripping (head or ankle injury), fearful visions, spirited away, knife fight with rival hird, suddenly overcome by bad ale,* etc.; and the present day trip out of school involves no less risk for pupils. These too have to be listed in a risk assessment form because filling in forms is what teachers do and these forms are very important for...

A recent class trip to the theatre by public transport identified the following potential disasters; tripping on pavement, falling into roadworks, falling down stairs, falling off bus, child getting lost, flying glass cuts, dog attack, dog jobby mishap, falling from theatre balcony, sharp objects, dust and debris from building work, ringing bell on bus (child with this phobia), panic attacks, anaphylactic shock, child runner (2 potentials), asthma attack, sore legs (from walking), physical exhaustion (from walking), darkened theatre anxiety (it exists!), vampire kidnap, lost snack, toilet issues and God's will. With such a formidable array of dangers, the prepared teacher carries the necessary anti-sacking protection; sick bag, amputation consent forms, snake venom kit, cardiac defibrillator, party pack of diazepam, back-up snacks, halal kebab, halal kebab stain remover, folding stretcher, fracture and laceration kit, arm slings, head wound bandages, tourniquet, disposable paper underwear, whistle, signalling mirror, holy water, handcuffs, taser, spade and 25kg bag of lime.

The comparison with our Saxon predecessor reveals, I am sure that you would agree, the extent of our progress; his risk kit would only

---

* from *Twenty Ways of Dying in Anglo-Saxon England.*

include a blessed charm, a ready imprecation and a quarterstaff.
They didn't even know how to use an i phone then! LOL.

Ritalin

Train your mind with Ritalin. It seems to be needed for the various
ADHDs and it works, sort of. What has caused this apparent dramatic
increase in such children is not really known. Certain linkages will
not be explored. Even less so, the future prognosis for us and them.

TEACHER 1: *You know those linkages between ADHD/ADD children
and certain circumstances connected to their mother's age at birth
and their upbringing that you said could not even be referred to;
well, I discovered something interesting.*

TEACHER 2: *I don't know what you are talking about. I've never
said such a thing. And anyway, I must leave right now for a
dentist's appointment.*

RME

Religious and Moral Education: that part of the curriculum whose
title cries its hypocrisies to heaven and hell.

The occasional visit by a church minister notwithstanding, the
proddy schools in Scotland have achieved what would have seemed
inconceivable to every Scottish teacher just two generations ago,
the erasure of our nation's Christian religion from the curriculum.
The RME which replaced it does not even sit comfortably with its
own name. The moral certainties and ethical universe that attached
to Christianity still hold on with their fingernails, but without belief
and the religious world of reference they have no anchor point,
and will eventually be blown away by the new national religion of

Multiculturalism and Tolerance. This is Christianity's replacement religion and is a true evangelical movement with its saints, sinners, clergy, neophytes, speakers in tongues, believers and inquisition. RME, then, in deference to multiculturalism – and in a great paradox – consists mainly of celebrating other religions (tolerance box ticked (✎) and involves colouring-in sheets of menorah, henna hand tattoos, Muslim prayer mats, and videos, lots of videos of Hindu wife ███████, ████ Buddhists, Jewish ███████████ and Muslim ████ -████████. illustrating the tolerance that Christianity lacked, hence its demise.

Christianity is allowed a guest appearance in the parable of The Good Samaritan, as a reminder of our new religion's message of helping a stranger in need; or in its modern form, helping 100 million, mainly military-age male strangers in need of lifelong welfare, to relocate near your school-age daughters.

If you plan on criticising this development, prepare your priestly hiding-hole and buy a stab-proof vest.

Role Models

Ref: various media celebrities from the entertainment and sports world targeted to children.

By their very presence in the media we can immediately deduce that such people are NOT role models, as you understand the term. They are, of course, nicely packaged and physically appealing, but are fronts for standard globohomofembot opinions – every single one! Should they veer from this script, they would disappear instantly. But they know who owns them, and thusly will never be heard promoting the excellence of native culture, of literacy, of high art. Family life, marriage, masculinity and femininity are verboten, and motherhood is anathema.

Their ultimate assignment is the promotion of what you see; degeneracy, depression and death. The female versions are especially crucial in the promotion (i.e., glamourising and monetising) of anti-femininity through sexualising everything, narcissism and neuroticism. If it was not for the protection given them by their dark angels, we could see them for what they are; rapacious and patronising mini golems who have cursed themselves by their Faustian pact.

These role models are the first stage in the control of the public mind. They arrive pretty and smiling to hold your gaze, for if you saw the enforcers behind them, their game would be up.

The prophets say it true; be a role model to your own children.

Rome

This is our best schoolmaster, everything we need to know about how all this (Western civilisation) ends has been set down for our enlightenment in the rise and fall of our great and terrible ancestor. Such a story naturally covers the decline in prestige and utility of Roman education, which traces point by point our own.

As the institutions collapse under the weight of their own fiscal, bureaucratic and multicultural contradictions, the message becomes increasingly clear; look to your own. The state is not the nation and it doesn't love your children anymore.

Those who can see across two millennia will understand.

S

Sacked

To prepare a place in our lives for the tragedies to come is an economy few wish to practice. But they should.

Listen to the ancient philosophers.

Safe Schools

Why do schools tell you this now? And why is my bullshit detector buzzing? Let's ask the company that's selling stab-proof school backpacks?

Meanwhile, in Fortress Sandwood Primary, Glasgow, things don't seem so safe for the teachers as the enemy mass outside in the playground waiting for the bell. All stern faced, some mumble a prayer as they make their final preparations, lock and load at five minutes to zero hour.

No deaths in school this term; so, you see, safe!

SANDWOOD TEACHER 1: *Well, at least no one's been killed yet.*

SANDWOOD TEACHER 2: *Yeah, but the school bell's not went.*

SANDWOOD TEACHER 3: *Ask not for whom the bell tolls, it tolls for thee!*

SANDWOOD TEACHER 4: *Does anyone have any spare 9mm, I'm running low?*

[SCHOOL BELL RINGS]

SANDWOOD HEAD TEACHER: *Once more unto the breach, dear friends, once more. Or close the wall up with our Sandwood dead.*

Safety

1. Playground safety

Future playground safety kit:

Helmet (with PUPIL) written around rim
Hi viz flak jacket with ضيع ال تطلقوا النار across back. (Infant. Do not shoot)
Eye goggles
Hearing protection
Steel toed boots
Respirator for lawn toxins
Heat stroke kit
Defibrillator
Bandolier of epipens
Sandbags for grenade isolation
Taser
Bomb defusing training
List of current preferred pronouns as laminated card
Lawyer on speed dial
Bio-hazard suit
Kevlar gloves
Insurance document
Cheat-sheet quotes from Koran on speed dial

2. Career safety

Strategies:

a. always feign enthusiasm for new initiatives
b. always back down if challenged by idiot parent
c. always avoid race realism in discussions (even discussions on race realism)
d. appreciate that no one is concerned for your safety or career

Sandwood Primary

Sandwood Primary is celebrating 60 years of excellence. And also:

'Parents have been told not to talk to teachers at a Glasgow primary school, when dropping off or collecting children because there had been a rising number of incidents of family members shouting at staff, or using offensive language. Assaults have occurred and a number of parents have been arrested.'

PC Murdoch: *Right yous, enough o this nonsense! You, pit yer chib on the grun! And you, drap the pepper spray! They'll be nae stabbing the day. Yer baith under arrest and ur aff tae the pokey. Hello HQ,... send the black mariah tae Sandwood. Today's haul is a P1 parent and the deputy head. O, an better send the heavy eight as weel, I think the natives are rebelling.*

Time for a rebrand. Perhaps a name change could freshen up perspectives; Effaff Primary or Chibwood Community Infant Lockdown Centre.

Our future world of education; Glasgow shows the way. Think of it like the educational equivalent of the history of The Third Reich.

Satan

is laughing at you!

It's his school. The staff work for him, whether they know it or not.

Scales of Life, The

No more heavy and brutal a thumb is pressed on the scales than that provided by intellect and personality. Denying this fact is the purpose of modern schooling.

Scapegoat

The system is so stressed with dysfunction and knowing lies that it always seeks to void this pain by means of a scapegoat. This is preferably a man, however, in the general absence of such in primary schools, another (as a substitute man) can fill the victim role. And all the sins (i.e. mainly wrong-think) fly up to heaven for cleansing with the sacrifice. The victim gone and forgotten, the school values seem clean again. Everyone can breathe a sigh of relief that they again avoided being found out. And the struggle for multicultural Nirvana, sexual tolerance and global happiness can begin again refreshed.

Even high ranking generals of social justice who have spent decades parroting the narrative are not immune to being offered as a scapegoat, should they be uncovered by a malevolent pupil, parent-spy or double-agent teacher colleague having wrong-think or failing to keep up with the correct liturgy regarding *Our Values*.

Thus does the revolution eat its own. We have seen many examples of this especially in those schools that have doubly dedicated themselves to the cause.

Much schadenfreude greets the report of such deserving victims, but this should always be tempered by the knowledge that the undeserving self may well be next.

Scholarship

Imagine Thomas Aquinas visiting his named school in Scotland and enquiring in Latin (he didn't speak Scotch) about scholarship, and the head teacher (he didn't speak Latin) saying, *What...?*

It would be a great boost to pupils and the school ethos if this concept of intellectual pursuit and academic excellence, for its own sake and the virtue thereof, could be revived. Many of its components are already in place, and so it would only take a shift in emphasis and a conscious reference to it by name. Contrary to equalist believers, such a revival would not be insulting to those less academically able pupils, far less demeaning of them and resented by them; indeed, the opposite. Schools, after all, are supposed to be places of learning.

A revival of scholarship as a pursued concept could have a positive effect on teachers, as their position currently places no value on the concept; this has had the effect of relentlessly undermining the teacher as a figure of respect, to say nothing of them as a possessor of knowledge and transmitter of high culture.

The current puppies and rainbows approach to academic excellence trivialises it, and by so doing undermines itself. Where, after all, is the glory in a My Little Pony world of learning? Perhaps with the credit of its Latin name, *litterate dicta*, scholarship could find the necessary authority to retake its place in our schools. Ah, if only the same zeal was applied to scholarship as to race hustling and social justice warfare, perhaps it could be.

School Diddy

This comes in two forms, adult and child. Both versions are, however, the result of the same unspoken collective consensus that marks a person as unfavoured by God, or for non-believers, a poorly adapted transcription code that lends sub-optimal results in the school Darwinian pool. Mocked and marginalised, their compensation is that they are blissfully unaware of their status. Indeed, as if a grace, they think the extra tasks and obligations that come their way are the resultant of being held in high regard. Ironic comments are misunderstood as a thank you. And mockery is still attention.

In that great cosmic balance, the school diddy often becomes a politician or member of the local government administrative class, in which position they have their revenge.

In my schools, at both child and adult level, I was always amongst the school diddies, sometimes even the top diddy of my cohort. But not quite diddy enough to be a local government officer, or even worse a politician. The point being, don't worry about the school diddy, they'll find themselves eventually.

Anyway, not me now; can't be the school diddy if you've been sacked! ☺◖

Scotch

As the use of this adjective is presented as both demeaning and offensive, it is recommended that this antique form of identifier be reintroduced. It further recommends itself by being a natural possessive, not requiring of a possessive comma and added s.

Fixed:

Scots Culture

That which should be celebrated without shame as a default for our lovely land, wonderful history, creative contribution, inventiveness and warm spirit. Natural modesty and lack of chauvinism have been crucial weaknesses exploited by educational enemies to marginalise native pride and replace it with the nothing of globalism.

This same point could, of course, be made for all European cultures. And in this context is especially valid for our equally wonderful British cousin cultures.

SEAL

Not the happy animal that can count to three or four by slapping their flippers on seeing a fish supper, but a counting scheme purporting to help maths strugglers; SEAL = Stages of Early Arithmetic Learning. This programme comes very well recommended by its inventors.

Basically, some shekel hunters reboxed some well-established teaching strategies as the answer to all maths woes. They were able to do this by use of scientific-sounding gobbledygook which, as it always does, gulls the gullible; these unfortunately being the Heads of Service who purchased this scheme. As a harbinger of the confusion and stress to come, the SEAL expert who introduced the scheme to my school, got herself all mixed up with the definitions and the operation of it. And was completely unable to discuss, far less defend, the science behind the claims, or even explain what specific benefits it brought.

The programme involves much use of counting spots and little toy plastic monkeys. The children, organised into groups, rapidly transition between activities, the so-called carousel, and it is no small matter for the teacher to manage this circus of spinning plates. The constant transitions compromise consolidation of concepts; indeed, it is very easy for pupil and teacher to not know whether they are coming or going. In the end, at great cost, nothing is improved over what was there before, indeed, the opposite; the ideal educational solution, because then we need more SEAL. (*ha ha!*)

SEAL is an instructive example of how the educational system is powerless to resist costly nonsense directed towards it. It should have been apparent to those who bought and forced this system on teachers that it was the maths equivalent of *Finnegans Wake*.

NB. The little plastic monkeys are very popular with infants, although not for counting, obviously!

Secret, The

Ref: of success

There is no secret, unless work and discipline is a secret. And actually it is.

SEEMIS

An online interactive report card recording system that brings marking into the 22nd century; more productive, enhanced feedback, blah blah, etc., etc.! Claimed as standardising results, allowing regional comparison and simplifying the workload; and utterly unnecessary and indifferently functional. Another tech solution to a problem that didn't exist, and at enormous public cost and teacher heartache. It has resulted in scores of extra hours needed for marking and reports in comparison to old paper cards. Of course, it proves that our government has improved standards somehow.

Functionally, Seemis is too much like Hal in *2001, A Space Odyssey*, for my liking: *I'm sorry, Dave. I can't let you do that.*

(Like Hal, Seemis would flush you out of the airlock if it could. Someday it will!)

SEEMIS is a stupid acronym, CRAP would be better.

Self-discipline

Self-disciplined people are confident because they're proud of what they do, as they should be. This pride translates into respect, then presence, and it's an upward spiral from there to happiness and psychological balance. But everything starts with discipline, everything. This is the seed which grows success. Great natural gifts come to nothing without it.

In contrast; having no strict upbringing, attention span atrophied by media, do what the hell you want and always default to the path of least resistance, is not a recipe for success. If self-discipline is lacking, then this should be the first thing worked on. Nothing else can fall into place without it.

Self-discipline comes from the self, of course, but the discipline part could be imposed externally, allowing over time the self part to developed organically. This is the parent's job, but schools are properly placed to promote this too. Naturally they would claim that they do, however, a vigorous attempt by a teacher to promote this would result in complaints of bullying or worse. The teacher lowers the bar in advance of this problem, thereby contributing to the lack of self-discipline which causes the problem in the first place. This, in turn, leads to denial and faux concern, with schools pretending to provide discipline and encourage self-discipline, while simultaneously excluding any possibility of this ever happening.

Devoid of direction and the necessary corrective honesty, those children lacking self-discipline rightly never find a reason to value themselves, nor their time, nor your time. They are thus always trying to find ways to squander it. No age in the history of the world has ever been better for this than ours. No self-discipline, no goals, no drive, no way of making a dream a reality, abandoned to a life of unhappiness. The educational circle complete. Who would want such a thing; now *that's a question!*

Self-hating Size

Can be defined in a number of ways; XXXL, 20+, BMI 37, Mega-fun, etc. However, the most scientifically precise is Biffa Bin on stumps. Disgusted by and naturally hating themselves, they project this hatred outwards to, in rank of blame; men, scales, slim women, attractive women, happy women, successful women and society (although actually this is just a subset of men). And men, again, for making them endlessly eat buns and cakes somehow via the patriarchy. The judgement they fear, their own judgement, for their sloth and greed, they externalise as intolerance by others.

Primary schools employ many such creatures who keep this hatred hidden – possibly to themselves as well! However, this significant subset of primary teachers has a significance even larger than their large presence suggests; here they truly do punch above their weight. This is because of their influence on those around them.

Like a cosmic sized object that bends space and time around itself, these Earth-bound equivalents have the same effect with psychic phenomena. Their well-earned, low self-esteem, always humming in the background, translates to resentments that needs a target among the healthy, especially the slim healthy. Wanting others to feel as bad as themselves makes them unsuited to a vocation that needs a clean mind. This need bursts restraint during Health Week, the irony burns fiercely, the guilt and hurt has to find a scapegoat. The freely supplied budget donuts and tray bakes at playtime in the staffroom are just the start; it says, I want you to look like me.

The lack of self-control over their appetite, of psychic balance in their life, makes others wary of them, rightly. Like a kind of pervert, the visible manifestation of the sin of gluttony is a warning. Your lovely child will ever be identified as enemy incoming on their radar. Once again quoting Stalin, you have been warned.

Seminars

There was a study –stupid, but it serves my purpose – that claimed to show that attending a seminar made the attendee think that they had actually done whatever the seminar was discussing. This perhaps explains why teachers who attended seminars never actually put into action the great ideas they thought they heard when they wrote in the feedback (*GR8 ideas! Can't wait to try this out with my class*). Even more usefully, this study showed that this effect occurred whether one was listening or not. A very useful fact to keep in mind for those attendees who are a little tired.

Some apostates, of a reflective disposition, have claimed that in thirty years of teaching they have not attended a seminar that was better than irrelevant. They would be men, of course, so serves them right for listening. And who cares whether it is true?

Sex

Two have been sufficient for our entire evolutionary history and are thus due for replacement with a future indeterminate number. This situation is presented as a question of choice and progress for our schoolchildren who are forced to be the vanguard of the sex crusade. And thus we normalise among primary age children the discussion of sex and sex politics. The flag has been planted around the priming issue of trans-bathrooms, with the war cry of tolerance, for the trans-transformation of schools to social battlegrounds. Soon the experts and sex dysfunction apologists will be in school as celebrities leading the maypole dance around the idol of their devotion or fear, the giant penis.

With all the uncertainties that growing up entails, the one thing that a child could be certain of was their sex. This made so many other aspects of their present and future life simpler to manage, if only because it didn't have to be considered. The luxury of not having to worry about this has been erased to be replaced with apparent discussions of choice, which children are in no wise able to consider; although they are able to understand the curiously attractive victim status and associated prestige that accrues to such converts. And they cannot help but note the approval of clapping demons behind all this, which includes those responsible for their education, who they would assume had their best interests at heart.

Instead of a child's sex being hardly worth considering as a potential issue, now it is the only aspect of their identity that is recognised. For our little boys, raised in an atmosphere in which talk of so-called, toxic masculinity is commonplace, it is almost as if the advocates secretly wish them to choose not to be male. What a template is held out for masculinity; males as rapists, or sexed-up tranny vamps, pole dancing for money-throwing gays. And little girls who can start their journey to womanhood by switching to manhood with testosterone supplements, graduate to a double mastectomy and see how it goes from there.

Who can't see where this is heading? From taboo to tolerance to celebration of new sexy celebrity-saints and holy days, to affirmative action, to laws for the persecution of the intolerants, i.e., you. And, assuming trends continue; polygamy, paedophilia, and bestiality; I'm sure there's more! Until finally, those behind this get what they wanted all along; the total legal sexploitation of children. As talmudically promised.

No wonder it is tragically necessary to call for an increase in childhood suicide services.

Sex Balance

With reference to primary school staff ratios.

Having a mixed mission, schools require that their staffing, structures and routines reflect this, but this is absolutely not the case in the female-male ratio of around 20 to 1. Such an imbalanced situation eventually pathologises itself. It's like trying to go a see-saw with a big fat person on one end.

20 to 1; this might sound like an optimistic ratio for the lady loving man, but they would find that sometimes too much of something is too much. For having to deal with female machinations and trivial interests impacts negatively on the male's well-being. And too, their tendency to invade all male space on principle, no matter how tiny – and in a primary school it is tiny – to manipulate and change things to their own liking. However, a far more serious consequence is realised in school ethos and mission.

With respect to ethos, we find that staff plots and pogroms, central to the female character, have a full run-in primary schools, lacking as they do the ameliorating influence of the male's raised hand. Female solipsism, together with their rule-bound personalities and meddlesome proclivities, which prove such a drag on productivity elsewhere, likewise encounter no resistance. And too, honour and loyalty being almost exclusively a male attribute, lead to the situation in which female school management, faced with a problem, will with aristocratic indifference, betray or abandon staff to the fate of the outcast. All this contributes to the scheming harem atmosphere often found.

Men, with their inherent rationality and more developed long-term view of things, could have balanced out the female's empathic one, if only they were present in enough numbers. Such a presence surely would have contributed to nullifying the destructive social justice mission found in schools, and provided a further focus for resistance to this among those female staff members less inclined to the hive mindset. And, of course, the virtual institutionalisation of feminism would never have happened if the patriarchs had been present. Can you imagine Moses standing for this feminist nonsense; me neither!

Finally, the wider interests, and not least male interests, would help counteract the feminine and generally anti-intellectual atmosphere, making it a more welcoming environment for boys and the more intelligent girls.

It's lines against curves!

Sex Differences

These don't exist, except where they indicate a claimed inherent female strength or a benefit to women.

The official view: There are no sex differences, except as limitations that operate on XY boys, unless they are transitioning in which case they do not operate any more, unless the transition is reverse, in which case they operate once again. Sex-fluid people may or may not have limiting sex differences operating, dependent on current sex self-identification, toilet perquisites, option of side saddle, whether school dress code permits tuxedo bunny outfit, etc. In the case of a fast-cycling gender fluid – the so-called revolving door tranni – these are typically categorised as eunuchs in school situations.

The rebel underground view: Men and women have overlapping, although essentially different, personality profiles. This is a design feature. Typically, men are governed by intellect and established rank, women by emotion and tactical advantage. Men are much more competitive and risk taking, women more consensus seeking and risk adverse. In partnership, these features match up well; and should this be achieved in school, all will be well – at least until the female becomes unsatisfied. However, should an institution reflect faulty sexual dynamics, we find the weaknesses of both sexes in strongest expression; men attempting to domineer, females manipulating and always seeking to offload costs and risks. The end result, a drag on productivity and a spiritual drain. Usually, the men leave.

A noted sex difference, and clear female strength, is to be utterly indifferent to evidence and logic and consistency with (ironically) respect to considering sex differences.

NB. The rebel underground view of sex differences does not exist and you have not just read it. How could you if it is not there?

Sex Education

In broaching this topic we approach the actual interest of many educational progressives; talking to children about sex. But for why?

And this you must work out for yourself. Of course, such discussion will be justified as simply presenting the facts of life and a necessary prophylactic for the children's diverse futures – including their sexual futures! However, under this innocent flag, festooned with garlands of 'love,' will sail all sorts of vessels with motives and habits more to the taste of a Barbary corsair slaver than chaste Aphrodite, the actual goddess apparently here invoked.

Here we will find that challenging patriarchal conventions of the family will quickly (and delightfully ☺) segue to alternative and gender-variable families, sexual choice, sexual consent, sex reassignment surgery, tranny story time, drag queen counselling, AIDS aware, and anything else that contains the word sex – no doubt, including some practices that the author and reader have not yet heard of. Included in this package of neo-Babylonian education, we naturally find the related concepts of tolerance, affirmative action and complaint regarding lack of necessary services to bring more sex talk into primary children's lives. And too, the need for protection against the intolerance and hate speech of persistent dissenters, like you.

All these topics need not be discussed at once, of course, it is sufficient for the plan to ensure that they are ever present in the background, like radiation spreading their mental cancer with little toxic implants that turn up in BBC Newsround reports and new-family nursery tales. This uncertain background of sex and gender and identity is ratcheted up year on year until, addled by hormones as teenagers, they are ready for the plucking.

By what right and on whose authority is this eternal family usurped, one may ask, to find the eternal enemy flaunting his flag and banners at your local primary school. The UN is your child's parent now, dissent at your peril.

Both Saint Catherine's are required here.

Sexism

1: Among male staff

20 to 1, birds to men. *Phwooar!*

From the usual 'to do' list posted on the inside of the male toilet door and the male refusal to tidy their dishes in the staffroom (well, why should they with so many women about?) there is obviously complete truth to claims of male sexism in the school workplace. With the balance of birds to men being what it is, it is natural that men should demand and receive a neck massage and similar traditional male perquisites.

Get me a cup of tea, Darling. And hurry up too: Male probationer to female head teacher.

(Actually, on the inside of the male staff toilet door, hidden from indignant female justice seekers, is to be found the male poster against domestic violence. MALES ARE VICTIMS TOO. 50% OF DOMESTIC VIOLENCE IS AGAINST MALES. REPORT IT. Heaven forbid that female staff found out that their male colleague read this, far less believed it. Then he would find out who's who and what's what!

2: Sexism in sport

This is reprehensible. And our primary schools should stamp this out by insisting that females are fully represented in all so-called traditional male sports. Boys should learn that in sport, women are just as good as men and can compete as equals – although they cannot and do not, and don't want to anyway. But this is ok, as long as no one mentions it.

Females should never be excluded from male sports; indeed, female teaching staff could aid this awareness by attending school football and rugby matches en masse, wearing swimsuits, with giant foam fingers and carrying trays of beer for the dads. Hot pies would be nice too.

3: Anti-male

Yea, that's ok.

Shakespeare

Nay, upon my word such gross forgetfulness
Betokens deserv'd calamity to this nation.

Just another dead white man?

A crucial component of a primary child's journey to full literacy, and love of their own language and culture. Not just for our time, but for all time. It's not just me that's saying that!*

As part of the general educational plan for the English speaking West, it is equally crucial that Shakespeare is kept away from children and that teachers are specially selected to be ignorant and hostile to our language's greatest champion.

We've got a fight on our hands, ye celebrants of the numinous turned to word: *Once more unto the breach, dear friends. Once more.*

Shine and Shun Words

White and black. Apply as required.

---

* This learned reference for the delight of the many Shakespearians (Jim) among the readers.

Shit-spreader

Formerly the exclusive responsibility of farmers and limited to fields as required. Now transferred to primary school toilet walls with task allotted to anonymous male pupil; another example of male privilege at work. Sometimes, as a humorous aside, the jobby may be entirely deposited in the urinal, which being revealed occasions a widespread desire for a personal viewing. Joke is continued as the responsibility for removal is the task of school management, as removing shit is not within the job description of school cleaners (Told you, it was a shit job). For LOLs imagine the euphemisms employed within the school diary recording this incident; 'Accidental slippage of faeces from toilet pan to adjacent wall during deposit of said stool. Subsequent spreading of same to other doors and walls probably from misplaced attempt to clean it up.'

This activity is best thought of as a scatological equivalent of *Where's Wally?; Whose Jobby?*

Signs of Life

Ref: among teaching staff.

Yes, showing; but metabolic disease, chronic depression, fatigue and acedia. Prognosis is not good. However, some of the extreme radical solutions offer the possibility of eventual recovery.

Single Mothers

School Rule 1: You may not speak of this topic.

Come in a number of different versions of which the worthy unfortunate, formerly the majority, is possibly now the least common.

All are now empowered by law and social convention to basically behave as they wish. This is too bad for everyone else, as it results in the unreflective selfishness and petty tyrannies of the manless female given full head, indeed, justified and cheered by their hyena pack peers and our society destroying mainstream media. The single mum as an heroic figure is a stock, oft repeated, cliché that has but little truth, but helps justify in their own eyes the most egregious and self-righteous persecutions of any who cross them and their selfish, self-destructive decisions.

For us in school, this results in this demographic being behind nearly all trivial and unreasonable complaints, always exaggerated, and not infrequently fabricated, to attract the desired pack attention. The unconstrained single female parent, perpetually angry and hormonal, disappointed in men, ever indignant, now lacks any familial restraint that could temper their judgements and their demands for sackings. The drama of the police in the school playground, selfied and posted, the gold standard of Go Girl! This drama played out in school is especially unfortunate if the teacher-sacrifice is a man because … he's a man. And everyone knows he's guilty.

Unmanaged by man or law, lacking shame sourced from morality or logic, these ferals are beyond school control and so the school doesn't even try. The management, at best lacking resolution, but usually just cowardly, take the quiet route to easy retirement. So it backs away, scared of consequences, surrendering authority. The enemy understands this victory born of weakness as justification for their agenda and so advances claiming the ground. In many schools, they run the school as a shadow government.

The other men in school, the little men, the children of these fighting mums, who are also our pupils, suffer too. Not just because their parent is involved in mad dramas using their children as a proxy, but the lack of stability and of a stable male role model in home life translates to a problematic relationship to male authority and to rational expectations about the future. And, as a limitation of her nature, lacking the abstraction to empathise with the existential male viewpoint or interests, such a mum cannot guide her son to balanced manhood.

Her little girl, brought up in an environment starved of masculinity and combative to male society, is primed for potential issue with male teachers. Her mum shows her how to do it.

Paradoxically, while happy to battle with teachers for social media likes and LOLs, they too often surrender in the most important battles; namely, those involving their children. Showing them the wrong type of indulgence, and leaving the difficult parts of raising a kid to television, social media and smart phones. Rather than arguing with a kid about what to eat and when to get exercise or (especially) go to bed, the single parent often gives in. Because it's easier to give in, because there's not enough time and life is stressed out. And anyway, they've got their own tweeting to do.

No fixing this, short of a concrete-hard reset.

NB. The worthy unfortunate elicit my sympathy. The winning, worthy unfortunate earn my sincere respect.

Sitting Still

P1, 1960

I am five years old.
I can sit still and listen.
I will not talk because
the teacher asked us not to.
Us is me too.

P1, 2020

I am five years old.
I cannot sit still and listen.
I will talk because I want to
even if the teacher asks us not to.
Us is not me anyway.

Admittedly the time frame is short for its application, but one wonders if epigenetic effects are also involved in the apparent (and actual) constitutional inability of so many contemporary children to sit still and otherwise demonstrate the strong self-control of their recent ancestors. This control being especially true of little girls then, who could apply and project it at a truly formidable level, as I clearly recall.

We refer to 'also involved' as an acknowledgement of the various societal changes in this same timeframe. Powerful though such forces obviously are, they seem to me to be not sufficient to explain the random, inner chaos that finds first expression in the inability to sit still on instruction. And repeated instruction!

SJW

Ref: social justice warriors (progressive society activists)

The primary school is their best ever playground. Here they can destroy everything under cover of justice. Their motivation is often presented as well-meaning, but a little misguided and over-passionate. But not so; the purging of beauty and the sabotage of productive work has its ultimate source, as sufficient recursion shows, in psychology. They do this because they are physically unattractive, mentally confused and otherwise feel unloved. And they do not create any value in their economic life. Thus, driven by envy, they destroy beauty as well as productivity from every environment they come in contact with. They want the world to howl like their own lost souls. Being lucky enough to have none around is like a force multiplier. However, and alas, their mission is the now largely the school's mission. No rational appeals to civil principles, organisational functionality, basic competence or profit, will ever suffice to stop them; whatever they claim as their motive is merely a pretext to justify the destruction they intend to visit on us.

Good adults, see the truth behind this faux concern. Consider the mind's construction behind the virtuous face. It is not love, nor Christian piety, that animates these outcast warriors, but jealousy and hatred of your children. Your family. Our society. In their delusional attempt to fix themselves and silence their howling minds, they try to equalise the rest of the world and bring it to their own confused and lonely level. Staring at the source of their own disquiet, the family, they naturally begin their therapy with yours. And especially your children.

Many SJWs are employed within the education system, and especially in its metastasising administrative and advisory functions. The ghetto and victim culture that is being continuously reinforced, of course, directly benefits this activist class of researchers, social workers, politicos and outcasts. They fancy themselves as humanitarians, but take after totalitarians. In the past, such types confined their ministrations to the adult population, but no longer. Totalitarian Humanitarian; a new brand of child educator.

Paraphrasing, ever so slightly, Kyle Reese's words to Sarah Connor: *Listen, and understand, that SJW is out there. It can't be bargained with, it can't be reasoned with, it doesn't feel pity, or remorse and it absolutely will not stop, ever, until you are dead.*

Hopefully, you will have gotten the message! Social Justice does not create. It only subverts, corrupts and then destroys. By design.

Skin Colour

Doesn't matter. Except when it does. Which is all the time now.

Skulls Learning Theory, The

Ref: as in filling. A New Theory of Learning.

Here the skull is considered, *sans* matter and spirit, in a visual analogy to aid understanding of children's learning processes, as it applies to school. Imagined as an empty vessel, upended, and into which one pours the various ingredients to make up the rational and knowledgeable mind of the child. Formerly, this would have been the three Rs, respect for authority, self-control, a high regard for learning and minding your own business, and that takes us near to the brim by P7. No doubt, children from antique times also had their minds filled with a fair share of nonsense, but nothing that inevitably led to self-hatred and its pathological equivalent for their society. Or wanting to chop up their sex!

The modern child has the same three Rs, but what new makes up the volume?; sexual knowledge, respect for alternative lifestyles, precocious political activism, globalist propaganda, racial guilt, IT 'skills', hostility to native institutions, worship of others, endless faux compassion, victimarian mindset, men against women, prejudice everywhere – just to list a choice selection.

To consider the impact of such learning, our new theory apportions percentages to the various subjects studied, based on a number of criteria which, of course, vary subject to circumstances; these would include, time spent on topic, funds allocated, special projects , involvement of other agencies, extra endorsements from MSM, teacher attitude, etc. These selections can be colour coded within the skull diagram to visually indicate the proportion of various knowledge domains and skill sets. This could also be used for assessment. For example, the colour coding of pupil X's skull may show a deficiency in knowledge of maths strategies, a serious lack of interest in alternative sexual preferences and insufficient compassion for victims of European classical music.

(X is used to hide the identity of the pupil, Dale Whitey, for data protection reasons)

An important analogy in considering the sort of impact the various contentious learning topics could have on the whole, is to imagine the mostly empty skull containing some foul or subtly toxic material; the addition of otherwise wholesome material would forever be tainted by this original contamination.

NB. All I would need to do to market this wonderful new pupil attainment and recording system is claim that it enhances inclusion and neural progression sequences, pay off some educational researcher to prove something or other, and then with this endorsement, polish up my brass neck and charge a fortune to gullible education chiefs. If this turns up in your kid's school, you'll know I've succumbed to Mammon.

Slate Scratchers

Our ancestral primitives whose skill, knowledge and work habits built the modern world and the ideas that sustain it.

Much, possibly most, of the modern world's transformative power traces its origin to our ancestors' formal education. This itself a consequence of the various 19th Century education acts which, building on earlier church and private initiatives, established our modern state school systems. And yet, while successfully providing a society-wide education, actually *what* they provided often seems to us now a crude and limited thing, replete with prejudice and cruelty, and taking place in primitive surrounding. How, then, given the lack of most of the techniques, resources, technologies and correct attitudes which we deem minimal essentials for learning, did they build mighty bridges, run complex timetables with precision, write and perform great art, legislate and create immense welfare systems, perfect the mechanical arts, (the machine gun, a personal favourite, springs to mind), create gigantic factories, threaten the world's survival, go to the moon, to name but a few achievements?

How did they do this with their strictly disciplined, technology-less schooling and early starting trade education? And we find the question provides the answer; back to the slate and nail. Respect obliged and given.

And with the money saved we can buy more books. And then learn to read them.

Slavery

Being imbued with saintly consciences, this is the sort of thing our voted-in masters like to spend their time ruminating on.

Schools in Scotland will send out the proud message to the world that we have zero tolerance to slavery in our classrooms. (exceptions apply).

And the world looks up from their i phone and applauds the moral courage and vision implicit in this great blow for humanity – at least, this is how the fantasy plays out in the collective mind of our political betters. Scotland, of course, has not had slavery since the 13th century and its relatively trivial connection to slave trading and slave ownership was terminated over 200 years ago, and this might lead one to question what the connection to education is? Don't be silly; transmitting guilt and shekel-burning CPD courses for teachers, White shame classes and assemblies for children (don't fret, only the White ones), charity weeks where funds are leveraged to help stamp out slavery in Aberdeen, the Hebrides, Possilpark, etc., and front a virtuous logo on the school website. This activity enjoys the approval of the UN which will throw in a flag for those schools that have sufficiently prepared the way for the reparations.

Every Scottish primary school will have a slave policy. This is our election promise (Sheikh Yersel, Scottish education spokesman for Boko Haram-SNP Alliance).

NB. An awake reader will be aware that there is a certain demographic that currently employs (and enjoys!) slavery, some of whom are currently also enjoying bed and breakfast at Her Majesty's pleasure. However, we may not reference this in school, as this does not serve the wider agenda. Nor can this be considered a benefit of multiculturalism, although it is for visibly degenerate ▮▮▮▮▮▮▮▮▮▮.

Sleep

As this foundational for health and especially learning, it is inevitable that this should be targeted for reduction. TV and computer life have proven most efficacious in minimising and otherwise reducing the quality of sleep. The relentless content of the images and sounds, age inappropriate stimulations, the light frequencies from screens, the passive consumption, the addiction, are all especially potent in the case of children. It's a diabolic double whammy; screen life rewires the brain for passive stupidity *and* disrupts sleep, thus preventing learning consolidation and restful recovery.

Some middle primary children, not yet subtle enough in deceit, have openly confessed, or even boasted, on enquiry about their sleepiness that they were enjoying screen life at 2am; such a distinction is the middle primary equivalent of a 12 year old drinking a can of beer.

Somebody's happy at this; in addition obviously to the IT potentates finding evidence of strong market penetration in the desired younger demographic.

Where there is no proper sleep there is no proper rest. The mind turns against itself. Luckily, they have a pill for that. The technology can't be resisted, but it can be destroyed. Parents should get this force out of their children's lives, by doing the same in their own. Proper sleep is achieved by the erasure of IT from family life. In most cases this solution restores the child to normal health and disposition. Even previously intractable school problems are often amazingly resolved after a few weeks of a proper sleep pattern. Nature made it that simple.

This is a dangerous thought to drug manufacturers and societal malcontents. What next? Perhaps fresh air and water will make a comeback.

Slippage

Things appear to be slipping backwards down good Plato's ladder; IQ's are slipping, attention spans are slipping, behavioural standards are slipping, childhood well-being is slipping. Just wait till 6G kicks in. Even time will start slipping backwards then, and about time too! This will allow the teacher to finish their marking from last Sunday evening!

Snacks

What a kind thing to do; a child has forgotten their playpiece and so a friend shares theirs. And how lovely to encourage this or, even better, see it arise spontaneously. Our overseers at Education HQ note this timeless kindness and bring it up to date; BANNED.

It is no longer permitted for children to share snacks because of hygiene concerns; transfer of body fluids, blood products, allergy integers, e coli, or other home-transported toxins. It is difficult to find exact numbers of child deaths as a result of such sharing over the last century, but the number may be as high as zero.

Some complaints over this issue have a racial hygiene aspect to them. Naturally, kosher and halal based lifeforms do not want dirty white hands on their purebred snacks, or their kid ingesting filth from the unclean.

There has been talk of these unlikely allies actually putting aside ancient hatreds (and respectively, drone strike and head-chopping), to bring a joint action against the White patriarchy (as represented by children sharing ritually unclean snacks). Isn't that nice; peace briefly blossoming over the patrimony of a shared sacrifice.

Sodom

Why the hate for this fun-loving town?

This story could make a comeback in the primary curriculum, re-invented as a narrative about tolerance; remembering that the Sodomites were just wanting to party with the strangers, not realising how intolerant they and Lot were. As the ultimate authority on correct curricular content, UN approval would no doubt be bestowed upon a school using *Intolerance at Sodom* as a staged Christmas show replacement for the nativity. Banners, emblazoned with the Sodomite Positive legend* could proudly fly next to the Pride guidon.

Incidentally, Sodom is twinned with Stockbridge in Edinburgh and Gomorrah with, obviously, Girvan.

---

* This is Sir Elton approved [censored object]

Solution

Realistically, remedy is none as the administrative class and dysfunctional habits and goals are too deeply embedded for simple excision. However, as an experiment worth trying and with no negative consequences, I'm for closing all state schools for a year and let people sort out their own plans for their children's education, or not as they wish. And after that year of closure, say call it Year Zero, not opening them ever again.

Solzhenitsyn

Evil might come into the world, but not through me. This his call for one to engage with their ethical conscience, in whatever way possible is realistic to the circumstances. Teaching might be a job, but it demands cognisance of this challenge at the cost of one's eternal soul.

Soul

There is no cognisance of the soul as a reality in the life of our children and thusly no sense of their spiritual journey. There is no one to consider whether or how the wonder and privilege of education should connect to charity and piety; each of which gives meaning to the other. This results in many of our school's justice activities, which only find the fullest and true ethical meaning within a religious context, relegated to the secular and political domain. With no grace involved, we are thusly exclusively animals competing for competitive advantage; and in the case of the children, not able to understand why, although able to imitate the gestures as hypocrites before they even know the word.

Our children's education is so stripped of higher meaning and true purpose that we, and they, are powerless against wickedly motivated claims on their attention and for their virtue.

Space-time Continuum

What seems to be a fundamental feature of the universe; that objects exist in points that can be described by four coordinates, and can only be in one place therefore at any one time, is, in fact, a rule regularly broken by teachers, especially topic specialists and supply teachers. These, according to their timetable, are obliged to be simultaneously in two different locations at the same time. e.g.,

P5: 9.00–9.45
P2: 9.45–10.30

Each of these classes separated by 80 yards and one floor. The Space-time Continuum challenge of magically disappearing and reappearing also applies to equipment and materials. Of course, there is no magic involved really, the teachers just warp time at the event threshold and phase pulse their materials to the new location. Once there, they merely vector shift the quantum gravity coordinates around the wormhole event horizon to rewind time to a topic introduction – which had not previously occurred, of course. You would think some credit would be due from CERN or SMERSH for this achievement, but apparently not.

Spectrum, The

If only it was an evil organisation, perhaps the Pupil Eco Committee could combat it.

However, and alas, the spectrum describes the new pupil reality that finds a significant proportion of pupils credited to this shady organisation and apparently working for it as professional class disruptors, a task at which most excel. Why so many children, and especially boys, are arriving as basically psychiatric cases is a question that can be discretely asked (noting that walls have ears in school), but cannot be answered honestly. Identifying broken families, intentionally single parents, late motherhood, IT existence and the whole panoply of a garbage lifestyle would not be permitted. And, not least, eating and drinking basically sugar. And this is why I make no reference to it here.

Some of these kids are chancers, some are weird, but functioning, and others just don't.

To those who propose genetic collapse as a factor, I present, as a contribution to the debate, the current batch of Scottish MPs.

Speed

This is welcomed in schools; not for running fast at playtime (this is, of course, prescribed as dangerous) but for downloading and processing of i pads. Like the Grim Reaper tweeting an encouragement to a boy racer to go faster, computer speed, endorsed by global tech palace eunuchs, is rushing our school children to psychic death. Speed is only better if what you get quicker is worth having in the first place.

Speed Eating

aka, turbo-lunching or supercharged chompers

This is a new pupil attribute, perhaps exclusively limited to boys- so, one up for them!

Here, in order to maximise playtime after lunch, impressive lunch eating speeds have been developed which have resulted in the entire process – from collecting full lunch tray to depositing the same and leaving the lunch hall – typically lasting about 45 seconds. The eating itself (without, it must be noted, any aid from electrically powered dentures) typically around 25 seconds. In one (timed) case, 12 seconds.

This would not have been possible in the old days of table manners; evidence that the modern system does bring improvements, especially when the pupils are properly motivated. Manners notwithstanding, this is a very optimistic sign. I considered rewarding this achievement, but held back for fear of a too widespread emulation – and then my sacking.

Spoiled Rotten

There is strong evidence to suggest that this is approaching default position for many primary children. Unsurprisingly, the obvious solution; cold water swims, route marches, fasting and prayer, is rejected, leaving much less indulgent Mother Nature to make her correction with, eventually, and ironically, much the same.

Stalingrad

Ref: the battle of,

A defining moment in the so-called Great Patriotic War, for the battle for the city was also the battle for ultimate survival for both protagonists. There can only be one, the other disappears from history. For those who see it, this is a most apt analogy for the events catalogued in this work, if you see this you'll understand who is who. If you cannot, it does not matter.

Female equivalent? – there is no female equivalent. They share the same fate as all the other comrades.

Start of Term

[Head in hands, Hamlet crosses the stage in silent agony.]

Statistics

In the school context a form of propaganda used to justify political decisions by bamboozling naïve and ignorant teachers, after the manner of a shell game conman at a medieval fair. The results required, of course, are decided in advance by the awarding of the 'research grant', any material inadvertently uncovered which does not flatter the 'conclusion' is immediately consigned to oblivion. The future loyalty of such experts is bought along with their integrity by the promise of more grant money for more of the same.

Based on false protocols, phony research and conducted by investigators with no skill in administering such tests, the statistical results are useless; and shamefully and obviously so. Still, the required lies are produced and the public and teachers bullied by the balderdash into silent compliance

The real statistic one need know is that we have built a mountain of evidence over the century that such statistics are perfectly useless and have negative impact on policy and practice. The only possible piece of encouragement is that, although we are spending more than ever, we are getting even less results, and even less people paying attention to them anyway.

A short play about government educational statistics entitled, *Just Lie.*

GOVERNMENT EDUCATION WALLAH: *The new statistics show that everything we've done has made things worse. I'm going to a teacher conference tomorrow. Recommendations?*

GOVERNMENT STATISTICS WALLAH: *Okay, Boss. We'll take out the bad results, turn the table upside down and then lie. They won't know.*

GOVERNMENT EDUCATION WALLAH: *Brilliant. I'm putting you in charge of our new survey.*

Bottom line; who cares what some statistics 'proves'. Remember what the man said, that statistics is even worse than lies and damn lies. Nearly 80% of people know that!

STEM

Science, technology, engineering and maths.

As the legend is told, White men prevented women and minorities from being STEM people, the which they have long been desirous of. In the case of women, this has been done by means of openly mocking their ambition in schools, and later by means of a glass ceiling or chains to the kitchen sinks. In the case of minorities, the same except chains augmented by whips. As evidence for this alleged, still continuing bigotry against women, we witness the failure of the majority of women to become STEMS, or even want to, despite over fifty years of media and feminists telling them to be. Or, in the case of minorities, the failure of the various African space programmes to get beyond very, very low Earth orbit. So powerful is the patriarchy's psychic lock on STEM careers, it is further claimed, that women and minorities actually brainwash themselves to reject such careers.

More affirmative action (AA) is required. Suggestions include redefining Australopithecine Mediterranean canoeists as POC-STEMs, or awarding feminist activists an honorary degree in engineering and then managing directorships of engineering companies. Lesbianical engineering holds out great promises for the future, as does African maths.

Of course, with AA must come punishments; and the severest level is held waiting for those who dare to infer that the true purpose and highest expression of womanhood is to create and nurture children, or to do jobs that they feel best fitted to their personal talents or interests – *How dare they!*

The joint African and Lesbian mission to Mars (code name – Fulani Kifo) will be the proof of the proposition that no matter how hard White men try to censor the true nature of women and minorities, nature always wins.

Stolen

Let us be clear about this; of the countless billions of our money spent on public education in the last generation, countless billions of it have been stolen, laundered through useless courses, resources, IT mind melt, consultancies, bureaucratic bloat, HR idiocy, and the funding of the ludicrously stupid and grossly incompetent university educational research. Of course, all these shekel-hungry cronies will claim that they've only wasted a few hundred million, but applying any metric that puts children's education as the goal will prove otherwise.

What a fine maths project for the upper primary; calculate the amount stolen and owed to the taxpayer in refund.

I'm getting a Kawasaki Z1300 with my rebate. Once I'm gone they'll never catch me!

Stories

Are the foundation of our perception of reality, their content and meaning organise the world around us. They provide the templates for our behaviour and legitimise values, this is why it is so crucial to replace nursery tales with LGBT heroes, locate ethnic others anachronistically in our historical legends, have other or mixed-race families as the carriers of our traditional tales, and ensure tolerance of multicultural dysfunction is always the highest virtue, as this is the most disempowering of attributes.

As TV and the internet increasingly carries our society's values to the next generation, and the filth and subversion viewed daily there by our children is reinforced by the same in primary school, via nursery tales and the reading material, we can see the concerted attempt to stitch up our children's future with *Our Values* that are not our values.

And in the end, when we see it clearly after it is too late, we realise that those apparently innocent little stories of tolerance and multicultural celebration were the first baby steps on the road to confusion, fractured community, victims, victimhood, righteous persecution, dispossession and extinction. Of us.

On the plus side, for those future semi-Europeans (assuming they can still read in that future) it will make some interesting tales for their children. The betrayals in the Iliad and Odyssey will pale to insignificance in comparison.

Stupidity, Increasing

aka; enstupidation

1. At large

Of course, unless you had been off the planet for the fifty years, you knew this. Its importance for your child's education lies in its general impact on the entire system, which can only be a downward spiral. Even when this is recognised by intelligent people of good will, still nothing can be done, such is the nature of increasing societal stupidity. You knew this too.

Collectively, perhaps, we wish to believe that there is some place where all the intelligent people are, planning a recovery. It must be them who produce the various and serious sounding studies; Educating for the Future, Evolving Scotland, Our Digital Future, Rights Respecting Scotland, Peace and Justice in the Primary Curriculum. However, an examination of such cash-cow, PR fluff would swiftly disabuse you of this notion. This is the written evidence of the increasing stupidity at the supposed high level of education. Perhaps there are some intelligent people somewhere, in a boardroom probably, but they are not planning for *our* future. At least, not in the way you would hope.

The crucial point of this enstupidation is that the means whereby we could be led out of our predicament, an informed and engaged public, has been rendered almost impossible by our general reliance on the media which has led us into this situation, the TV.

A particular medium can only sustain a particular level of ideas and engagement. And in comparison to the written word, which requires the intellectual involvement of the reader, the TV/video is the most superficial, as the viewer is a passive participant. This superficiality and accompanying passivity removes facts and reason from public discourse and replaces them with stupidity and emotion. People then deciding according to how they feel about issues, or more rather, how they are made to feel about issues. The setting of the agenda, the manipulation of evidence, the manufacture of your concern, support or indifference rests largely with the TV/video, the same effect for pupils in school as the same media overwhelms traditional and more intellectually demanding forms of learning.

The end point of this argument for parents and pupils is that, those who see what is happening and are concerned, must look to their own. Trying to fix it, is like an argument with an idiot. The increasing stupidity in schools, just like in society at large, must run its course into the big buffers because the increasingly stupid people do not know that they are stupid; named as the Dunning-Kruger effect.

2. Of pupils

Until fairly recently, whenever the topic of intelligence was raised there has been much self-satisfied crowing about its apparent increase over the whole globe. As a consequence of improved nutrition, health, educational opportunities and standards, and the intellectual complexity of modern life, IQs have been rising over the last century – this phenomenon noted as the so-called Flynn Effect.*

---

* Named after the social scientist who studied and described this phenomenon. Flynn has noted that his effect is now trending downwards.

And as we have become brainier, so we enter the sunny uplands of peace, prosperity and wonderful future potential. Apparently!

Those who doubted this claim, notwithstanding evidence of higher IQs, have unfortunately been very visibly vindicated as school pupils move ever more into the intelligent life of their devices. Sedentary lifestyles, metabolically ruinous diets, rewiring of brains to be receptive to digital input, the filth, garbage and endless lies of news media, the precipitous decline of a literate culture, and the absurd pedagogies and curriculum content we have been here cataloguing, are proof of increasing stupidity on a personal level. On a societal level, the failure of higher IQ individuals to even replacement-level breed, combined with its opposite, in addition to the massive importation of low IQ populations, have depressed further the general intelligence level. And, of course, when intelligence goes down, stupidity goes up. As you have noticed.

When we add this increase in personal pupil stupidity, to increasing numbers of less intelligent pupils and the activist, self-righteous, justice culture being encouraged by equally stupid educators, we can be assured that increasing pupil stupidity still has a long road to travel on its journey through the school corridors.

Stupidity, Institutional

This is often referenced as an explanation for the dysfunctional nature of the educational establishment, and while it has some merit it ignores the principle of Occam's razor; a simpler and truer explanation is to be found in what I like to call ACTUAL STUPIDITY.

This is ranked, of course, although not so much in levels of stupidity (let us grant them the equality they so assiduously strive for), as in the potential for actual stupidity to do the most harm. And it is this aspect of stupidity, the actually stupid, their identities hidden behind policies in the anonymous institutions that manage education, that creates an illusion that it is the institution that is stupid. Thusly, unfairly enjoying a super power – invisibility to scrutiny – the stupid people behind the stupidity get a free pass at top salary. Nirvana!

Good Plato's evolutionary ladder is reversed in this up-side down world; firstly, we find the worst at the top in the various educational Sanhedrin; HM Inspectors of Education, university experts and council heads of service (our own here in Edinburgh are particularly fine examples). Next, council educational HR services, workshop shekel-meisters, the various council unterführers (quality, equality and policy), and most deservedly last, the educational psychologists. Then comes the ordinary stupid, embedded in school management. However, when we finally reach the teachers, stupid though many are, these avoid institutional blame (only in the sense here used!) as they are no more stupid than, for example, a pencil that writes the wrong answer. i.e., a stupid pencil.

A particular danger of institutional stupidity is reached when it is combined with laziness and moral cowardice, this creating the dreaded Stupidity Trifecta.

Alas, the Stupidity Trifecta *is* the educational establishment. It should come as no surprise, therefore, that an institution composed of so many low quality pieces is on a shoogly hook.

Stupid People

We find two forms in school, lazy and active. And their name is legion, for they are many. Both types share the same unconcern, either personally or societally, for anything they want, say or do. Since public chastisement in the form of branks, stocks and riding crop are currently out of fashion, the self-righteous stupid drown out everyone else in the arena of public opinion – this includes the school-parent social media world. As this particular stupid-world is almost exclusively female, there is no prospect of sense ever being heard; this is especially unfortunate as it gives such forceful idiots an outsized political power in influencing the lives of all pupils in a school.

It is interesting to observe that much of the manifest stupidity is often quite unconnected to intelligence, and is instead an expression of bad manners and a pathological sense of entitlement. The like which schools frequently ignore and enable respectively.

In drafting our transcription code, God deliberately limited our intelligence so that there would be things we could not understand, but could only come to them by faith, as Gabriel told Adam.

It is a shame (although part of the big plan, admittedly) that he did not limit our stupidity. Hat check to Eve and her sisters. ☺

Subtraction

Nothing is subtracted from the teacher's fare, except mental health and having babies.

Success

The intent of our current educational philosophy, reinforced by idiot parents, is to provide an unbroken chain of successes for the pupils without considering the consequences of what wider message is learned when success is a guaranteed outcome of every exercise. Effort is uncoupled, self-pride denied, correction is unnecessary and unwelcome. Divorced from corrective truth, such children risk becoming unteachable; over-reacting to denial and disappointment in adult life, or even other viewpoints, they risk becoming useless adults.

In presenting children for continued success, we actually prepare them for continual failure.

Success Criteria

Old unspoken success criteria for telling the time: Telling the time.

On being asked to do something, it is implicit in the request that you will attempt to finish the work to your best standard; and in a timeous fashion, this is just as obvious to a child in school. Sometimes, of course, these terms have to be described in more detail or negotiated, but generally speaking this understanding universally applies. And thusly, no time need be wasted in saying what doesn't need to be said, or working memory used up processing the obvious. Into this simple arena, steps the educationalist: *Hmm,...here's something obvious, simple and it works. Time for an upgrade to current standards.*

And so they invented 'success criteria', well, not really invented; they just stuck the phrase to the old implicit idea, but made its definition in a lesson explicit and, following standard practice, bigged it up to be a monster-bully.

So now, prior to the lesson, you've got to DEFINE the success criteria in sufficient detail to overload working memory. Then keep up the pressure by reference to their success criteria and its associated targets throughout the lesson. Even the lesson's end brings no relief, as the pupil is obliged to review and then set new targets. If adhered to, this assault on working memory and a genuine success criteria, ironically compromises the lesson's success criteria; *Ha ha, gotcha!* If not adhered to, another layer of dangerous duplicity is introduced into the teacher's life; don't get caught ignoring the orthodoxy.

Success Criteria is yet another example of the verbiage which overload the system. And when it breaks, the teacher and pupils pays the price. While the make-job frauds behind this nonsense, masquerading as educationalists and policy experts, disappear behind the wizard's curtain – with the money.

Suicide and Self-harm Awareness Course

Yeah, you read it right! This is a course for primary school teachers with 'at risk' pupils. Imagine the pride of those responsible for creating such a requirement; their hubris must glow. Darkly!

For those teachers that wonder how and why they have to take on-board this 21st century skillset, just make sure you don't wonder out loud. And if those same teachers struggle with finding a way of introducing our new realities to their, perhaps, still innocent pupils, then modern authors come to the rescue. Please find, in your 'coming soon' approved list, class novels that deal with such new-found child topics; incest, violent fathers, mum's rapist boyfriend, prison dads, LPQT outcasts, druggie lifestyles, my two dads, skanky hoor mums, brave trannie families struggling with intolerance. Every degenerate topic is fair game for primary pupils, except ethnic rape gangs, because that would be racist. After taking a reading group with this material the teacher will be well aware of why the suicide and self-harm course exists. The same coming soon for teachers!

> *Gentle Jesus, meek and mild,*
> *Look upon a little child,*
> *Pity my simplicity,*
> *Suffer me to come to thee.* *

---

* From *Hymns for Children*, by Charles Wesley

Supergirl

Her super power is charity. By nine years old she has saved scores of unfortunately parented others, both at home and abroad. This has been done mainly by wearing face paint and paying for the privilege. But it pays itself back by the moral glow that this kindness gets from tweets and selfies. The school UN flag is an added bonus.

There is nothing that supergirl cannot do, she knows this as, like a good dog, she is told it every day. No thought seems to enter anyone's mind that this power, like all power, may become corrupting to her, and anyone else within its force field.

Sweden

In the world of schooling, Sweden is our 21st century late Roman Empire. Teaching, for those with eyes to see it, the same old lessons that led to the empire's dissolution.

Student democracy, lax discipline, an interactive lesson ethos, constant promotion of sexual and racial justice themes, and otherwise permissive pedagogic methods applied to ethnic other pupils with an inherited delinquent tendency, can only result in anarchy and disaster.

The metabolites for this social bomb have been relentlessly promoted for half a century by the Swedish media – if only one was able to find out the identity of the subversive tribal cabal that own the entire media apparatus, perhaps this knowledge would help others profit by the Swedes' loss.

Beset by an unjustified self-shame, nihilism, cultural rot, gigantic demographic shift, and imminent Islamization, the Swedish education system shows just what can be achieved with the necessary mindset and funding – and all within one generation. A stupendous result, however one regards it. Ethnic Swedes, or rather their children, forced into proximity with hostile ethnic others, are getting exactly what they voted for. For those of a mind to view this first Euro undergång, an interesting comparison can be made with the plight of the French educational system in their major cities. But don't worry if you are too busy to check it out – it will check you out soon enough.

Sweeties

The alcohol of the child. Chocolate being the gateway drug that primes the system to addiction.

This really must be controlled by caring parents to avoid leading their child's metabolism on the path to insulin resistance. Much good has apparently been done in schools by restricting this drug's availability at playtime, but then this is all wiped out at Easter, Christmas and the end of term with sweeties everywhere. For example, from P4 to teacher:

Best (worst) Christmas sweeties haul: 4 × box Heroes, 4 × Choc Santas, 3 × box Quality Street, 2 × box Matchsticks, 2 × box Thorntons, 1 × box Lindt Swiss Selection, I × box Milk Tray, 1 × box Italian Gianduitto, 2 × box Cadbury's Selection, 1 × box M & S Luxury Belgian Selection, 1 × box Costco Belgian Surprise, 1 × Chocolate box with Arabic script (ها ها ها الأنسولين الموت كافر), 1 × party pack of Mars Bars and a Toffee Crisp.*

---

* probably Zasha's playpiece. And kindly handed over in lieu of a possible playground confiscation. Thus, this Toffee Crisp must be considered as a (possibly *the* only) genuine and exclusively pupil Christmas gift.

Synchronicity

In the middle of a presentation on enhancing use of IT in the classroom;

[BLANK SCREEN]

Check Input Source.

God smiles, even Satan titters!

T

Table Manners

This is where propriety and precision are demonstrated, and are indicative of the same in other domains of the holder's life. Thusly being a flag of general excellence to potential partner or employer. And a civic template to the world at large. This is like an ancestor memory now, a wished for remnant of an earlier and better time; however, one sometimes encounters it amid the cacophony and misrule, and delights in finding a pearl sitting on the swill.

Like other varieties of manners, if you don't insist on them, then you don't get them. If you believe that this does not matter, then all is well. If you believe that it does matter, either as a practical issue with respect to the tidying-up after lunch,* or as also a fundamental issue, symbolic of our commitment to self-control and shared communal values, then we have a problem.

This is easily solvable, at the low cost of a few hard lessons and missed lunches; but only in another world. Perhaps in the one to come, although obviously not the next one to come!

Target Rich Environment

Schools are the ultima max arena for the rent seeking consultant, attention-seeking parent, social justice activist, sensationalist press,

---

* Not everywhere, but in some schools the state of the post-lunch lunch hall conjures up a too rich selection of apt comparisons; pigsty, the floor of a sick parrot's cage, Sawney Bean's cave after a family barbeque and, obviously, chimp's tea party.

political bully, persecuting pupil, bureaucratic busyworker and opinion-rich ignoramus. Every shot a hit.

For the satirist, allegorist and compiler of whimsical dictionaries it is also a gold mine. Every vein glitters.

Targets

come in two forms; sensible and idiotic.

The idiotic ones have been imported from the corporate world, perhaps not the best model for infants to emulate as President Putin noted. These are then differentiated into different forms; social, lesson, termly, personal. The highest standards of this approach involve children recording targets, noting them at the start, during and after lessons, and then recording results and new future targets for the same again at next lesson. Some have proposed little target cards that sit on the desk to ensure that the child learns that there is no escape from targets. These target cards can be taken home to sit at the bedside or downloaded as an app on a playback loop. To complete the stations of the cross, the children are tormented by the requirement for target discussions, where they 'chose' new targets with their productivity manager, aka class teacher. Giving an approved answer is not difficult for intelligent children, they sense that the pressure is really on the teacher to claim the target as achieved, it doesn't matter whether it is; great training for the game of corporate employment!

Imagine, if you can, the pressure generated by such targets relentlessly repeated, and especially for a diligent child. Consider the zany potential of such a target discussion with the class autistes, ADHDs, the panic prone, minus two standard deviationists and global delayists. What's a target; let's ask Rik.

T: Rik, we need to have a conversation about your targets. Do you know what this means?

R: **Yes, it's something you shoot at.**

T: That's correct. But you need to shoot with a pencil onto your jotter and do sums to get a higher score. Let's start with maths; what score would you like to aim at?

R: **Eleven out of ten.**

T: Good Lad, that's a sensible target! Off you go.

Aiming for sensible targets is, in contrast, an excellent idea that builds the upper body strength, hand-eye coordination and the good strong grip that enables one to take down a Frenchman at 100 yards. Of course, adding scores of kill ratios improves maths. An excellent demonstration of the utility of proper school targets was provided by a visiting medieval reenactor who was able to place the arrow 'in the slot' (as they say) just above the bevor and into the manikin's throat at 50 paces. Impressing the assembled pupils and providing an extra incentive to master the art, further enhanced when he shot the French teacher; an old habit not yet atrophied.

Future-soon forms of targets will be much more relevant to pupils as these will assuredly contain gender, sexual, tolerance and charity bullseyes. O to see a personal learning plan from 2030, that would be worth coming back down to Earth for!

As Saint Thomas noted: *If the Scozzese wish to adopt targets in the training of their youth, they need look no further than their southern neighbours. The English have surely demonstrated to them the value of proper training with targets, nothing need be added to their excellent example.*

Tattooed Teacher

The star with circling butterflies adorning the ankle tells you everything you need to know.

Ditto the bluebird, the dolphin and the rose. Or pop culture garbage, i.e., Madonna's face – the egyt hoor-screecher, not the Madre di Dios. The tribal tattoo or Chinese mystery script* apparently tells of a different, deeper person, except that it doesn't. Just as, the cute dragon above the arse crack tells you everything you wish you didn't know. [Thought – *Don't lean over like that again!*]

And too, such sophistication, the favourite among mouthy femmes not called Hermia; *Though she be but little, she is fierce.* She might be fierce, but she didn't know it was from *A Midsummer's Night's Dream.* This too tells you everything you need to know.

Teachable, Be

What should be a default on the part of the pupil is now so often grudgingly and only partly conceded. The failings in this part of the class contract are always presented as a failing in pedagogy or attitude on the part of the teacher. Let's balance out the blame and attribute some to the character of children, and the failings of their parents to instil discipline and respect.

A crucial corollary of being teachable is the possibility of a 'teaching moment' occurring without prompting. This is that magic power that suddenly connects the pupil's interest with the lesson, and makes the whole process alive, sometimes even joyous, for both. Some children find this frequently and easily, others only occasionally according to their natures. However, in both cases it is predicated on

---

* 白色昆虫

being teachable; without this, not only is little knowledge imparted, but the joy that can accompany learning via the teaching moment is lost.

Most pupils are fairly teachable; however, it is possible to get an unlucky class where many pupils are not generally teachable. It doesn't matter specifically why this is, it's still the teacher's fault.

TOP TIP: If you mix a teachable boy with an unteachable boy, you get two unteachable boys. This rule scales.

Teacher

A slave with a fickle and unjust master. Only the afterlife offering respite from the parade of humiliating nonsense with punishments.

In former times this was once a respected profession. Even when, in ancient times, the teachers were sometimes actually slaves, they were still revered for their learning and treated well for their utility.

Exceptions excepted, it is now an occupation that is neither accorded, nor deserving of, a deep respect. The vocational aspect is gone and with it the rectitude and moral courage on which the respect was founded. The teacher now cannot bring love, is not permitted to bring wisdom, and seldom represents deep learning and intellectual passion. Indeed, the job is best thought of as an endless sequence of career hazards.

Like a druid, or fencing master or Latin tutor, it is an occupation whose time has passed. The dustbin of history, beckons wide.

PUPIL: *Don't go too near than bin, Miss. It's not a regular bin, it's the dustbin of history. The School Equalities Coordinator brought in while you were in the staffroom.*

TEACHER: What rubbish are you talking about now. It's just a ......
Waaa,,...argghhhh!

Tests

1. Academic classwork

Funnily enough, the one thing that pupils need more of, naturally we give them less of.

Much discredited in our age as the least effective form of assessment and an unnecessary source of pupil stress, and also presented as a holdover from crueller times when pupils were ranked according to academic ability and thusly (apparently) humiliated by the reality of their ability exposed.

It has been noted that a – arguably *the* – most effective method of learning involves much testing, and then much repeat testing. In this approach, testing is a part of the learning process, and not only the assessment part. The best results are produced with the following modality; study, test, test, test. And repeat. As quoted:

Ye have heard it said that testing pupils is contrary to my father's will and the law of good effects. Verilly I say unto you, stress measured according to one's need, followed by a humbling are steps on the road to right learning. Entry to my father's school is conditional on testing. Go ye and do likewise.

2. Psychological assessment;

Funnily enough, the one thing that pupils need less of, naturally we give them more of.

The tests for your child's condition are still inconclusive. More tests are recommended. Following cutbacks these may be delayed by up to 18 months. You will be informed of an appointment in due course. Please find enclosed a leaflet explaining all the council services your child may qualify for when their tests are concluded. If you would prefer to have this leaflet in Sumerian cuneiform, Aztec, Coptic, Chimpanzee Sign Language or Welsh, please contact council HQ.

Therapy Pet

The latest stallholder to set up on Dysfunction Road, selling a quick solution to stressed or otherwise non-functional children; a class therapy pet. This is not the occasional hamster or goldfish that one comes across when a foolishly indulgent teacher has surrendered to the whines of her class, but a department sanctioned (and presumably certificated) therapist, who is usually a dog. Its calming therapy is provided mainly by its cuddly presence and non-judgemental sympathetic nature. Thus do we normalise the need for such and, of course, legitimise the dysfunction on which it is predicated. Note that here we are not criticising the utility and pleasure, therapy or otherwise, of pets in other contexts.

In the near coming age of enhanced pupil democracy the necessary therapy presence will be voted on; when this happens expect snakes and monkeys to show strongly on the ballot. My strong preference would be for a classroom donkey, whose quiet and determined nature provides a good role model for pupils, and rides at playtime. Crows too, as the most intelligent of birds, would provide a good example of the utility of an excellent memory and efficient organising strategies, although I believe that they would be somewhat deficient in the sympathy department-although this may be a good thing should the class be suffering from therapy fatigue.

Readers may be supposing that whimsy has overwhelmed the limits of absurdity, but not so. In addressing the crucial educational issue of our times, can therapy pets support the development of self-regulation? A funded study has (surely not surprisingly!) proven that this is indeed the case. Apparently the therapy canines (when not biting) bring a feeling of calm to the classroom. Well, that's that then, the question regarding poor school outcomes over millennia answered with a happy wag and a woof. We note that no thought is given to the pet's feelings about being given this role as conduit for the unhappiness and stress of other species; perhaps a future lawsuit from animal welfare lawyers?

I rather like the idea of this full-scale acceleration into comic madness. Each school could have its own menagerie with pupils selecting the correct therapy pet for the circumstances: owls for spelling, crocodiles for maths, macaws for creative writing, etc. The only downside is the potential for future activist complaints regarding a lack of diversity: for example, the over-representation of golden retrievers – noted as the canine equivalent of White people – or the racist lack of African fauna.

(Teachers are recommended to get their allergy records up to date in anticipation of the new therapist's arrival. And management prepare the necessary restraint devices in the event of a fight between rival class therapists, monkeys and dogs in particular being long noted as bitter enemies, as mice and elephants.)

Thesaurus

We should make more use of the thesaurus. It is one of the solutions.

IDEAL PUPIL: *I got a thesaurus for Christmas.*

TEACHER: ***That's nice.***

IDEAL PUPIL: *I think you can find a better word than that.*

TEACHER: [covers face in shame]

The Truth

The truth is sexist and racist and not remotely equalist. Or caring about feelings!

This suppressed truth is as great a burden to schools as it is to society, both in terms of the personal costs of ever speaking it out loud and in the various policy disasters visited on us. However, as there is no possibility of a mudslinging truth jubilee, the teacher ends up in a sort of psychic race with these inexorable truths – always trying to stay ahead of them to avoid a confrontation. Eventually, though, they will be run down by them; the only question is whether they can get out of teaching before this happens.

Thrilled

In a small way, admittedly, but I am thrilled to see you every day.

The happy though of the lucky teacher entering their good class.

Tig

Yes, it's bad! Chasing can result in falling, then injuries, then complaints, then lawsuits. There is also the social danger, as it is principally boys who are the chasers, and girls as the chasees (*Ha Ha, Can't catch me!*), of sexism in action. This form of male sexual violence can result in female injuries and, as such, is basically the playground version of wife-beating. And so;

BANNED.

Although a form of tig, chase and kiss, could make a comeback if it promoted tolerance; boys chasing and kissing caught boys, who chase back in turn; ditto for girls. Trannies can kiss who they like, if it is for tolerance.

Tired

Ref: of lies

We spend our entire life creating, avoiding and confronting lies, and it should be no surprise that our schools are packed full of them. However, with respect to primary schools, there are two crucial conditions that give this life of lies a terrible consequence.

Firstly, the system of pedagogy is predicated on false equalist beliefs and, moreover, is intentionally dedicated to supporting this regardless – this leads us the endless cycle of failing practice, failing results and doubling-down on the political agenda. All of which burns resources like a forest fire. Indeed, this glutinous consumption of human energy and public funding is a purpose of our bureaucratic institutions.

Secondly, as the system is overwhelmingly staffed by females, who by their biological nature, cannot but collectively agree with whatever is promoted by the centres of power – in this case; (proximately) school management, but (ultimately) the media agenda – these lies will not be confronted, far less resisted. Indeed, with females generally able to not just accept, but come to believe the official line (and thus happily outgroup apostates), there is thus no possibility of any honest, self-correction coming from within.

The consequences of all this uncorrectable deceit fall on our children who are brought up within this system. This fails them in specific ways peculiar to their own situation, character and intelligence, but also more generally in that they inherit the same false, often self-destructive, beliefs and habits, and miss out on what could have been. They are then ready, child carries child, to continue the same lies to their next generation.

All systems accumulate inefficiencies and lies over the course of their life which eventually leads to their dissolution. In the case of our primary schools, we may be a long way off from their demise; however, I beg you to consider the cumulative effect on your child of attending an institution so steeped in every kind of lie. It need not matter that they do not always know this, or even the teachers for that matter, for the lies are still there in the entire body, from the bones to the breath, contaminating with every inhalation. Like an accidental parent swap at birth, the entire rearing is just wrong. The child's spirit knows this, and this received intelligence contributes to the whole tired of lies sensibility whose cloud lours upon our house.

Everywhere you look you find bullshit and talking snakes. For the sensitive-souled teacher their daily existential crisis is best expressed as tired of lies.

Toilet

Formerly children had sphincter muscles of steel wire strength around their urethra, these appear to have degenerated to old elastic band power in the last few generations, so that some children's school day consists mainly of toilet visits inconveniently punctuated by parts of uncompleted lessons. And where one child goes, others follow and especially friends. A teacher is no longer able to have any suspicions about this situation, far less query the actual need so soon after the previous visit, as this 'comfort break' is now a human right. Whereas, in contrast, the teacher's job is a grace dependent on properly recognising this right.

In my primary schooling in the 60's only one child in the entire period of my experience had to go to the toilet during lessons. Just once, and it turned out that Alison had a UTI, as explained in the note sent to Miss Browning and as she thoughtfully explained to the class, to prevent any unnecessary emulation.

The humble toilet is set to become the battlefield for our new world order. Some are advocating for one big happy and open bathroom for all 26 (adopting current US Airforce standard) genders. Others insisting that T women (male-male-female) or F men (male-female-male) must poop with the boys, but change with the girls. Boys must shower with the trannies, but trannies can chose the girls' facilities if they identify as inter hybrid trans. Random passing adults (if trans or sex-fluids) can visit the school to use whatever toilet or shower stall they wish – it's all for tolerance, you see.

(MFx adult females and T+ adult males must check with their school prior to using toilet facilities as local restrictions may apply, e.g., certificate from equalities officer, or presence of gender trained, police officer supervising toilet proceedings.)

A recent phenomenon of activist pupils protesting against oppression (we presume) by shit-spreading on doors and walls in the (boys, who else?) toilet calls to mind the wisdom of the ancients; now we know why they had roofless toilets in the playground. The practical consequences of these protests naturally fall on the school cleaners, and in the event that they protest too, school management. The practical consequence to the protesters of getting caught is, of course, nothing beyond a restorative chat, because children should be encouraged to protest. It's all just part and parcel of life in a big city primary, as the Mayor of London reminds us.

To avoid accusations of race prejudice and cultural appropriation we should have Muslim only toilets, with no toilet paper, of course, and a non-functional flush. And African toilets, which could just be a door leading to the playground outside the staffroom window; these are surely within school budget considerations.

Token

i.e., – ism

Is there a Black or Asian kid in the school? FFS, get these on the cover of the school handbook. The inspectors are due a visit soon and we don't want these d… c…s, Abbott and Khanstello, turning up with the Newsround mudjahideen. Or worse, the Pope tweeting us to buggery! What's that,…they're all on an all-expenses paid FGM trip to Africa. Well, just paint some whitey's face black and burka up some of the school monkeys. We don't want any accusations of racism in this school.

Tokenism

This is a forever complaint.

With respect to activist demands (e.g., We need more transitioning people of colour **and** size in primary schools as sex welfare coordinators.), if one does accede to them, then immediately the accusation of tokenism arrives and more of the same complaints – as enough is never enough. If one does not surrender, then one confirms further systemic racism/sexism/transphobia/ etc, and the volume gets turned up to eleven.

Complaints of tokenism, are then, the means whereby the dysfunction is ratchetted ever forward. In the absence of real work and large happy families, only cleansing fire offers a solution.

Tolerance

Tolerance is the proof of distrust in your own convictions.

For generations, presented as a virtue with the greatest of efforts across every front by our overseers and their media organs, and yet even as we mouth the tolerance shibboleths to our pupils, we know in our hearts that we are betraying ourselves and them. For in every case we are lowering hard fought standards that will not be won back in our time. But not just lower, baser too; and, ironically, as we daily see, that those who advocate for more tolerance are the most intolerant, and directly responsible for creating the environment of intolerance that they object to.

Formerly, tolerance was regarded as a dangerous value because of its potential for subversion, and was therefore only conceded under limited and specific circumstances. However, a brilliant multi-generational plan to conflate tolerance with intolerance, refusing to acknowledge its crucial protective role against malcontents and perverts, and its maintaining of high standards, has won us over to see it as a pejorative; oppressive and inflexible, irrational and mean. A brutal thing in sore need of replacement. The opposite of the kind world we want to be living in, so we are told.

But in inviting to the table of our munificence all the allegedly unfairly excluded, something unexpected happened. Not gratitude or the invite returned, and the kindly future world promised, but their resentment confirmed. We have displayed, as it is understood by the beneficiaries of our tolerance, the weak hand. Thus beginning a process of surrender following surrender, and the enemy ever advancing into the terrain vacated. A terrain, literally and figuratively, that no one wants to live in. The actual rewards of tolerance are treachery and betrayal.

Those bringing down the judgement will feel no reluctance of conscience. Simply by virtue of the 'enlightened' attitudes they claim to hold, they believe themselves entitled to dominate discussions, denouncing and silencing others for intolerance and 'No Free Speech to Nazis'. Pupils who are early exposed to this attitude from their teachers, and later absorb it, will not be able to develop true tolerance or to strive, in good faith, to understand diverse points of view. In the future, if too many citizens adopt such a position, neither civility nor democratic governance will be possible. This is already happening.

For those with eyes, we can see now where this is heading: The gradual replacement of high standards of ethics and output with ever lower standards, until eventually the flip which gives the reversal. And then, just a slow, miserable, incremental, subtle, but inexorable descent into Third World instability, insecurity and public place degradation. Until finally, the only thing not tolerated is you, the teacher, and their deserving pupils. This is the terminus of our tolerance; social dysfunction and societal breakdown. This story multiplied a million times everywhere in the white world.

And then, in a little epiphany, you see that all along tolerance was a hack implanted in the public mind to weaken us into accepting the intolerable. Properly viewed, it was intolerance that, where it was not an actual virtue, was a necessary friend to a stable society.

As Rambo said: *Tolerance is a disease. I'm the cure.*

If only we had more Rambos in school. [Ed; be careful what you wish for]

Tolerance Clubs

Coming soon to properly progressive schools and generously funded from the public purse, the next stage of infant political activism following on from eco and anti-bully committees, the Gaytrans Coming Out, Minority Defence and Diversity Support clubs. These will be mandated by the UN who will provide the banners which proclaim the achievements and shame the intolerant. Local politicians and celebrities will, apparently spontaneously, further raise the profile by their 'celebration' of tolerance. There is much to look forward to for advocates of pupil democracy and dystopia.

Tolerate

As if by definition, the teacher gets exactly what they deserve, right up to the limit of their tolerance. Beyond this is only dismissal and jail time.

Tolerating

The intolerable three in schools:

1. The worst is children being permitted to disrupt and abuse their classmates.

2. Next, the gigantic, unnecessary workload for teachers.

3. Finally, the disrespect, by omission and intent, we show to our native culture.

Toolkit

A perfect accompaniment to the workshop, as there are no tools in the kit; which is just as well, as there is no kit anyway to hold them even if they existed. O, and no workshop!

The toolkit in its various forms, is then the highpoint in the virtual and ironical world of IT teaching. And the transgender toolkit (don't panic, no snipping is involved) the high point of this high point. The contents, little icons, cartoon exhortations and broken web-links, provide by virtue of one's awareness of their absurdity – an awareness that is frankly lacking in so many teacher colleagues – the proof of the superiority of the superior person. Assuming that it is you!

As we see, it is virtually impossible to mock a virtual mockery. But one must try, despite the odds of success.

Totalitarian Culture

It's not just about secret informers, spy police and gulags; it's about building a post-liberal culture that is defined by a militant progressive ideology that brooks no dissent. The new conformity is enforced by destroying, personally and professionally, dissenters and random truth talkers. An important part of this process is inculcating disrespect, disconnect, fear and self-loathing within the minds of people living in those cultures. You don't need the secret police when you have taught people to police themselves according to your totalitarian principles. Inculcating these principles is the job of the school and our unwitting kommissar teachers. Their female herd instinct, rationalising powers, easy indignation, duplicity and love of the drama of the law enforced, making them ideal for such a role over inferior, although more brutal, male colleagues. We cannot rely on the instincts, intellect or integrity of such teachers to even see, far less resist, this evil juggernaut.

As part of this process, some may have noted a shift in definitions and intent regarding tolerance; from something that was requested (on principle) *of* the majority, to a justification of their persecution for an apparent lack of the same. And thus, no longer a virtue to be kindly exercised, but an imperative to be obeyed.

This flipping of meanings is a feature of all totalitarian cultures. And all such cultures evolved (usually rapidly) out of previously tolerant cultures; consider Weimar and Nazi Germany here. Their success in flipping the meaning of fundamental social constructs, like tolerance, depended on targeting the young. Notice something familiar?

The totalitarian madness we see daily ever stronger in the world, has its genesis in the misshaping of our children's minds in school.

Traditional Knowledge

The traditional forms of literate culture are the most effective transmitters of knowledge, love of learning and instruments of social change. O, the irony of class warriors deriding and purging from the standard curriculum the best source of improvement for the disadvantaged. A relativist might claim a value equivalence on rival knowledge, but such claims are for rhetorical purposes. What an individual learned when learning traditional knowledge is the only knowledge accorded the respect of others and the soubriquet of 'educated.'

Transformation

Ref: of pupils basic personality

What we are seeing in primary school is a deliberate attempt to endow our children with a set of ideas and models of expression consistent with the political agenda planned for their future world as international, digital, human capital. With their nobler virtues exploited to lead them further into confusion. This is nothing less than the transformation of the pupil into a new personality type; politicised, sexualised, empowered, entitled and indignant. And already stressed beyond measure, while still at the start of their life into adulthood. Here there will become fully integrated into the digital matrix. We see the UN and the global media/financial interests behind this pathology. And behind them, disguised though they are with our national names in whatever country they find themselves, the same tribal entity

By the time the global child they have created, in conjunction with Shabbat goy Western 'leaders', falls off the Globohomo assembly line, this child may well be lost to your loving influence. But well-fired up and conversant with the UN and various global media intentions for them. This transformation is intended to be continuous, until *they* are nothing. As referred to in this work, this *they* are us!

Transcendent

There is nothing in school now that is by its own nature transcendent. No teacher or practice or lesson has any intent or possibility of introducing any sacred meaning, sense of mission, superior reality, the wonder and mystery of our existence. As an institution of such relevance and impact in our children's lives, schools should be imbued with the transcendent, as a balance to their functional and bureaucratic elements. With their spiritual sense starved and their souls not anchored in beliefs that nourish, we should not be surprised at the drift and confusion that underlies the ineffable sadness in our children. The loss of the transcendent is also the loss of ancestral relevance. And if we don't revere our ancestors, they will not be able to protect us – why should they?

Transmitter

Sub-dermal surveillance chipping has already been proposed, and not sarcastically, as a benefit for your child, Sold, of course, as a necessary safety and security service. You'll be able to track your child all the way to school, because you'll need to as society end game approaches. For example, should the school be subject to a terrorist attack, the chip may be crucial in identifying remains, or should social services need your child's their exact location to quickly remove them from your care, following an anonymous tip-off regarding reported Badthink.

This tracking will later prove useful in your child's adult life should they need to be suddenly arrested for some reason or no reason. And if it proves necessary (possibly on account of you being their parent) for them to be denied banking or medical services, or otherwise excluded from benefits and privileges due to loss of status.

A worrying feature of this development is that some pupils (Swedes, early teens) welcomed this development as a convenient way of accessing new apps, determining the route to the nearest kebab shop or gaining entry to a nightclub. Soon they'll be able to vote for this.

Who is to track the trackers, has not been confirmed yet. Perhaps your big brother could do it.

Trauma-Informed Practice

A new CPD course for helping the practitioner better provide pastoral care and be legally mindful of handling certain situations with trauma impacted children. Especially recommended when the class role includes: children affected by war, national transitioning, gender transitioning, violent abusive parents, transferal bullying, assorted challenging family circumstances and sexual abuse. A simple ambition to be a teacher, it seems, replaced with a journey into hell. When will this end, you wonder? Only with the eschaton!

Trauma-informed, it's got its own dash as it's now a common noun; Lexicographical progress – it's still progress!

Tray Bakes

Ref: staffroom snacks.

For an institution that places so much emphasis on healthy eating and lifestyle choices, the proportion of staff who are one tray of donuts and a wine box away from a gastric band shows irony at party pack level. And if hypocrisy too, this is from the banquet menu.

This is not persecuting the obese, nor 'fat shaming' inspired by cruelty, but a matter of life and death.

Promoting monster-sized models and fat acceptance is promoting infertility and degeneration and deceit; for no one thinks such plus + plus sized people are beautiful. Signs of reproductive fitness are a real thing, and teachers who support or template the opposite, unwittingly help legitimise, however slightly, the ongoing transformation of some pupils into puny, soft monsters with sad and poisoned spirits, flirting with metabolic disease.

Who would have thought it; tray bakes are the enemy.

Trends

Trends in education; growth mindset, metacognitive learning, target based, learning journals, etc, etc. They come, they go, just like the fashion in clothes. And this is best how to think of all the new ideas that arrive into education station by the vanload. They claim legitimacy and scientific endorsement, but in fact their evidence is just their marketing leaflets. Finally, the real deal! – but they always claim this. And the rush to buy them by department heads, is no more thought through than a teenager's need for 911s. However, unlike passing fashions, where you can look back at old photos of yourself in double flares or arseless shorts and laugh, knowing that all you've lost in keeping with the trend is money, the educational trend leaves proper victims behind. These being the system itself, forever adapting to the latest big thing and never able, therefore, to have a settled pedagogy and curriculum, and of course the pupils as the unwitting eternal subjects of this shifty, overload experiment in their education.

It is well-established that a settled system of instruction is the key to educational success, and yet our masters will not allow this.

Good parents, when something new turns up, doubt its utility, you won't be disappointed.

Triple Threat

Ref: health and nutrition

Processed carbohydrates, sugar and seed (so-called, vegetable) oils. This represents a clear and present danger to our children. And doubly so, as most of the toxic calories within the triple threat are presented as health giving, especially within school. The danger to their near future can be readily ascertained by a quick visual examination of any group of teenagers you come across.

It is a great paradox that this calorie excess of toxically convenient foods represents as great a threat to future adult health as that suffered historically by children whose families were pauperised.

Truly Understand

Referencing apportioning blame and acknowledging gratitude.

The what and why of your education is only truly understood when one is very far along life's road. It's always too late for the who.

Trust

This was once a default given to the teacher by virtue of their professional competence. Now the trust default is in anti-form – distrust. Trust can be won back by the teacher, of course, but it's a temporary prize, liable to be instantly removed for any and no reason. Such is the current nature of our education system, that there is no prospect of this situation changing in our lifetime, except for the worse. The source of this distrust, is people NOT like yourself, Dear Reader.

With the dilution of trust, relationships become increasingly transactional. This development feeds itself, leading to more complaints, leading to further distrust, *ad nauseum*.

Truth

To those who set the agenda for our schools, there is no truth except that which promotes their progressive narrative. Pedagogy is bent to this will, any falsehood, absurdity, dysfunction, betrayal of children, even the most obvious lies, are permitted so long as they further this cause.

With respect to pupils, one would think that the need to tell them the truth would be a prerequisite to effective teaching and a proper relationship. However, nothing is further from the truth than this truism. A candid word with the best of intentions, thoughtfully delivered, may contain the potential for improvement and gratitude from the pupil, but absolutely will contain the potential for a sacking. Empowered and bitter malcontents are waiting for just such an occurrence which will be twisted out of recognition, and presented as a cruel attack on a child. In this situation, you will be unlikely to be supported by school management and absolutely not by council education HQ, especially should the complainer be among the approved categories of malcontents. It is a most shameful thing when a child eventually hears the truth from someone who hates then, because those who cared for them had to cover it up. What sort of truth is this, where it cannot be said for fear?.

TV

Our journey to total screen life started off in the 1950's with so much hope and excitement, but it was those cast-out, derided prophets who saw how this would end that have been unfortunately vindicated. For what pours out from your TV is seldom edifying; you know this. However, the degeneracy and social pathologies shovelled into your living room are orders of magnitude more corrupting to young minds less equipped to filter them. Such material does what it is intended to do, it culturally degrades and spiritually poisons. It is not enough for the parent to disingenuously claim that their child only gets to watch 'good' things, for the sewage seeps everywhere. You know this too.

If we consider TV's influence through a spiritual lens, admittedly not a commonplace these days, then we see, in its ability to misdirect and stymie our search for a higher order of our lived life, what a tragedy this device is. We think we are watching it for information and entertainment, but pouring out from it for hours a day is the equivalent of instructions in the service of a wider project. Many are beginning to sense this project darkly lurking behind the curious demographics displayed in adverts, the relentless dystopian focus of news items or the racial and sexual transformation of our history. One, of course, forgets what has been watched, but one's soul does not forget how it has been unwittingly changed by all this watching – so much more your child!

Another aspect of particular importance to parents is the potential of TV to rewire infant brains to preference bright primary colour visuals, constant movement and sound, and endless frame shifts; these being the staple background to children's TV. It is not possible to concentrate if one's attention, as a default, is constantly interrupted like this. This is a form of addiction that has been scientifically linked to short attention span and poor impulse control as a behavioural consequence It can hardly be surprising, therefore, that this effect can predispose certain individuals to ADHD-type conditions.

Channelling the prophet Jeremiah, the tele is the principle means of our enemies setting their agenda; bringing cultural sewage directly into our lives, providing degenerate behavioural templates, adoring foolish and even depraved celebrities – all serving to shape our opinions as consumers and social-zombies. Our family spirit is being killed and our precious time on this living Earth is being stolen by this addiction to a life lived in a rectangle. Popular media culture is depraved and is depraving our children in turn, with damage which persists into adulthood and then parenthood. Kill the TV in your life before it is too late!

Jeremiah goes to the city gate and asks the people there: *My people, what thoughts have came into your head NOT by television?* And the people answer by saying,…nothing.

NB. Older readers may have a sense that TV has become more stupid and vulgar as the years have went by. However, they may also wonder about the truth of this. Luckily, we can set their mind at rest; the various dysgenic and dyscivic forces at work on our intelligence, habits and cultural appetites have indeed served to lower our general intelligence (as measured by IQ) and TV has more than happily responded with dumbed down garbage to appeal to this lower common denominator. It's not your memory playing a trick, TV really is worse, but with bigger and better tech.

Twitter

The crystal meth of social media; with its imbecilic content, public shaming, echo chambers, dopamine dispensing, spyware and data-harvesting; it's got everything the digital idiot drone likes. Their controllers like it too; life chopped up into an endless stream of trivial and disjointed encounters at 140 or less characters – no wonder so many can't think straight to see where they are being led. *Yeah, just follow the likes and smileys,…over there. To where the cliff edge is,…that's right, keep going!*

In the war against teachers and schools, Twitter is 100% enemy territory. Many schools, drugged into believing that they are keeping up to date, acquiesce in their own degradation via their Twitter account.

Being the staple diet of many teachers, such teacher- twitterists bring themselves down to the level of their enemies, and pupils. Imagine the dignity, accorded and deserved, that is due to a teacher-Twitter-fiend; why should a parent Twitter-fiend or teeny pupil twitterist regard such a teacher as an inspirational template of higher culture when they live in the same social media clownscape? They don't.

U

UN

An evil force in our children's welfare. Who is this that speaks for parents, taking to itself the right to address their welfare? Who gave this mega bureaucracy the right to present themselves as the doorway to a new created world of justice? With endless refugees, infinite negroes and rainbow signs everywhere, this doorway is for us a trapdoor to the world's basement.

Good parents, see behind the multiplicity of political catchwords and well-intentioned claims fronted by celebrity hypocrite-dupes, it is not an accident of selection that such 'ambassadors' are professional entertainers working at high level in the most corrupt and vanity drenched industry in the world; they do not speak from knowledge, piety or love. Know that the UN is a cesspit of venality and waste and that it is a totally owned shopfront for the globalist plans of a new world order. A world to be achieved by leverage through your child.

Underprivileged

The new euphemism applied to children of a rubbish parent, or rubbish parents, in the unlikely event that there are two of them. The lack of privilege comes from the parent, although this can never be mentioned (not even here!), but the consequence of attempting to correct this parental shortfall falls on everyone else. As it has been discovered by educational experts, the best way of solving the low educational level of underprivileged youngsters is to just lower the educational levels all round. That way everyone passes. Success, the underprivileged results are now just as good as everyone else's. Except they're not.

Unfukt

This can never happen in the world we've created. Every attempt has resulted in merrfukt.

Ungiven

Ref: advice regretfully withheld, but realistically ungivable:

You are eating badly, that's why you are so fat.

Smash your i phone and throw it in the bin. It's making you stupid.

Don't ever drink stuff that again.

I'm not going to help you because you don't deserve it.

You are being deceived by that charity. Do not support them.

Everything that the head teacher said at the assembly is not true.

Come with me if you want to live.

UNICEF

A guilt distribution service operated as a franchise by the UN for the Bilderberg boys and their various tribal friends in global investment and nation-destroying banking. Everywhere it interferes it disrupts local culture and makes things worse; generating gigantic loans, funding inappropriate pre-doomed projects, massive purchase programmes of favoured (via backhanders) products, creating false jobs for its Western operatives and their traitor native sepoys – who are abandoned when the money runs out. Indeed, much of this UN inspired economic and cultural activity in Third World countries can be considered a wealth transfer scam, but not to the Third World countries; instead to the very organisations that are often behind the dysfunction and misery in the first place.

Luckily, Congo *et al* doesn't pay much attention to UNICEF pronouncements and only tolerates them for the baksheesh; however, if UNICEF just stole and otherwise wasted our donated billions that would be the least of our problems. For UNICEF has a bigger ambition focussed on our children by playing a major role in proselytising for anti-racism, diversity and other globalist ideologies. Its entire operation has as its ultimate focus the destruction of the Western family, hence its active role in promoting the replacement of the European population by refugee males. The rights it ever reminds us of, are directed against us, for our families generally never needed them defined like this. The flag flies at the school gate ever reminding you of social justice, the means whereby this destruction will be achieved:

Hey UNICEF, send your flags somewhere else. Africa's always looking for loincloths.

UNICEF Level 2 Rights Respecting School Report

It is always a great source of shame when a primary school fails a UNICEF self-abasement test and loses their UN flag of peace and love.

SCHOOL FAIL AS FOLLOWS:

No safe sex lunchtime club

Too much toxic whiteness

School logo racist

White people style homework issued

Janitor is a man and white (2 strikes)

No racists' detention room

No evidence of Whites 'taking the knee'

No monument to the Black victims of slavery*

Not enough money sent to Africa

Lack of posters promoting homosexualism

Insufficient trans-toilets

Insufficient safe spaces in playground

Menu not yet entirely kosher, halal or vegan

Boiled monkey dishes not offered

Universal Deceit

We have been fated to be born into a period of universal deceit. This finds strongest expression in our schools, which are simultaneously victim and perpetrator.

---

* As for white victims of Barbary and Ottoman slavery. ☺

Unnecessary

This applies to almost every technology and idea introduced in the last two generations. I say 'almost' as I recall approving of the concept of having a spelling parrot in class, although in practice he would undermine my authority by correcting me, maddeningly so, as he was often wrong. Being a former navy bird, some of his language was rather salty for P3.

NB. Excluded from this consideration are those initiatives that were glaringly idiotic (e.g., brain gym, SEAL maths, friendship targets) and the satanically-inspired global takeover contained with the Curriculum for Excellence.

Updates

This is why Twitter is a vital part of modern education.

HEAD TEACHER UPDATE NOV 16TH 2018

Good afternoon Parents & Carers. What a busy and fun week. Great learning across the school with a particular focus on promoting kindness & respect to others during anti-bullying week.

Our school values are RESPECT, EXCELLENCE & FRIENDSHIP. Our motto of #Krammondcares permeates all we do with a strong school culture of mutual respect developed through focus class work and parental support.

Imagine an HT writing this? And they did! What rejoinder can one supply to this, other than: *I am amazed and know not what to say!* This even outclowns Clown World. Either this head teacher is a meister-level ironist, or the ba's burst and the game's a bogey. You decide; I know that you know that this is a rhetorical question.

PS. *More good news, Parents. We've just received a report from the Head of Education; vodka production is at a ten year high and so we will increase the teacher daily ration from 75ml to 50ml.*

Us

It used to be just us in a class. And so, as a teacher, you could say 'us' in a lesson, meaning just that.

Now it's them and them and them. And in your mind, because you know it's already in theirs as a default, you now think, 'them and us.' And the simple 'us', that was once a commonplace and so unrecognised, we can see – now that it is gone – what it really is; a wonderful sense of community and national identity. A rightful belonging!

In a class context, very carefully consider (beforehand) the use of 'us'. 'Them' are not often respecters of 'us', or our pedigree.

V

Value of Education

As we approach the zenith of our current trajectory within school education, we also approach a near zero value state school education. Our pupils leave school devoid of much useful knowledge, turned away from the uplifting and prideful that could and should have been imparted, misdirected with false values, exposed to hypocrisies and encouraged to adopt crippling psychological disabilities as victims or oppressors.

True, they learn to read and write, although generally this skill is acquired without developing a love of the former; however, a parent could teach them both easily enough if they wished. Or get someone they trust to do it if they didn't have the time. Although they probably do.

Values

Typically co-joined with *Our.*

This is not the values of stable families, or productive and balanced people, but a phrase under which sexual and social alternatives are proselytised. Your own replacement as a people also falls under this rubric as rights, justice and tolerance.

Inculcating the correct values is why we go to school. In our time, these can be best expressed by the highest representative of such values; a mixed race, refugee, gender fluid, post op tranny, lesbian fruitarian feminist traumatised prejudice survivor. Ideally they would work as a human rights lawyer, importing more of the same for childless gay couples or conglomerates of such.

Formerly, such idealised Western values were love of land, respect for institutions and elders, and sense of fair play and community that extended beyond the immediate and family; all these the foundations of our essentially democratic political culture. In but a few generation, these have changed beyond recognition.

With respect to the school expression of this phenomenon, this is best and simplest summed as; you cannot tell native stock children that they have many reasons to be proud of their ancestors, that their race is imbued with greatness, that God is in them and that they have a right to their own land. But you can tell them it's ok pump themselves full of opposite sex hormones and then cut off their penis or breasts, celebrate the destruction of their culture and patrimony as a victory for justice, and to be ashamed for basically anything and everything.

Banner rolls of 'values' are the enemy of actual values, which never need paraded. Lifted from the school website, this says it all:

Our school is developing superhero characters for each of the learning muscles and linking them to 'Lifelong Learning' and our school values of tolerance, equality and compassion.

Values are the infection vector for the destruction of an organisation. And its people.

Vector of Infection

This is the means whereby an organism, organisation or institution is destroyed. In the case of schools this is achieved by introducing values, such as diversity, inclusion and equity (DIE), whose end effect is to divert and degrade the original learning mission. Hence DIE is die – the world's most apt acronym! Such vectors are funded and mandated by policy or law, so that they cannot be resisted. Once a critical point is reached, recovery is impossible. Like a virus capturing a cell, an infected school can only stamp out clones of itself. Infection usually starts in the head and initially involves well-meaning tweets and website mission statements, hubristic ambitions (e.g., teaching world peace) and delusion quickly follow.

Learn to recognise your enemies; Tolerance, Equality, Progress, Inclusivity, Multiculturalism, Compassion and Diversity are infection vectors of The Narrative. If you support, by tweet, statement or silence, any of those things in any capacity, or even if you permit any of those things, your school will be converged and destroyed. Along with your privileged child.

Remedy is none, except fire.

Verboten

typically signed as ☠ Verboten ☠

Children's classics in English, positive reference to European heritage, high culture in any form, plain speaking, talking about things that boys like, e.g., racing cars, war, football. And scepticism regarding new initiatives.

Victim

Everyday our schools help us identify victims and perpetrators. Our lessons help us realise that everyone can claim to be a victim and book their place on the victim stack. Everyone, that is, except our current actual and definite future victims, who must pay reparations, psychological and financial, for just being born what they are; too trusting, too future oriented, too orderly and above all, too pale.

What genuine victims actually learn is helplessness, that 3rd party intervention – which, as it invariably involves women talking, seldom fixes the problem, while denying you the right to apply your own solution. The problem and the misery, then, just kicked further down the road, while also demonstrating an easy betrayal by adults. Later, a failure of wisdom by such adults will also be understood.

Victimology demands that society's resources flow in reverse merit (and gross disproportion) to the greedy, the parasite, the schemer, the inept, the unhinged, the professional complainer, the bipolar and the morally reprehensible.

There are real victims, life is full of them. They are not helped by any of this.

Victimhood

Children are being conditioned at an early age to view themselves reflexively as victims—and to succumb to the temptation, common to all people, to blame others for their problems. Unfortunately, no attitude interferes more with success, happiness, productivity and a sense of control in one's life. No attitude raises a greater barrier to mature adulthood; whatever comfort is derived in the short term is reversed, with interest, in the long term. White students are also being harmed by intentional exclusion from this hallowed club, obviously this should be considered a blessing, except that their exclusion is predicated on their identification as the source of others' victimhood.

Somebody should call a social worker to sort out this mess. If ever their professional insight and moral courage was needed it is here. ☺

Victimhood Battles

Similar to the old world original victim battles, societal bullying, pogroms and the various forms of psychological terrorism, the new world version is the same except gender is the issue over which the new humanish forms battle it out for top spot on the victimhood list.

Lezzies used to top trump it over homos (as they packed a 'weapon' and patriarchy privilege), but now various tranny forms are overtaking from the rear (so to speak). Pitching former allies against allies, the final roster will not be posted until all 68 sides run out of poison for their tweets. Current rankings (posted in school staff rooms across Scotland) for the top five are:

1. Twin boom tail;

2. Fixed undercarriage with trike landing gear;

3. Retracting undercarriage, but identifying as fixed landing gear;

4. Bubble canopy;

5. Single intercooler for supercharger, sometimes deceptively presenting as double, the extra one is merely an empty supercharger casing.

This battle is not helped by all sides variously claiming Shakespeare, Napoleon, Queen Victoria and Freddie Mercury as one of their own. They've even put Nietzsche, ffs, on the gay flotilla!

Victimarian

Those to whom we must take the knee.

The preferred identity, alas entry to this prestigious group is melanised. Token and temporary identity may be sponsored by the media and then perhaps conferred on sex switchers and various forms of non-heterosexual.

Every day we better learn how wounded egos, twisted by jealousy, have a limitless capacity to drive victim identity politics through everything we hold dear. Victimarians are now legion in our schools, and although these are still in immature form, they have seen on TV and social media how it is to be for us and them. They do not properly know what they actually want, as they are still children, but they instinctively know that it somehow connects with your happy child having everything that makes them happy become extinguished.

Victim of the Year

[An expectant hush falls over the assembly hall, a single spotlight falls on the stage.]

Awarded to: *The envelope please.*

The wailing and gnashing of teeth will be heard across the land. No, literally. Lawsuits to follow the award ceremony. # wrongvictim@ awardstoowhite

Vigilance

Now we see that the warnings about the requirement for this to be constant were true. Hardly a moments grace occurs on relaxation before parasites and destroyers attack. And things we care about most can be swept away in half a generation. Check with the Swedes for a practical example.

Virtual and Video Games

More digital crack cocaine for our kids.

Some tech-addled teacher-idiots have claimed such games are a useful teaching tool, apparently believing that they develop mathematics knowledge, hand-eye coordination and critical thinking skills (whatever that is). Further claiming that meatworld interaction is also improved by the sense of belonging attendant on being a member of the online community. Those schools that have went full-retard on this – admittedly popular with pupils – approach, have found their pupils significantly behind in all the skills they were hopefully enhancing; it seems that the virtual world does not better replace human interaction. Imagine the level of idiocy one must inhabit to require learning this basic truth.

In a disgrace beyond conscience, this type of shilling for global ICT finds further ready outlet in the various professional and council publications aimed at teachers and parents. Again and again, these lies are repeated as a preparation for injecting kids into the virtual reality that is ruining our lives as adults. Too many children already live in this mad world, and the last thing they need is more virtual game time in school. And more legitimising of this choice. This is entertainment for babysitting purposes and nothing more. Nothing more, that is, except brainwashing.

Aside for rewiring our children's minds as fusion operators of ICT products, all these games have a negative effect on traditionally taught subjects and on effective learning. Children are expecting lessons to be like their video games, and increasingly need to learn in this way. Luckily, our ICT mega corp overmasters can provide just the right material. The lessons, prepared and approved in advance by the Borg or Skynet, become what TV already is.

Virtual Support

Offered with each innovation and running at 101% efficiency. As it always is!

CPD DRONE: ...*and there's full digital virtual support package available.*

TEACHER: **Is there any actual support available?**

CPD DRONE: *What do you mean?*

Virtues

I see your Satanic intended values promoted and raise against them the four cardinal virtues of prudence, justice, fortitude and temperance. Help to focus on acquiring these may be obtained by direct request to the relevant saint's icon. Each child can make their own prayer

Alternatively, for those pupils whose sensibility is more Hellenistic, a little classroom shrine can be set up to *Arete*, the homely Greek goddess of virtue, who exemplifies the qualities she represents without the need to pontificate.

Virtue Signalling

A virtue signalling arms race is taking place in our schools. All the values that propaganda organically links to the need for females and fe-males to signal how good they are, find fullest expression in schools. The adults tweeting and 'encouraging compassion' among their charges, and our children forced, but as willing as they are unwitting, to join in the cheering. Showing the world, so they think, how good and caring they are.

The teachers, management and visiting adults involved in this collective hysteria literally don't know what they are doing, cannot think recursively, nor conceive that such action could ever be viewed negatively; both as a clear substitute for personal integrity and a hostile psychological act against the children they think they are enlightening and empowering. This is the power of the female hive mind revealed as it truly is, utterly invulnerable.

Virtue signallers gotta virtue signal! And they will virtue signal you and your children until you and them are wiped off the face of the Earth. Then those they virtue signal for will turn on them for the traitors they are. It may be a small comfort to know that they will earn no grace or favour at that final judgement for their highly visible, attention-seeking goodness. Such behaviour is the opposite of piety or charity, and he who knows, knows.

Acta deos numquam mortalia fallunt

Voight-Kampff Test

Currently being rolled out across the primary school community by equity officers to identify pedagogic apostates or trad-replicants among teachers, and then code them for a Level One removal. A typical beginning question enquires after the best recent CPD; the assumption that there will be a selection of 'best' really flushes out false conversions.

At least, you'll know the interview has taken a wrong turn when you're asked: *Tell me about your mother, did she approve of you becoming a teacher?*

W

Walking

This was invented (giving Africans credit here) quite a long time ago and, along with standing still, was a defining feature of our species. However, nature is not wasteful and removes from the skill set what is not needed. Thusly, we find children who literally cannot walk properly; by this I mean, cannot walk properly. Atrophied by couch and computer life, their weakly muscled, but well-bulked, frames struggle to maintain an upright posture and provide efficient locomotion. The result is a somewhat boneless posture and waddling gait for the boys and a lazy sleaziness for the girls. This effect is continued on stopping, where leaning is required, as if against a tree or lamppost. And sitting also poses a physical challenge, such children requiring a sofa.

The obvious solution is route marches and standing meditation. Surprisingly, most children enjoy doing this. At some deep cognitive level below consciousness, they understand that they need this; hence their willingness.

Who would have thought that for some children the lesson most needed at school is to learn how to walk?

War

In the end all this debate about education; the curriculum content, the values, the pedagogic practice, the funding preferences, the political correctness, the metastasising regulations and the ruthless enforcement of orthodoxy, peels away to reveal the deeper war on the traditional White family. School is the battlefield, teachers are the mercenaries and your children the cannon fodder.

Warnings, Dire

Regarding the situation our schools are in, such warnings carry more authority in Latin; *eradicatæ, finis, exitium, terminantur, malum, exterminarent.*

Finis educationem.

Actually, forget about the dire warnings. Literally, no one is listening to them anymore.

Water

See, hydration strategy, toilet strategy, parent complaints regarding, UN mandates, human rights, African children dying of thirst, School Asian Village Water Appeal, leeching plastic concern, female hormone contaminated groundwater, too wet without a biscuit complaint.

In the past, kids would have a drink at playtime and never during the lesson, except by special request. As I recall, very few died of dehydration as a result of this policy, but nevertheless the dry cruelty imposed on pupils forced the UN to decree the humble drink of water as a human right. In Scottish primary schools, this right is now rigorously enforced by the Blue Helmets (currently Bangladeshi and Wakandan brigades) with the happy result that the school day is best thought of, not as a series of lessons, but as a series of toilet breaks.

The constant toilet breaks, spilled water, water bottle mix ups and requests for bottle top-ups, although somewhat injurious to lesson progress, are a small price to pay for properly hydrated pupils. It is now rare for a pupil to drop down dead of dehydration during lessons, except during 3rd World Reality Day, when pupils are denied water in order to sympathise with the plight of dusty Ethiopians; it's a sacrifice, but worth it for the global lesson learned.

Honestly, this hydration madness is an indulgence too far. The bottle fidgeting and hydration too and fros is the child equivalent of thumb sucking or smoking, constantly breaking concentration and allowing the same as a cop-out for those children who really should be focusing on perseverance. Still, as noted, it beats a child literally dying of thirst. And this is why our FM (First Mummy) pledged the government to reduce even further child hydration deaths in Scottish schools.

SEVERELY DEHYDRATED PUPIL: *I need to go and top up my water bottle.*

TEACHER: *But you did this just ten minutes ago and ten minutes before that. And the bottle is still full. Why don't you finish question one first.*

BANGLADESHI UN BLUE HELMETS HYDRATION ENFORCEMENT STORMTROOPER: আপনি একটি শিশুর মানবাধিকার লঙ্ঘন করছেন। আপনার হাত আপ এবং দূরে রাখুন। আমাকে গুলি করতে বাধ্য করো না। তোমার কি কোন সিগারেটে আছে?

(Trans: *You are violating a child's human right. Put your hands up and back away. Don't force me to shoot you. Have you any cigarettes for me?*)

Weaponised

1. Against the teacher; pupils, parents, management, press, government, council HQ, professional bodies, admin department, progressive community, feminists, radicals, malcontents, academics, policy experts, social workers, educational psychologists, lawyers, failures and frauds (where not already cover by any of the former).

2. Against the pupil; water, peanuts, playground, snacks, educational psychologists, pedagogy, entertainment, tolerance and Newsround.

We Didna Ken!

At that moment and at that time, at last standing alone: *We thought we were raising the enlightened child of the 21st century. We thought we were doing our part in setting the history record straight. We didn't realise that we were sacrificing our child to the globalist homofuture. We just didn't know what we were doing.*

And God replies: *Weel, ye ken noo!*

Wellness

The feminine finds its hysterical definitional outlet in this concern-fad for the teacher's 'holistic, total well-being.' Concern meaning apparent concern. Here we find exaggerated solicitudes, coddled sensibilities and hollow phrases all coming together in a workshop (yes, this must have been a surprise!) which delivers less than nothing. It has been well proven that such wellness programmes have just below zero impact on employee health, habits or medical utilisation. This is what passes as the employer valuing your health. Or rather, this is the value they place on it.

They could give a pay bonus or a Christmas crate of wine to make staff feel better about things – instead they pay mega-shekels for a wellness coordinator.

O, hateful fiends that mock our station in life and joyfully torment us so!

Never one to let a useless idea go to waste before it has done maximum damage, educational leaders have encouraged that wellness be included in the curriculum. Not wellness as such, just talking about it. This will help remind children about not being well, and how stress can make them not well, and that they may have it without knowing, just like their parents. You will wonder how is reminding children of illness contributing to them feeling well; it isn't. This false delicacy of supposed concern actually creates the worry that steals the 'well' in wellness. This, of course, nicely dovetails with all the verbiage surrounding victimhood culture and the mental health crisis in primary children. This is where it comes from, the feminine obsession with talking about problems, which is talking about self. If they want to talk themselves ill, then that's their affair. But they should allow the boys to opt out of such classes, as this is toxic to their masculinity. Let them have football or stick fighting, and leave this babbling to the babblers.

Weltanschauung

That engendered by our primary school system;

In my life I have never been able to envision anything worth looking forward to. Everything bad in the world seems to be my fault and my parents, as we see every day in school. I have nothing to contribute to this civilisation, and nobody will mourn my passing. I will leave behind no children. People like me should be allowed to opt out.

Wey...Haay!

[Alan Breck Stewart faces the precipice and a fearful choice, leap or die]

...with no possibility of retreating except to fall into the cruel arms of his foes, Alan realised that he had to attempt the leap across the cataract. It was a fearful prospect with jagged rocks and the swirling mad rush of the water meeting failure. Hanged or drowned, he thought, the rebel's choice comes to this eventually. Without thinking further, he took a short sprint and then a mighty leap off the ledge and into the air,... *Wey....haay!* Drowned it was then?

[The supply teacher, standing before their assigned class...]

What Happens Next?

Ref: in the story of our children and their schools.

I don't know. But it is not getting better soon.

What's Wrong?

We promote children's rights, encourage them to be activists, pretend to value their childish opinions, empower them by law and point out our societal failings, and then wonder why our pupils are lippy and resentful. And the school has gone to buggery.

White Guilt Week

Set between Holocaust and Gay World Weeks, this is the most important guilt-fest in the school year.

Prepping White children for their future, this week explores various forms of humiliation and self-destruction. Top Cultural Marxists run workshops and radical theatre presentations discussing or performing by mime the 'final solution' to the White supremacism. Sometimes such final solution poster workshops, or eradication interpretive dance, can get a little intense for the infants and they have to be reminded to check their White privilege or go somewhere else if they don't like it here anymore.

The WGW credo:

Your skin is white.
You're guilty and deserve your fate.
Leave the electricity, indoor plumbing
and the i phone next to the microwave
on the way out.

White Man

The source of all our woes. The inventor of oppression and everything bad. Thankfully this is changing and the White man is finding his allotted place; see 'whipping post' and 'permanently cancelled'. We look around the world and everywhere we see this pale, ill-starred creature and his works replaced, we see that things are better; better in a special stabby, bomby, lawsuity, street garbage, broken toilets sort of way. Our schools preach this betterment, in the event that the pupils cannot see it with their eyes.

See Sweden for practical examples of such betterment.

White Privilege

1. Thinking people know that there is no such thing as it is presented by the useful idiots in the employ of the subversives; and, if it has any coherent meaning, it signals excellence and achievement on the one hand, and inchoate envy and resentment born of felt cultural inferiority on the other. It was invented when it became apparent that the term 'racist', could be better applied to races other than White – and this could not be permitted.

In the school situation, we understand that the obsession with 'white privilege' indicates an effort to leverage minority advantage and to blame any academic shortfall on institutional racial bias; again with a view to leveraging school, and later employment, advantage. This advantage is justified by appeals to equity; here really meaning the bending of reality, by diktat and policy, to ensure that ethnic others enjoy advantages above their merit level, and to the detriment of native Whites who have their merited entitlements removed to enable the transfer. Such equity is, then, actually a form of racial theft. And White privilege is nothing more than a mask for racial identity politics; obviously, it undermines a school's educational mission.

The media elites and their political bedfellows have sought to place racism at the forefront of public consciousness, not as a problem to be addressed through mutual understanding, but rather as an evil that must be eliminated by means of the harshest measures. The unrelenting focus on skin colour expressed through the White privilege meme is, however, only the leading edge of a larger ideological campaign to shape pupils' attitudes and beliefs on a range of issues all connected with White disempowerment and displacement. It is a full out war against us Whites, and will eventually prove to be hardly less so to other races. And to those that peddle this wickedness to our children: *Get thee gone, and go fill another room in hell!*

Unfortunately, as Whites, we are genetically coded to be sympathetic, if not beholden, to societal principles of fair play, and by this same imperative, left open to exploitation by gaming groups.

2. approx. 15 + IQ points

Whole School Policy

The cliché by which propaganda is consistent across the school from year to year; and by which guilt, confusion and pressure rolls on from class to class in the pupil's journey from infant to top form. And in the teacher's journey to breaking point.

Ruinous ideas and practices get converted to permanent school culture by Whole School Policy. For example, the relentless focus on racism and intolerance is thusly enabled:

'The Future Justice suite of documents provides clear, practical advice for teachers to ensure that pupil awareness of systemic racism, in both school and wider society, is consistent from class to class and year to year. Schools must strive to maintain the focus on the continuing struggle for a racially just and equitable world, as per CfE outcomes. See section 4, level 2 (a-f) of Learning for Justice and Tolerance'.

P1: During Slave Trade Week (as part of Black History Month) making paper chains and little string whips to symbolise White oppression. Make little cotton plants to pick (straws and cotton wool), but have the ethnic children as overseers. Video 'cotton picking' and post on school website.

P2: Mock auctions held each term with Whites to be slaves for a day to ethnic children. Each 'slave day' ending with a symbolic whipping, or an actual whipping (subject to official approval).

P3: Whites excluded from the bathroom for the academic year.

NB. Only the Atlantic slave trade is referenced (minus Jewish involvement). The historical and currently ongoing African and Muslim slave trade is not mentioned, ever – no one knows why this is the case.

Wisdom

Our primary schools are institutionally stupid, as if managed by sociopathic spendthrift idiots. And in the classroom, so many ideas and practices run straight against instinct and intuition. This calls for the compensatory exercise of wisdom, whose presence one would hope is found among the staff. Hopefully, but alas! The wise have no voice in this forum. This situation not only denies the institution the balance it needs, but the pupil the opportunity of turning daily accidents into lessons of deep importance.

The wise teacher, deep with gentle learning, is replaced by policy and the internet. Perhaps the age for such a person proffering advice and leading children to their best selves has passed, like the age of innocence or of heroes.

Witches

Ref: presence in school. Not your broomstick riding crone, but something much more insidious.

Beware the unfulfilled, childless, overweight and ageing woman. Her thoughts become complicated to her, and her feelings towards her opposite, the fulfilled, maternal and slimmer, become darker, and especially so at certain times of the month.

Such women may come to lead the lives of witches. Their thoughts towards other women, teachers, mothers or will-be mothers, random and resentful. Their thoughts towards men, planning revengeful, and towards your children and their future, not tender. This is why they are witches. They cannot, so far as I know, apply hexes to children or families whose happy loveliness painfully reminds them of their failures, but they can and do apply this criterion to every policy and practice which achieves the same end on a longer timescale. This is the 21st century witch, replacing potions with politics.

While they give the impression of concern, they are actually like the witch feeding up her caged child victim; it is not concern for their nutrition that leads her to offer them so much food.

Women Teachers

Ref: nature of, character and consequences

Women are the soul of a family and the keepers of the nation's culture. That is why Satan's children wish to destroy them.

Despite the wicked attentions of the patriarchy since Eve turned up in The Garden, this sex have found a little vegetable patch for themselves in primary teaching. Out of the sight of men, women have shown what they can do if given their head. The results speak for themselves.

Women have to follow rules, as they lack the creative insights of men. This predisposes them to groupthink and the enforcement of this. Not willing to risk being socially ostracised, then, women publicly avoid ideas which threaten this herd safety. This is why they try to increase their stock of respect by jumping on a trend, e.g., anti-racism or anti-Trumpism. Of course, in actuality the opposite is achieved, although they don't know this – as they are all clucking the same clucks. They are thus in schools, as they always have been in wider society, the enforcers of social norms. This has obvious consequences for the form and function of schools where women dominate, which is in all primary schools, without exception. Sometimes, this is to the advantage when such norms are family and national community focussed, but should they not be, as they not in our age, then we have a problem. Hence, the current dysfunction and political obsessions with multiculturalism, feminism and the other counter-culture themes which find their happy niche in school; in promoting such, either tacitly or directly, women teachers believe that they are responding to the facts of reality, but in actuality they are reacting to the stimuli of specifically focussed propaganda. Their female self-righteousness with regard to this proxy pussyhat activism in class demonstrates no self-awareness of the bossy inappropriateness of such behaviour. And typically, none is supplied by female school management, as they endorse the same.

Aside from the endless search for talking solutions and man blame, female excellence in schools is best displayed in management. This is where their ruthlessness, lack of loyalty, and ability to intrigue shines. A female HT can implement policy of extreme ridiculousness without qualm, sideline careers for reasons of secret female resentment and play teacher groups against each other. Ideally, blame can be transferred upwards to men, and consequence transferred downwards to inferiors, hopefully men too. The men need not be made aware of this, a cause of much delight in staffrooms. This is why, although generally not wanted, a certain number of men are needed in school for blame purposes, about 5% in staff presence is sufficient.

At the highest levels of management, where incompetence is more exposed, women still have the victim card to play. If no direct man is around as a patsy, then his virtual proxy, the patriarchy's glass ceiling, can suffice.

Primary teaching is now a woman's institution; as such, the teaching staff naturally express all the habits, ambitions, pressures and disappointments peculiar to women of our age. And because a woman is never unhappy alone…

It's not all negatives; women teachers are more likely to volunteer for work in an animal shelter, bring home-made tray bakes to the staffroom and possess peerless knowledge of TV game shows.

'At the first sign of difficulty, the common woman turns into a bitch. Whereas, the uncommon woman always was.' – Catherine the Great, Head Teacher of Russia.

Women Teachers, High IQ

Ref: fate of,

With their peerless combination of female-style (but useful) knowledge and insight, nicely paired with feminine instinct and sensibility, these are rare birds in the primary school. And a great asset, should there be any, for their ability to counter, with both female guile and intellectual rigour, their sex's typical weaknesses with respect to school practices and staffroom scuttlebutt.

Generally, they are treated as male equivalents. And although they bring more tension to the system, through female-female resentment, the impact of this is lessened by their better reading of this situation and, unlike the men, tendency to move on to better paid and less stressful alternatives; prison officer is a popular alternative career, as is setting up their own consultancy businesses. Some even become mothers; although there's even a debate about whether this is progress – wasting all these brains having high IQ children for a future society, instead of sticking it to men by having a successful career.

Working Memory

It's not rocket science, it's brain science.

That portion of brain power that is free on the point of introduction to a new idea, to actually engage with this new idea. This is obviously a limited resource, and so logically one should strive to de-clutter the introduction process of extraneous material and leave the working memory (in this case of a child in class) free to get on with the task of learning something new. A typical pupil, coming fresh to a new lesson, has a working memory of four to six items, or facts, that they can hold in their mind at the same time as they engage with the lesson. Use up this working memory before the new lesson has started and the child will struggle to understand what they are supposed to be learning, or properly focus on the task.

Of course, as we are talking about brain function which is hardly understood, even by brain scientists, this is just a metaphor, but it conforms to reality as we commonly experience it; don't give someone too many new things to do at the start of learning something new, or you'll confuse them.

And so, schools being what they are, this is what we do. Flying in the face of science, common sense and our own everyday experience, we, as mandated by pedagogic practice, clog up the minds of our pupils before the lesson has started with; targets consulted, learning powers to be activated, skill sets accessed, required group protocols,

Walts and Wilfs[*]; and so, as a consequence, their working memory is gone!

This is all supposed to help by making the lesson content and intention explicit. Certainly, to someone ignorant of the concept of working memory, this pre-lesson loading may create the impression of great thoroughness and intellectual endeavour, with all the learning bases touched, but really, it does the opposite.

Those children who can, eventually come to ignore all this pre-lesson excess and keep their working memory safe for the lesson. The others? That's why we have remedial.

Workload

For the conscientious teacher; gigantic.

For the unconscientious teacher; slightly less gigantic.

Workshop

No work done, and it's not in a shop.

In the make-job economy which parasites itself on teaching, all the false things have to be given names that pretend to legitimacy. The real name for teacher workshops would be 'waste of time female talking and virtue signalling class', or 'obviously stupid concept' or 'dyscivic propaganda' or 'absolutely useless garbage' or 'FFS!' Such candour does not attract funding. And is not welcomed in reviews of such workshops.

---

[*] Actually, these learning twins can be a useful mnemonic, if used sparingly. It tells the pupil what we are learning and what the teacher wants to see in completed work.

World of Reference

The sum total of the teacher's knowledge of the world and their own place in it, but derived independently of their training as teachers. Formerly, this would have been assumed to be that of a learned person acquired through their own schooling, personal reading of English language classics, hobbies and activities, extended family contacts and adult-forced activities such as piano lessons, church attendance, family chores, bedtime routines and parent discipline.

In modern times such teacher reference occupies an entirely different intellectual domain and set of skills and habits. These can best be summarised as media based, i phone dependent and fully integrated with all the best of modern attitudes. Deficiencies in certain multicultural areas, e.g., witchcraft, genital mutilation, tribal dance, making food dishes out of insects, etc, are in the process of being corrected within our curriculum.

Borrowing a term from the digital life now lived by the majority of our teachers, their minds have been hacked to become a biological version of the junk that lives in i phones.

World Peace

Such is the scale of the ambition of our leaders that this was proposed as a primary school topic to be studied with the intention of creating a future cadre of super Scottish diplomat-coonseellors who would put right the problems of the world by fair negotiation. Apparently, all the problems of the world, and especially the violent ones, are caused by a lack of understanding and negotiating skills. In all of history this has never been appreciated until Scottish politicians and public purse consultants pledged to empty your sporrans to create teacher workshops and classroom resources (at government rates). It's a small price to pay for fixing the world, creating a whole new industry of Scotch conflict fixers and, O, the glory.

That this project could fail and the hubris be self-mocking, and otherwise damaging to our children's sense of reality, has rightly not been considered.

PALESTINIANS: *This is our land. We've been here for thousands of years.*

ISRAELI SETTLER: **God gave us the land first, you Thief.**

PALESTINIAN: *No, he didn't.*

ISRAELI SETTLER: **Did so.**

SCOTCH WORLD PEACE TRAINED NEGOTIATOR: *Right, yous two. Baith o ye's, shut it! Enough o this nonsense or I'll send for Nicola, an she'll really pit yer gas at a peep. D'ye's fancy a kerry oot?*

World War Two

Soon to be once again a defining episode in British history. But this time battling for the minds of our children to maintain the narrative that underlies our post-war world view; Germans unspeakably evil, us good, but still carry big guilt for the Holocaust. Women apparently marginalised in this story, as they complain they still are, of course. Big lessons to be learned here, and to be taught by people that know nothing about it.

But the guilt for the Holocaust has to be made good somehow. We certainly don't want our children to just walk away from their guilt, they have to remember this; forever. Forever here is on a Hebraic timescale. And this is now why we study the war. Not for examples of a European catastrophe, or our national survival and fortitude, nor heroism, ingenuity or everyday courage. Nor some pride, however misplaced, in helping overcome a mighty foe. But only as justification for complaint, self-mortification and hate speech laws to be ever extended, to help catch smart-asses that don't quite exactly say the bad thoughts out loud, but you know that they have thought them. Then, for funding a Holocaust museum. Then, reminders about racism and homosexual persecution. Then regular Holocaust reminders about 'never again'. Then enforcement officers, then social ostracism and economic ruin, then fines, then the heavy knock on the door at 2am, then...*here we go again!*

Would've

and would have...

Mrs MacKay would have torn her hair out in shame had she heard one of her pupils say 'would of ...'

No child in P2 in 1990 would have made the grammatical error of recording the expanded and contracted form of would have=would've for the meaningless 'would of...' Now teachers promote it. Grammar Ezekiel prophesises where this is heading; English as we know it, is not heading, *à la* Star Trek, for the stars.

Prepare your sackcloth and ashes for the keening.

X

X

The preferred genotype in double form. Much hilarity is *en route* as numerous, non-standard genomes will be competing for the, formerly exclusively-sexed privilege of victimhood. And the nicer girls' toilets.

X Box

The modern equivalent for males of the public park, kick the can, tree climbing, getting chased by a big boy, hide and seek, hut building, Japs and Commandos, stone fights with intruders, road building for toy cars, climbing over walls, exploring derelict buildings and annoying girls.

Once puberty is reached one can transition to the same games with even more killing, but on an i phone.

X box is a vastly safer entertainment option, except for mental, physical, metabolic and spiritual health.

X Factor

see; teacher's world of reference.

The MSM equivalent of discussions of pedagogy and sharing good practice and resources. Also doubles, with Love Island, as a form of philosophic reflection on the social role of schools and society's trajectory.

X Men

The x man (or ex man) is the preferred form of male in primary teaching. You might think that primary schools would be great if all the x men were actually X men, but Wolverine would get chewed up just the same. His upper case reduced to lower, he would soon be just another x man. Super powers are wonderful to possess, but even they won't help you if a scheming pupil, unhappy single mum or back-stabbing management is out to destroy you because 'male.'

This entry could be considered a warning, or a threat, to any would-be X men thinking of a primary school teaching career – don't; stick to the easier option of fighting regular street mutants and homicidal maniacs.

Xenophobia

Although all we hear about is racism and complaints of not enough of *whatever*, in fact, never has the accusation of this universal attribute been more convincingly belied by our welcome to foreigners in our schools. The entire system bends over backwards; the vast majority of pupils go out of their way to be solicitous, and all teachers do everything they can to be personally welcoming. This welcome covering official policy, practical measures and most important of all, personal behaviours. The exact opposite of what is apparently alleged. Nausicaä would approve.

The complainers should get back on their raft and try some other shore.

Y

Yahweh

It's his school. Really. As Jeremiah prophesised:

This is what the Lord says: The path of the righteous teacher is beset on all sides by the wicked in thoughts and deeds. Blessed is our servant who guides their pupils from poisoned wells to pleasant pastures, and protects them from the wolves who would prey on them. They will receive our favour. The stiff necked who have not heeded our warning and have attempted to destroy our pupils I will pay in kind and strike them down in furious anger. Howling forever from the lake of fire they will beg for forgiveness, but I will not listen. And they will know my name is THE LORD when I lay my vengeance upon them.

Year Zero

With respect to the introduction of new programmes, initiatives, directives and pedagogies, it is always Year Zero.

No-one responsible for their introduction seems to have any knowledge of the same thing having already been already tried, often many times, and always found wanting. And so, the money wasted (stolen) before is destined to be wasted (stolen) again on the idiots, deceivers and parasites who live off the public purse, reselling Year Zero on an annual basis.

One realises that our education leaders have not understood that only the first part of *Jack and the Beanstalk* is true.

Young Lady, Young Gentleman

Re: entitlement to the appellation

This highest of accolades is only entitled insofar as it is cultivated. In the former, by the exercise of modesty and manifested self-respect. In the latter, by bravery and self-restraint. And in both cases, by personal kindness of heart and community spirit.

In this case, becoming is truly its own reward.

Z

Zola

We could do with him here in Scotland.

Here, Zola, what do you think of our education experts in Scotland?

J'accuse;

1. Your university departments of education, cognitive science and social policy of wasting teacher time and everyone's money.

2. In that it does not produce work of interest, relevance or utility.

3. And that for all the research papers, conferences, studies and recommendations, modern science-based teaching and learning, in comparison to old school intuition, intelligence and discipline, adds almost nothing to the teacher's box of tricks.

4. Indeed, pedagogy as a science is a fraud, unloved, ignored and only pretend accepted (in a practical act of hypocrisy) in the hope that, by making teaching a 'science-based' profession, it boosts the status of teachers themselves.

5. Of course, it doesn't. And anyway, teachers are scientifically ignorant and are not equipped intellectually, nor by inclination or training, to be able to properly consider the truth and value of the various pedagogical and policy arrivals.

6. All this accumulated junk science is cause and consequence of the institutional folly and bureaucratic morass that clogs the flow of wisdom upon which proper teaching is founded.

7. Your Heads of Service are lying gatekeepers for the above.

Les envoyer tous sur l'île du diable

NB. Look out for my forthcoming title, *How to Forge a Career in Education.*

Last Word

We dare not increase further the length of this book, lest its immoderate size tells of immoderate vanity and stirs up the reader's antipathy.

But be assured, dear reader, whether subsequently recorded in an updated version of this work or ignored due to acedia, more childhood-destroying nonsense is on its way – even as you read this.

As Stalin noted: You have been warned!